The
EVERYTHING®
Italian Cookbook

Dear Reader:

I was raised in an Italian-American family, with all four grandparents having emigrated from different parts of Italy. Throughout my childhood, I watched my parents and relatives bustle around the kitchen, preparing one delicious Italian meal after another. The difficult part of learning from these people was that none of them ever wrote down a recipe. The details were secure inside their heads and their hands just seemed to naturally know what to do. My aunt Gloria, in particular, guided me with copious amounts of patience and love, but her verbally delivered "recipes" often included instructions like "toss in a handful of flour" or "add some salt." In fact, Aunt Gloria specifically encouraged me *not* to follow recipes; instead, she stressed the merits of experimenting. Under her tutelage, I grew to accept and learn from my failed experiments and embrace and enjoy my successes.

   The best piece of advice I can offer you is to take risks in your cooking. Don't follow recipes to a T; go ahead and substitute yellow squash for eggplant or veal for chicken, and see what happens! Of course, substituting salt for sugar might not be the best idea, but use your judgment and be creative. I hope this book helps you create fantastic Italian meals, experiment with ingredients, and most importantly, have fun. *Mangia!*

Best of luck,

The EVERYTHING® Series

Editorial

Publishing Director	Gary M. Krebs
Managing Editor	Kate McBride
Copy Chief	Laura M. Daly
Acquisitions Editor	Kate Burgo
Development Editor	Katie McDonough
Production Editor	Jamie Wielgus

Production

Director of Manufacturing	Susan Beale
Associate Director of Production	Michelle Roy Kelly
Series Designers	Daria Perreault
	Colleen Cunningham
Cover Design	Paul Beatrice
	Matt LeBlanc
Interior Layout	Colleen Cunningham
	Holly Curtis
	Erin Dawson
	Sorae Lee
	Daria Perreault
Series Cover Artist	Barry Littmann

Visit the entire Everything® Series at *www.everything.com*

THE
EVERYTHING® ITALIAN COOKBOOK

300 authentic recipes to
help you cook up a feast!

Dawn Altomari, B.P.S./L.M.S.W.

Adams Media
Avon, Massachusetts

To my daughters, Jule and Quinn, and
my new granddaughter Mirabella, who inspire me every day.

An Everything® Series Book.
Everything® and everything.com® are registered trademarks of F+W Publications, Inc.

Published by Adams Media, an F+W Publications Company
57 Littlefield Street, Avon, MA 02322 U.S.A.
www.adamsmedia.com

ISBN: 1-59337-323-6
Printed in the United States of America.

J I H G F E D C B A

Library of Congress Cataloging-in-Publication Data
Altomari, Dawn.
The everything Italian cookbook / author: Dawn Altomari.
p.   cm.   —   (An everything series book)
ISBN 1-59337-420-8
1. Cookery, Italian. I. Title. II. Series: Everything series.

TX723.A48 2005
641.5945—dc22
2005015480

This book is available at quantity discounts for bulk purchases.
For information, please call 1-800-872-5627.

Contents

Introduction ∾ ix

1 Classic Italian Cuisine ∾ 1

2 Soups ∾ 13

3 Salads ∾ 31

4 Appetizers ∾ 49

5 Sauces ∾ 63

6 Flatbreads, Pizza, and Focaccia ∾ 79

7 Homemade Pasta ∾ 99

8 Risotto ∾ 139

9 Polenta ∾ 161

10 Frittata ∾ 179

11 **Meatballs and Sausages** ∾ **199**

12 **Meat** ∾ **245**

13 **Poultry** ∾ **245**

14 **Fish and Seafood** ∾ **265**

15 **Vegetables** ∾ **279**

16 **Desserts** ∾ **299**

Appendix A: Menus ∾ **315**

Index ∾ **317**

Acknowledgments

I would like to thank the following people with all my heart: Aunt Gloria, who gave me the greatest inspiration to cook and experiment; my daughters, Jule and Quinn, for their unending love and support; my mother, Theresa, who cooked hearty meals from scratch every day; my father, whose specialty was fried pork chops and potatoes; Aunt Ada, for her fresh roast chicken with potatoes; Aunt Josephine, for her fried chicken and pasta and soft-boiled eggs; Aunt Viola, who taught me how to make ravioli; Aunt Babe (Amelia), my sanitation teacher; Aunt Angie, for her attention to detail; Aunt Tessie, who made incredible desserts; Kate McBride, for her writing and editing support, her friendship, and her fantastic Minestrone; Patti Rosenbloom and Lianne Haney, who remind me that I am never alone; the Pagliaro and Altomari families, and the Motluck and Rathjen families, for their assistance with research and recipe development and testing.

Introduction

When most Americans think of Italian cuisine, they probably picture something closer to what is actually Italian-American cuisine—a big departure from authentic Italian food. The Italian families that immigrated to America years ago brought with them their treasured family recipes. But subsequent generations were forced to adapt and alter these dishes due to the unavailability of particular products, differences in kitchen setups and tools, and other discrepancies. Hence, the pizza sold at American pizza parlors is nothing like the authentic focaccia from which it likely descended.

The purpose of this book is to give you a feel for authentic Italian cuisine; however, compiling a comprehensive collection of recipes to represent the food of Italy is an enormous task. Italy is broken up into several regions, each of which has its own unique character that is dictated by geography and culture. In addition to these regional differences, there is also a distinction between the food of Italy's home kitchens and that of Italian restaurants. From one place to another, you will encounter different spices, different vegetables, and different meats, but they all contribute to the general Italian palate.

In this book, you will find many recipes that are considered "authentic" Italian cuisine, such as Osso Buco, Pasta e Fagioli, Zuppa di Pesce, and Bruschetta. You will also see some recipes for traditional Italian dishes, but with a slight twist. These might include the addition or substitution of a new ingredient not typically associated with that dish, as in Citrus-Braised Halibut, Turkey and Cranberry Sausage, and Pork and Apple Meatballs. And there are a few dishes that are usually associated with other cultures that are given here with traditional Italian ingredients or a typically Italian flair. Some examples of these dishes are Chicken Terrine and Fish Casserole, both of which are based on French recipes. You will also notice shallots in many of the recipes. Shallots are not a traditional or typical ingredient in Italian cuisine, but they can be used in place of onions in many recipes for a fresh, distinctive flavor.

Though some of these recipes are already altered from their original state, you should feel free to further customize them to your own tastes and the tastes of your family. You can add and subtract ingredients to make foods creamier, sweeter, more colorful, or more nutritious. It is not only okay to substitute or vary ingredients in recipes, but it is also fun and fulfilling to do so. No recipe is sacred, and cooking is all about experimentation!

In Chapter 1, you will find information to guide you through some specific processes of Italian cooking. There are tips for preparing dough, helpful hints for making your own sausage, definitions of particular cooking terms, a list of basic ingredients to have on hand, and much more. The only other thing you need is a kitchen! So, put on your apron and read on. You're about to embark on an exciting and mouthwatering Italian journey!

Chapter 1

Classic Italian Cuisine

Italian cuisine is largely based on family tradition and is characterized by fresh ingredients and simple preparation. While these traits unify the country's general tastes and methods, traditional ingredients and cooking styles vary in Italy's separate regions. The foods that are common to one area can differ greatly from those of another area, depending on the availability of fresh ingredients and various cultural differences. The history and the unique geography of the country have also served to infuse the cuisine with a unique blend of both "peasant" and "patrician" elements.

Regional Differences

Today's Italian cuisine is the result of the slow integration of the many different regional traditions and food customs. When the regions of Italy were unified in the mid-nineteenth century, only about a half million Italians out of the total population of 25 million were able to speak and understand the national language—instead they spoke their own regional dialects.

The same kind of separation was also reflected in the food of each region. However, the slow unification of the regions into one nation and the increased interaction and travel between the different parts of Italy caused both the language and the cooking styles to integrate. While the traditional food customs of each region still exist in the kitchens of Italian homes, restaurants offer the more unified "national" cuisine—a collection of favorites from the various regional cultures.

Extra-virgin olive oil comes from the first pressing of the olives, has the most intense flavor, and is the most expensive. Use this for salads and for dipping breads. Virgin olive oil is from the second pressing. Less expensive than extra-virgin, it can be used for the same purposes. "Olive oil" indicates it is from the last pressing; this is the oil to use for cooking since it does not burn as easily at high temperatures.

Since the history of Italian food is so rooted in the regional cultures, it is interesting to take a look at the main regions of the country and what kinds of food products and dishes each one is known for. The most important regions in Italy to examine for culinary reasons are the following: Abruzzo-Molise, Apulia, Calabria-Lucania, Emilia-Romagna, Liguria, Lombardy, Naples-Campagna, Piedmont, Rome-Lazio, Sardinia, Sicily, Tuscany, Umbria-Marche, and Veneto. These areas can be split up roughly into three categories: northern, central, and southern Italy.

Northern Italy

Emilia-Romagna is one of the most famous regions of Italy when it comes to food. Parmesan cheese—possibly the most famous Italian cheese—comes from the capital city of Parma and the province of Reggio. The trade name Parmigiano-Reggiano is protected by law and should only be used on authentic cheese products produced in this region. Emilia-Romagna is also famous for its pork and pork products, especially a variety of seasoned sausages known as "salami," including mortadella, prosciutto, pancetta, coppa, zampone, and Bologna.

Liguria, which mostly occupies coastline, is sometimes called "the Italian Riviera." Seafood dishes from Liguria include cioppino (seafood stew similar to bouillabaisse), capon magro (fish salad), and baccalà (dried salt cod). But the most famous dish by far is Genoa's pesto, the traditional sauce made from fresh sweet basil, garlic, pine nuts (pignoli) or walnuts, ewe's milk cheese, and olive oil. Traditionally, these ingredients are mixed into a smooth, very aromatic sauce using a mortar and pestle. Pesto is classically served over trenette pasta.

A multitude of Italian dishes are instantly recognizable as having their origins in Milan, the most important city in the region of Lombardy. For example, risotto, minestrone, costolette (veal cutlets), and osso buco (stew with veal in tomato sauce) are all well-known dishes from this region. You will often see dishes originating from this area referred to as "alla Milanese" (in the style of Milan).

FACT

When the Tuscans were looking for a way to use stale bread, they rubbed cut garlic cloves on the bread slices, brushed them with olive oil, grilled them over hot coals, and sprinkled them with salt. Bruschetta (plural is bruschette), which comes from the word *bruscare*, meaning "to toast/roast," can also be prepared in a toaster oven or hot frying pan.

Piedmont is a northern region that shares the Alps with Switzerland and France. The delicate white truffle is the pride of Piedmont and is an important ingredient in many of the dishes of this region. Fritto misto (mixed fry), bagna cauda (hot garlic dip with anchovy), and fonduta (Piedmontese fondue made with fontina cheese) are classic dishes famous in this region.

Food historians say that the more formal Italian cuisine originated in Tuscany (Florence, in particular) in the sixteenth century at the court of the Medici. Florentine specialties (alla Fiorentina) such as baccalà (dried cod), bistecca (steak), and anguilla (eel) are all examples of the fine art of Tuscan cooking.

The region of Veneto has both mountains and coastline, so the cuisine varies in character according to where you go in the area. Rice and polenta are popular dishes, and the art of cooking fish is also prized among Venetian chefs. Famous dishes are risi e bisati (rice with eel), risi e bisi (rice and peas), brodetto di pesce (Venetian fish soup), baccalà mantecato (creamed salt cod), and fugazza di Pasqua (Easter bread).

Central Italy

Abruzzi-Molise is a mountainous region that stretches from the Adriatic Sea to the high peaks of the Apennine Mountains. The most famous dish of the region is maccheroni alla chitarra—long fresh pasta noodles served with tomato sauce flavored with sweet peppers and pork fat and sprinkled with pecorino cheese. *Chitarra* means "guitar" and refers to the guitar-shaped wooden implement used to cut the fresh pasta. Sheep are raised in the mountains, so lamb is the main meat of this area. Lamb is usually roasted, fried, or cooked "alla cacciatora" (sautéed with red peppers and tomato sauce). The local shepherds are also "masters" of cheese making; pecorino and scamorza (smoked mozzarella) are the two most famous cheese products of the area.

In the region of Rome-Lazio, specialty dishes include bucatini all'Amatriciana (pasta in a tomato sauce with onion, pancetta, and a dash of cognac) or bucatini alla carbonara (pasta with a creamy egg and cheese sauce), gnocchi alla Romana, saltimbocca (a fillet of veal rolled in ham and flavored with sage, cooked in butter, and served with a Marsala sauce), and abbacchio al forno (roast lamb) or abbacchio alla cacciatora (lamb with an anchovy and rosemary sauce).

Sardinia is the second largest island in Italy (after Sicily). With its rocky terrain the land of Sardinia is not conducive to growing anything. Hence, the region is famous for its bread, which Sardinian women bake lovingly in large ovens. Otherwise, most dishes of note are seafood based. Burrida (the famous fish stew of the area), calamaretti ripieni (stuffed baby squid), and spaghetti alla rustica (country-style spaghetti with anchovy and oregano sauce) are famous Sardinian dishes.

In Umbria-Marche, the cooking is known for its use of the prized black truffle. Specially trained dogs and even pigs with a highly delicate sense of smell are sent out to search for these hidden treasures buried in the soil. Also famous for their pork dishes, Umbrians cook the meat in the oven or roast it on spits. In the classic dish arrosto alla ghiotta, a cooking pan or dish is placed under the spit to collect the fat drippings from the roasting meat. White wine, vinegar, lemon slices, sage leaves, and black olives are placed all together in the dish. As the boiling fat drips into the mixture, it releases an aromatic vapor that is infused into the roasting meat as it rises.

Southern Italy

Apulia, which makes up the heel of Italy's "boot," is famous for its pastas and fresh vegetables. Fish and seafood dishes are also common, and oysters, fish soups, mussels, and squid stew are favorites. Apulia is also one of the richest wine-producing regions in Italy.

FACT

There is a new product that comes in handy when certain fresh herbs are not in season (or you don't have them on hand). In the freezer section of your local market you can find chopped fresh herbs, such as parsley, basil, cilantro, and oregano, in large spice jars. You can open up the jar, use as much as you need, and pop it back into the freezer.

Most of the region of Calabria-Lucania occupies coastland. For this reason, the population traces its origins back to many different races that once visited the coastal towns, including Greeks, Arabs, Albanians, Spaniards,

Normans, and even Turkish pirates. The land away from the coastline is exceedingly fertile and this region is characterized by vast olive groves and lush plantations of jasmine, lavender, roses, mimosa, sweet peppers, eggplants, and citrus fruits. The famous Italian sausages luganega and soppressata come from here as well. Luganega is made with a mixture of pork spiced with sweet peppers and chili, and soppressata is lean meat and lard seasoned with salt, black pepper, and sweet peppers that is stuffed into casings and hung over a chimney or fire to be smoked. Calabria is also famous for its exports of figs, honey, almonds, and dried fruit.

Pizza and spaghetti are the main attractions in Naples-Campagna. Folklore has it that pizza was born on the streets of Naples two centuries ago when street vendors sold baked wedges of dough with hand-pressed extra-virgin olive oil drizzled on it and topped with chopped garlic. This became known as pizza Napoletana. In 2003, the *Washington Post* reported that "in Naples, pizza makers are trying to get an EU patent on Vera Pizza Napoletana made with dough fermented overnight on marble counters, cooked over a wood fire with a sauce of fresh tomato and buffalo mozzarella."

It makes sense that Sicily, Italy's largest island, is famous for its seafood and fish dishes. Sardines, tuna, and swordfish are central to Sicilian cuisine, and even pasta dishes are cooked with seafood. Tonno alla cipollata (tuna fried with onions), seppia (cuttlefish served in its own black sauce with pasta), and pesce spada alla Messina (swordfish cooked in oil with tomatoes onions, olives, capers, and tomatoes) are classic Sicilian dishes.

The Classic Italian Meal

The "classic" Italian meal is composed of the following elements: a first course (a soup, a pasta, or a risotto), the main course (meat or fish with a vegetable), followed by salad, and ending with the dessert. Of course, this order is not a hard-and-fast rule. Sometimes the pasta can be a separate course following the first course that is served prior to the main part of the meal. Likewise, the risotto is often used as a side dish to the main meal, instead of as a first course. In many homes the salad may be eaten prior to the main meal instead of after it, and obviously, pasta can often be served as a main dish all on its own. While a formal Italian restaurant may offer the full menu of traditional courses, a family will often customize the order to accommodate their time, mood, or budget.

Basic Ingredients

If you're going to be preparing authentic Italian food, you're going to need several basic ingredients. The fantastic thing about Italian cuisine is the astounding number of different dishes that can be made with a few fundamental items. However, it's important to always use fresh seasonal ingredients—local produce is best, if available. Stock your kitchen ahead of time with the basic nonperishables and make quick specialized trips to the market for fresh produce, meat, and dairy products.

Here is a list of basic ingredients that appear in most Italian recipes:

- **Flour:** there are many varieties besides all-purpose white, such as durum wheat (semolina)
- **Eggs:** freshness is very important—observe dates on cartons and dispose of eggs when the date has passed
- **Milk**
- **Unsalted butter**
- **Fresh fruits:** pears, figs, apples
- **Fresh vegetables:** tomatoes, onions, potatoes
- **Fresh fish and seafood:** cod, shrimp, mussels
- **Fresh meat:** chicken, veal, pork,
- **Fresh herbs:** parsley, basil, oregano
- **Olive oils:** pomace, virgin, extra-virgin
- **Spices:** salt, pepper, garlic salt,
- **Nuts:** almonds, pecans, walnuts
- **Honey**
- **Sugar:** granulated, brown, confectioners'

In Italian cooking, you will go through a lot of spices, olive oil, and flour in a short time. Always keep extra supplies of these items in your pantry, and find a local market where you can get these basics at affordable prices.

Cooking Techniques

The techniques used in the Italian kitchen are not much different from the basic techniques you would use to prepare any other cuisine. Again, the method of preparation may differ from region to region for the same food, and often the method chosen has to do with the freshness and availability of the particular food item. It is not uncommon to find the method of preparation in the title of a recipe. For example, Vitello al Forno (page 236) is veal baked in the oven and Cavolfiore Fritto (page 280) is fried cauliflower. There are several different techniques used to make the dishes in this book. Some foods are made in the oven, others are made on the stovetop, and some employ both methods.

On the Stovetop

To bring the contents of a pot to a boil you must keep the pot on high heat until frothy, popping bubbles arise. You will often need to bring water to a boil and then add food (whether pasta, rice, or vegetables) and lower the burner to medium heat while the food cooks. Simmering is slightly different from boiling. When you are instructed to "simmer" something in a recipe, you are usually heating a liquid or partially liquid mixture at a low to medium-low temperature. A simmer is like a slow, calm boil—there should be small, rolling bubbles instead of frothy, popping ones.

There are a few very basic "nevers" by which a true Italian cook abides. Never overcook pasta. Never buy grated cheese in a jar or plastic container—only use fresh-grated Parmesan or Romano. Never use bottled salad dressing. And of course, *never* buy prepared tomato sauce in a jar or can. Make your own!

Braising (*brasare,* "to braise") indicates first searing the item (browning the outside at a very high heat), and then partially covering it with liquid and simmering at a low heat. Stewing is very similar to braising. When stewing ingredients (*stufare,* "to stew"), you have the option of first searing the item, but it's not required. Then the item is completely covered in liquid and simmered slowly.

When you sauté (*saltare*), you cook an item on the stovetop in a very small amount of fat on high heat. This is a moist cooking technique—the fat used is usually oil or butter. Often, the item is lightly dusted with flour, as well, to create a batter or breading. The item is quickly cooked and browned on both sides. Steaming is also a moist cooking technique and is accomplished by rapidly boiling liquid (most commonly water) in a perforated pan with a lid. The lid is kept secure throughout the cooking to trap the steam.

Poaching can be accomplished in a shallow or deep collection of liquid. Items are generally simmered in a flavored liquid (usually stock). *Al cartoccio* means wrapping and cooking food in parchment paper. The more commonly recognized French term for this is *en papillote*. To do this, the food is encased within parchment paper and cooked, either in the oven or in liquid on the stovetop. Sometimes aluminum foil is used in place of the parchment paper.

Frying

Frying (*friggere*, "to fry") can be accomplished several ways. You can pan-fry, deep-fry, or stir-fry food. Pan-frying is similar to sautéing, but items are usually breaded or battered and larger amounts of fat are used in the cooking. Deep-frying is much like sautéing and pan-frying in that items are almost always coated with either flour, breading, or batter. However, the amount of fat utilized is far greater than in either sautéing or pan-frying. The item being cooked is completely submerged in fat and cooked with high, moist heat. Stir-frying, although not an authentic Italian practice, is a helpful moist cooking technique. Very similar to sautéing, it quickly "fries" items, but there is even less or no fat, and items are cut into very small pieces.

In the Oven (al Forno)

Roasting (*arrostire*, "to roast") is cooking through indirect heat. Foods that are roasted are often placed on wire racks so that hot air can completely surround and thoroughly cook them. Baking (*cuocere*, "to bake"; or *al forno*, "baked") is similar to roasting. Often dessert mixtures are placed in baking vessels (pans, pie dishes, etc.) and these are placed in the oven. Hot, dry air circulates around the food. Broiling is a dry direct-heat cooking method using high heat, in which the heat comes from above the item. Grilling (*grigliare,* "to grill") is just the opposite: it is dry, direct-heat cooking in which the heat comes from below the item. When broiling or grilling, you can quickly marinate or moisten the product with oil or a vinaigrette before cooking.

Basics of Sausage Making

You have two choices when it comes to sausage making: You can grind the meat yourself or buy the meat already ground. You can buy desired cuts of meat and fat and chop them to your preferred consistency with most food processors or a meat grinder. However, ingredients and equipment must be ice-cold throughout the process to ensure food safety and thorough mixing of the meats and spices. Also, be sure that the processor or grinder is completely cleaned and sanitized before and after each use.

When grinding meat in a food processor or a grinder, you should grind to "hamburger consistency." Grind meat and fat separately, and keep the two separate and chilled until instructed to mix. Mixing meat and fat together later in the process ensures that each ingredient maintains its individual flavor profiles and characteristics.

ALERT!

When working with raw meats (as when making sausage or meatballs), you want to be sure your hands are clean and you're working on a clean surface. Don't chop raw meat on a wooden cutting board; gel-plastic boards are easier to sanitize. And always clean knives and other tools that have come in contact with raw meat in hot, soapy water.

Whether to form the mixture into patties or stuff it in natural or synthetic casings is your choice. There are special attachments available for use with some grinders for stuffing sausage mixtures into casings. When stuffing casings, pack each casing fully, but at the same time be sure not to overstuff. Avoid air bubbles that can become trapped in the casing. You can use a sanitized needle to vent trapped air bubbles (professionals have "teasing needles" for this specific purpose). Overstuffing and air bubbles increase the risk of breakage or bursting during the cooking process.

You can also customize your sausage to accommodate your particular tastes and budget. Less expensive cuts of meat can be used for sausage recipes if you're looking to save money, and you can use less fat in any recipe and increase the content of lean meat for healthier sausage. Test the flavor of your sausage by thoroughly cooking a tablespoonful of mixture, tasting it, and adjusting the seasonings accordingly. Dried herbs are often used because they impart a more intense flavor profile in sausage. Fresh herbs can be used, but you'll need to double the amount called for.

Making your own sausage involves quite a bit of work, but the results are well worth the extra effort. The quality and taste of homemade sausage is far superior to most store-bought varieties, unless you are buying from a local butcher shop where the sausages are made fresh.

Chapter 2

Soups

Chicken Stock 14

Beef Stock 15

Vegetable Stock 16

Fish Stock 16

Stracciatella 17

Chicken Orzo 18

Zuppa di Pesce (Fish Soup) 19

Minestrone with Meatballs 20

Tomato Soup with Fried Pasta Garnish 21

Lentil Soup 22

Hearty Fish Soup with Pesto 23

Cioppino 24

Pasta e Fagioli (Pasta and Bean Soup) 25

Bean and Sausage Soup 26

Dandelion Egg Drop 26

Garlic Soup 27

Vegetable Broth with Roasted Rigatoni 28

Pasta with Rich Broth 29

Chilled Beet Soup 29

Pork Soup with Acini di Pepe 30

5–6 pounds chicken meat
    with bones
3 yellow onions
1 bulb garlic
6 parsnips (or substitute
    3 large carrots)
3 large leeks (whole)
4 stalks celery
2 cups mushrooms (optional)
5 sprigs fresh thyme or
    1 tablespoon dried
½ bunch fresh parsley or
    1 tablespoon dried
1 tablespoon olive oil
2 cups dry white wine (not
    cooking wine)
1½ gallons water
3 bay leaves
½ teaspoon peppercorns

Chicken Stock

You can prepare this broth for use in a specific recipe on the day you plan to cook, or you can make batches ahead of time, let cool completely, and freeze them for later use.

1. Rinse the chicken in cold water and pat dry with paper towels. Peel and roughly chop the onions, garlic, and parsnips. Clean and roughly chop the leeks, celery, and mushrooms. Clean and dry the thyme and parsley.

2. Heat the oil in a large stockpot over medium temperature. Lightly brown the chicken. Add the onions and leeks, and let wilt. Add the garlic, celery, parsley, and mushrooms; sauté for 5 minutes.

3. Pour in the wine and reduce by half the volume. Add the water, bay leaves, and peppercorns.

4. Bring to a simmer and cook for 4 to 6 hours, uncovered.

5. Strain the broth through a fine-meshed sieve, and discard all the solids. Use immediately, or let cool completely and freeze for later use.

Removing Fat from Chicken Stock
It is a good practice to prepare chicken stock one day in advance of using it for a soup recipe. Chilling causes the fat to rise to the top and congeal, so store stock overnight in the refrigerator. The next day, you can remove the thick layer of fat to reveal pure stock.

Beef Stock

*Try lining the strainer with cheesecloth before pouring
the soup through. In addition to straining out all the solids, this is
helpful in removing any fat from the meat.*

Makes 1 gallon

5–6 pounds beef with bones
5 yellow onions
2 shallots
1 pound carrots
1 bunch celery
5 sprigs fresh thyme or
    1 tablespoon dried
½ bunch fresh parsley or
    1 tablespoon dried
1 tablespoon olive oil
1 cup red table wine
1½ gallons water
3 bay leaves

1. Remove the beef from the bones. Rinse the beef and pat dry with paper towels. Peel and roughly chop the onions, shallots, and carrots. Clean and roughly chop the celery. Rinse the herbs and pat dry with paper towels.

2. Heat the oil in a large stockpot over medium temperature. Brown the meat on all sides. Add the onions, shallots, carrots, and celery; sauté for 2 minutes.

3. Add the wine and reduce by half the volume. Add the water, thyme, parsley, and bay leaves. Bring to a simmer and cook for 8 hours, uncovered.

4. Strain the broth through a fine-meshed sieve, and discard the solids. Use immediately, or let cool completely and freeze for later use.

4 pounds yellow onions
1 pound carrots
1 pound parsnips
1 bunch celery
1 bunch fresh parsley
½ bunch fresh thyme
4 bay leaves
Fresh-cracked black pepper
2 gallons water

Vegetable Stock

This basic vegetable stock is easy and great for use in many soup recipes.
Keep some stored in your freezer so you can use it anytime.

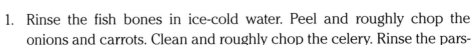

1. Peel and roughly chop the onions, carrots, and parsnips. Clean and roughly chop the celery. Clean the parsley and thyme.

2. Place all the ingredients in a large stockpot and simmer for 2 hours, uncovered.

3. Strain the broth through a fine-meshed sieve, and discard the vegetables and herbs. Use or let cool completely and store for later use.

Makes 1 gallon

4 pounds fish bones
3 large yellow onions
2 large carrots
3 stalks celery
½ bunch fresh parsley
8 sprigs fresh thyme
3 bay leaves
Fresh-cracked black pepper
2 gallons cold water

Fish Stock

Do not use oily fish bones like those from salmon or tuna.
Light whitefish bones are a better option for this stock.

1. Rinse the fish bones in ice-cold water. Peel and roughly chop the onions and carrots. Clean and roughly chop the celery. Rinse the parsley and thyme, and pat dry with paper towels.

2. Place all the ingredients in a large stockpot and bring to a simmer. Cook over medium-low heat for 2 hours, uncovered.

3. Strain the broth through a fine-meshed sieve, and discard the solids. Use in recipes as needed or let cool completely and store for later use.

Stracciatella

This is a basic chicken soup, Italian style.
You can customize the recipe by substituting certain ingredients—use escarole
instead of spinach or try sweet sausage instead of meatballs.

Serves 10

3 pounds bony chicken pieces
(neck, back, wings, etc.)
3 yellow onions
2 carrots
2 stalks celery
1 bulb garlic
½ bunch fresh parsley
2 sprigs fresh thyme
2 tablespoons olive oil
1 cup pinot grigio
8 cups Chicken Stock
(page 14)
4 cups water
2 bay leaves
½ teaspoon peppercorns
½ meatball recipe of choice
(see Chapter 11, page 199)
4 cups fresh spinach leaves
6 eggs
¼ cup fresh-grated Parmesan
cheese

1. Rinse the chicken pieces in cold water. Peel and roughly chop the onions and carrots. Clean and roughly chop the celery. Peel the garlic and leave whole. Clean the parsley and thyme, and leave whole.

2. Heat the olive oil in large stockpot over medium-high temperature. Add the chicken pieces and brown for 5 minutes, stirring occasionally. Add the onions, carrots, celery, and garlic. Brown for 3 more minutes.

3. Pour in the wine and reduce by half the volume. Add the stock, water, bay leaves, and peppercorns. Reduce heat and simmer on low for approximately 3 hours, uncovered.

4. Meanwhile, prepare the meatballs and drain on a paper towel. Set aside.

5. Clean spinach. Steam spinach in a vegetable steamer or in a large covered pot of boiling water (2 inches deep) with colander or strainer for approximately 2 minutes.

6. Strain the soup through a fine-meshed sieve, and discard the solids. Return the pot to the stovetop and heat on medium-high. Stir in eggs and simmer until cooked. Add the meatballs, spinach, and cheese right before serving.

Discarding Solids

When making any chicken-based soup, the reason you discard the chicken and the vegetables after cooking is that their flavor has seeped into the broth. The solids are basically flavorless at this point, so they are discarded.

3 pounds bony chicken pieces
(neck, back, wings, etc.)
3 yellow onions
2 carrots
2 stalks celery
½ bulb garlic
½ bunch fresh parsley
3 sprigs fresh thyme
2 cups fresh mushrooms
3 cups fresh escarole
2 bay leaves
10 peppercorns
8½ cups Chicken Stock
(page 14)
4 cups water
1 cup pinot grigio
1 teaspoon. olive oil
2½ cups cooked orzo pasta
¼ cup fresh-grated Romano
cheese

Chicken Orzo

*Orzo is a good pasta choice for using in soup. It is a small
oval pasta that retains its texture in the hot broth.*

1. Rinse the chicken pieces in cold water, and pat dry with paper towels. Peel and roughly chop the onions and carrots. Clean and roughly chop the celery. Peel the garlic and leave whole. Clean the parsley and thyme, and leave whole. Clean and slice mushrooms. Clean escarole and remove leaves from head.

2. Place the chicken pieces, onions, carrots, celery, garlic, parsley, thyme, bay leaves, peppercorns, stock, water, and wine in a large stockpot. Simmer on low heat for 4 hours, uncovered.

3. Meanwhile, sauté the mushrooms in large sauté pan at medium heat with the olive oil. Set aside. Steam the escarole in a large covered sauté pan with ½ cup of chicken stock. Set aside.

4. Strain the broth through a fine-meshed sieve, and discard the solids. Add the mushrooms, escarole, and orzo to the broth just before serving. Sprinkle with the cheese.

Zuppa di Pesce (Fish Soup)

This "fish soup" is great served with a loaf of crusty Italian bread.
Make sure there is plenty of bread for dipping.

1. Rinse all the seafood in ice-cold water. Peel and finely dice the onions and carrots. Clean and finely dice the celery. Peel and mince the garlic. Clean the parsley and thyme, and leave whole. Shell and cut lobster tail into bite-sized pieces.

2. Place the onions, carrots, celery, garlic, herbs, bay leaves, and peppercorns in a large stockpot. Add the Fish Stock and Old World Gravy, and simmer on medium-high heat for 10 minutes, uncovered. Add the shrimp and scallops, and simmer for 5 minutes. Add the calamari and clams, and simmer for 5 minutes. Add lobster, and simmer 1 minute longer to reheat lobster meat.

3. Remove the herbs and peppercorns. Sprinkle with the cheese, and serve.

Serves 10

1 (1½-pound) whole fresh cooked lobster
¾ pound fresh whitefish
1 dozen large uncooked fresh shrimp with shells
¼ pound fresh sea scallops
¼ pound fresh calamari
1 dozen littleneck clams
3 yellow onions
2 carrots
2 stalks celery
¼ bulb garlic
½ bunch fresh parsley
2 sprigs fresh thyme
2 bay leaves
½ teaspoon peppercorns
6 cups Fish Stock (page 16)
6 cups Old World Gravy (Long-Cooking Tomato Sauce) (page 64)
¼ cup fresh-grated Parmesan or Romano cheese

4 yellow onions
2 carrots
½ bulb garlic
2 stalks celery
1 tablespoon olive oil
3 pounds veal bones and
*   meat*
2 cups chopped tomatoes
8 cups water
4 sprigs fresh oregano
½ meatball recipe of choice
*   (see Chapter 11, page 199)*
½ cup green beans
2½ cups cooked pasta of
*   choice*
⅓ cup fresh-grated Parmesan
*   cheese*

Minestrone with Meatballs

Minestrone soup can be made with various vegetables,
rice or pasta, and almost any kind of meat. Use what is fresh
in the market or what you have on hand, and your minestrone
will come out different, but delicious, every time.

1. Peel and roughly chop the onions, carrots, and garlic. Clean and roughly chop the celery.

2. Heat the oil in a large stockpot on medium and brown the veal bones. Add the onion, carrots, celery, garlic, and tomatoes. Add the water, and simmer for 3 hours, uncovered.

3. Add the oregano. Simmer for 30 minutes, uncovered.

4. While the soup simmers, make the meatballs, and drain on paper towels. In a small covered saucepan, steam the green beans in small amount of boiling water for 2 minutes. Strain beans.

5. Just before serving, add the meatballs, green beans, and pasta to the soup, and sprinkle with the cheese.

To Absorb Excess Grease

To absorb excess grease from your soup, drop a lettuce leaf into the simmering broth. As soon as the lettuce soaks up the fat, remove it and throw it away. This trick will not work as well with thicker recipes, like stews and sauces.

Tomato Soup with Fried Pasta Garnish

Make Parmesan curls by scraping your vegetable peeler against a hard hunk of Parmesan cheese. These curls make a great garnish for many Italian dishes.

Serves 10

2 yellow onions
1 bulb garlic
8 tomatoes
¼ bunch fresh basil
½ bunch fresh parsley
¼ cup olive oil
8 cups Vegetable Stock
  (page 16)
½ recipe Deep-Fried Pasta
  (page 135)
½ cup Parmesan cheese curls
1 tablespoon capers, rinsed
Fresh-cracked black pepper

1. Peel and dice the onion. Peel and mince the garlic. Clean and cut the tomatoes into small wedges. Clean the herbs and pat dry on paper towels. Slice the basil and chop the parsley.

2. Heat the oil in a large stockpot on medium for about 3 minutes. Add the onions and sauté for about 2 minutes. Add the garlic and sauté for about 2 minutes. Add the tomatoes. Reduce heat to low and add the vegetable broth. Simmer for 1½ hours, uncovered.

3. Add the herbs and simmer for 30 minutes, uncovered.

4. While the soup simmers, prepare the Deep-Fried Pasta.

5. Serve the soup in individual bowls with clusters of fried pasta. Sprinkle each serving with the Parmesan curls, capers, and pepper.

Serves 10

½ pound pancetta
(or substitute ¼ pound
prosciutto or ½ pound
bacon)
3 yellow onions
2 carrots
2 stalks celery
½ bunch fresh parsley
3 sprigs fresh thyme
2 tablespoons olive oil
2 cups dried lentils
12 cups Vegetable Stock
(page 16)
2 bay leaves

Lentil Soup

*Pancetta is salt-cured pork—the Italian version of bacon.
It is usually sold in a large rolled form and can be purchased in Italian
delicatessens and some specialty supermarkets.*

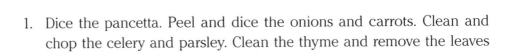

1. Dice the pancetta. Peel and dice the onions and carrots. Clean and chop the celery and parsley. Clean the thyme and remove the leaves (discard the stems).

2. Heat the oil in a stockpot for 10 minutes on medium temperature. Lightly brown the pancetta for about 4 minutes. Add the onions and sauté for 1 minute. Add the carrots and celery, and sauté for 1 minute. Add the remaining ingredients and simmer for 1 hour, uncovered.

3. Discard the bay leaves, and serve.

Why Brown Veggies First?

Why cook vegetables in oil before adding to liquid? Because the rigid cell walls of many veggies lock the flavor and nutrients inside—only lipids can dissolve these walls. Carrots, for example, are high in fat-soluble beta-carotene. To extract this essence, the carrot must first cook slowly in fat or oil to dissolve the cell walls without burning the carrots. If veggies are just thrown in with the liquid, the broth will be bland.

Hearty Fish Soup with Pesto

Although pesto is usually used as a sauce over pasta,
it also has many other uses. A dollop in any stew, sauce, or soup
will add the fragrant flavor of garlic and basil.

Serves 10

2 pounds boneless, skinless halibut
4 shallots
3 pounds carrots
2 bunches leeks
½ bunch celery
½ bunch fresh parsley
3 tablespoons olive oil
4 cups Fish Stock (page 16)
2 bay leaves
About ¾ cup Traditional Pesto (page 71)

1. Clean and large-dice the fish. Keep chilled. Clean and peel the shallots and carrots. Thoroughly clean the leeks, celery, and parsley. Medium-dice the shallots, carrots, leeks, and celery. Chop the parsley.

2. Heat the oil in a large stockpot on medium temperature. Add the fish and vegetables, and sauté for 5 minutes.

3. Add the stock and simmer for 1 hour, uncovered. Add the bay leaves and parsley, and simmer for 30 minutes, uncovered.

4. While the soup is simmering, prepare the pesto.

5. Ladle the soup into serving bowls and garnish each with a spoonful of pesto.

2 pounds king crab or snow
    crab
2 dozen littleneck clams
2 dozen mussels
2 pounds skinless sea bass
    fillets
1 bunch parsnips
2 bunches fresh leeks
1 bunch celery
5 pounds plum tomatoes
½ bunch fresh parsley
4 sprigs fresh thyme
1 bunch kale
2 tablespoons olive oil
12 cups Fish Stock (page 16)
2 bay leaves
2 tablespoons saffron
Fresh-cracked black pepper

Cioppino

*This Italian seafood stew is a hearty dish that can be served
as a main meal. Accompany a steaming bowl of this with
a fresh loaf of Italian semolina bread for dipping.*

1. Clean the shellfish and fish in ice-cold water. Keep chilled. Peel and
    chop the parsnips. Clean and roughly chop the leeks, celery, tomatoes,
    parsley, and thyme. Clean the kale, and remove and discard the tough
    center stalks.

2. Heat the oil in a large stockpot. Add the seafood, parsnips, leeks,
    and celery. Sauté for 5 minutes. Add the fish stock, tomatoes, parsley,
    thyme, and bay leaves. Simmer for 30 minutes, uncovered.

3. Add the kale, saffron, and pepper just before serving.

Saffron

*Saffron is one of the most expensive food ingredients in the world. In
Italy it grows in the Abruzzi region and can be purchased in either
threads or powdered form. Saffron is used to give both flavor and color
to food and must be used sparingly, not only for the expense but
because too much of it will make the food taste slightly medicinal.*

Pasta e Fagioli
(Pasta and Bean Soup)

You can presoak the beans overnight to make the cooking faster, or you can use a good brand of imported Italian canned chickpeas (see step 4 of the recipe).

Serves 10

1 pound dried chickpeas
4 gallons Vegetable Stock
  (page 16)
4 shallots
1 bulb garlic
2 celeriac (celery root)
2 pounds plum tomatoes
½ bunch fresh parsley
2 tablespoons olive oil
2 cups cooked bite-size
  pasta of choice
½ cup fresh-grated Asiago
  cheese
Fresh-cracked black pepper

1. Sort through the chickpeas, discarding any stones. In a large stockpot, simmer the peas in 2 gallons of the stock for approximately 2 to 3 hours, until the beans are tender. Drain.

2. Peel and finely chop the shallots, garlic, and celeriac. Clean and chop the tomatoes and parsley.

3. Heat the oil in a large stockpot over medium temperature. Sauté the shallots, garlic, and celeriac for 3 minutes. Add the tomatoes and sauté for 1 minute. Add the remaining stock, the chickpeas, and parsley. Let simmer for 1 hour, uncovered.

4. Just before serving, stir in the pasta (and beans, only if canned are used). Sprinkle each serving with the cheese and pepper.

Shocking Pasta

When a soup recipe calls for pasta, never add the uncooked pasta to the pot to cook along with the soup. Instead, cook it separately, and shock it with cold water as soon as you drain it. It should be cooked only al dente, because it will cook more in the hot soup. Add it to the soup just before serving.

Serves 10

2 pounds hot Italian sausage
3 yellow onions
4 sprigs thyme
1 tablespoon olive oil
2 gallons Beef Stock (page 15)
2 pounds cooked cannellini
    beans
About ⅔ cup store-bought
    roasted red pepper purée
About ⅛ cup Roasted Garlic
    Paste (page 70)

Bean and Sausage Soup

To make it easier to cut the raw sausages, freeze them for about 30 minutes before you slice them. Just let them thaw a little before cooking.

1. Cut the sausage into slices about ½ inch thick. Peel and finely slice the onions. Clean the thyme and remove the leaves (discard the stems).

2. Heat the oil over medium temperature in a large stockpot. Brown the sausage for 3 minutes. Add the onion and cook for 1 minute (do not brown the onions).

3. Add the stock and simmer on low heat for 1 hour, uncovered. Add the beans and simmer for 30 minutes, uncovered.

4. Ladle the soup into bowls. Garnish each serving with about 1 tablespoon of the red pepper purée, ½ teaspoon of the garlic paste, and a few thyme leaves.

Serves 10

2 pounds fresh dandelions
1 bunch leeks
6 eggs
1 tablespoon olive oil
2 gallons Chicken Stock
    (page 14)
⅓ cup fresh-grated Romano
    cheese
Fresh-cracked black pepper

Dandelion Egg Drop

Dandelions are hard to find but worth the effort for this dish. However, you can substitute any green (kale, escarole, spinach) if your local market does not carry dandelions.

1. Thoroughly clean and slice the dandelions and leeks. Beat the eggs in a bowl and keep chilled.

2. Heat the oil over medium temperature in a large stockpot. Wilt the leeks for 2 minutes. Add the stock and let simmer for 30 minutes, uncovered.

3. Add the dandelions and eggs, and stir constantly for 2 minutes. Remove from heat.

4. Sprinkle each serving with the grated cheese and black pepper.

Garlic Soup

To make your own crostini, cut off the crust from day-old Italian or semolina bread. Slice the bread very thinly, and either fry in oil or butter, or brush the slices with olive oil and toast in the oven.

Serves 10

2 shallots
½ bunch celery
4 sprigs fresh parsley
1 tablespoon olive oil
1 cup Roasted Garlic Paste
  (page 70)
2 gallons Vegetable Stock
  (page 16)
Homemade crostini

1. Peel and mince the shallots. Clean and thinly slice the celery. Clean and mince the parsley.

2. Heat the oil in a stockpot over medium temperature for about 2 minutes. Add the shallots and celery. Whisk in the garlic paste, and sauté for 1 minute. Add the stock and simmer for 1 hour, uncovered.

3. Sprinkle each serving with the parsley, and serve the crostini on the side.

Wonderful Wooden Spoons

When cooking soups, stews, and sauces, the most intense, delicious flavors often concentrate on the bottom of the pot. Wooden spoons gently loosen soluble concentrated juices from the bottom of the pan, without scraping up metal shavings or burned solids. They are also gentle on your metal cookware.

Serves 10

4 large white onions
½ pound parsnips
½ pound carrots
1 bulb garlic
1 bunch celery
1 bunch fresh parsley
6 sprigs fresh thyme
¼ cup olive oil, divided
2 bay leaves
4 cups vegetable juice (such as V8)
4 cups Vegetable Stock (page 16)
Fresh-cracked black pepper
½ recipe cooked Stuffed Rigatoni (page 121)

Vegetable Broth with Roasted Rigatoni

Roasted rigatoni is used as a garnish instead of the standard crackers. It is crispy enough to add texture, but putting it in the hot soup softens it enough to eat.

1. Peel and finely dice the onions, parsnips, and carrots. Peel and mince the garlic. Clean and chop the celery and parsley. Clean the thyme and remove the leaves (discard the stems).

2. Heat 1 tablespoon of the oil on medium-high in a large stockpot. Add the onions, parsnips, and carrots. Sauté for about 5 minutes or until lightly browned, stirring constantly. Reduce heat to medium and add the garlic and celery. Sauté for 5 minutes.

3. Add the parsley, thyme, bay leaves, juice, stock, and black pepper. Reduce heat to medium-low and simmer for 1½ hours, uncovered.

4. Fifteen minutes before the broth is finished, preheat oven to 350°F. Toss the Stuffed Rigatoni in olive oil, and place on a baking sheet. Roast the rigatoni for about 10 minutes, until golden brown.

5. Ladle the broth into serving bowls, and divide the roasted rigatoni evenly among the bowls.

Season to Taste

If something seems to be missing from your soup, it's usually salt! Salt brings out the flavor of soups. Unless you have specific health issues requiring you to limit your salt intake, season for ideal flavor. Don't stop adding spices until it tastes perfect.

Pasta with Rich Broth

Pastina is tiny star-shaped pasta that can be added to soups or cooked on its own and served with butter and grated cheese. Pastina with butter and cheese is a favorite dish of Italian-American children.

Serves 10

2 pounds chicken or turkey (bone-in)
Fresh-cracked black pepper
1 tablespoon olive oil
2 gallons Chicken Stock (page 14)
2 bunches fresh escarole
3 cups uncooked pastina
½ cup fresh-grated Asiago cheese

1. Rinse the chicken and pat dry with paper towels. Season with the black pepper. Heat the oil in a large stockpot over medium temperature. Brown the chicken on all sides.

2. Add the Chicken Stock and simmer for 2 hours, uncovered. Strain the broth through a fine-meshed sieve and discard the solids.

3. Bring the broth to a simmer. Clean and slice the escarole. Add the escarole and pastina to the broth. Cook for about 3 minutes, until the pastina is al dente.

4. Sprinkle each serving with the Asiago cheese.

Chilled Beet Soup

The natural sweetness of beets makes this a tasty soup. Always take special care when puréeing hot liquids—it is safer to cool them first.

Serves 10

2 pounds fresh beets, with tops
1 white onion
8 sprigs fresh thyme
1 gallon Vegetable Stock (page 16)
1 cup plain yogurt
Fresh-cracked black pepper

1. Peel and chop the beets. Peel and finely dice the onion. Clean the thyme and remove the leaves (discard the stems).

2. Simmer the beets in the stock with half the thyme for 1½ hours, uncovered. Let cool slightly, and carefully purée.

3. Ladle the soup into serving bowls. Garnish each with a dollop of the yogurt and sprinkle the onion, the remaining thyme, and pepper over the top.

2½ pounds pork meat
(bone-in)
½ bulb garlic
½ bunch fresh oregano
1 tablespoon olive oil
2 gallons Beef Stock (page 15)
1 cup dry red wine
2 cups fresh spinach leaves
½ recipe Acini di Pepe (page
109)
Fresh-cracked black pepper

Pork Soup with Acini di Pepe

*Browning the bones and meat before adding the stock is an
important step when making a meat soup. The small bits of meat that stick
to the pan during the browning process help flavor the broth.*

1. Remove the pork from the bones and finely dice the meat. Peel and
   mince the garlic. Clean the oregano and separate the leaves from the
   stems (discard the stems).

2. Heat the oil in a large stockpot over medium-high temperature. Add the
   pork meat and bones, and brown for about 10 minutes.

3. Reduce heat and add the stock, wine, garlic, and oregano. Simmer for
   2 hours, uncovered.

4. About 30 minutes before the broth is finished, steam the spinach for
   1 minute in a covered saucepan with ½ cup boiling water. Cook the
   Acini di Pepe according to the recipe's instructions.

5. Remove the bones from the soup. Just before serving, add the spinach
   and Acini di Pepe, and sprinkle with pepper.

Cheese Curls
*You can make cheese curls by scraping a block of hard, fresh cheese,
such as Parmesan or Romano, with a vegetable peeler. These curls
make an attractive and tasty garnish for soups, as well as pasta and
vegetable dishes.*

Chapter 3

Salads

Fresh Tomato Salad 32

Caesar Salad 33

Antipasto Salad 34

Fresh Mozzarella and Tomato Salad 35

Cannellini Bean Salad 36

Aunt Gloria's Italian Green Bean Salad 37

Wilted Kale Salad with Roasted Shallots 38

Lobster Salad 39

Bread Salad 40

Grilled Tuna Salad 40

Savoy Cabbage Salad 41

Celeriac Misto 42

Fresh Crab with Arugula Salad 43

Baby Greens with Apple and Mascarpone 43

Fig and Gorgonzola Salad 44

Cheese Tortellini Salad 45

Christmas Eve Salad 45

Hearty Cold Antipasto Salad 46

Eggplant Arugula Salad 47

Chilled Marinated Whitefish 48

Citrus Green-Bean Salad 48

2½ pounds fresh tomatoes
1 pound Vidalia onions
About 20 fresh basil leaves
2 tablespoons fresh basil tops
Extra-virgin olive oil
Fresh-cracked black pepper

Fresh Tomato Salad

Use beefsteak tomatoes or plum tomatoes for this recipe,
and only prepare this dish when tomatoes are in season.
Also, use only fresh herbs. If you cannot find fresh basil, you can
substitute ½ bunch oregano for a different but still delicious flavor.

1. Clean and wedge the tomatoes. Peel and finely slice the onions. Clean and gently slice the basil leaves, and clean the basil tops.

2. Mix together all the ingredients. Serve chilled.

Choosing Tomatoes
In season, use ripe vine tomatoes. Off-season, use quality canned rather than greenhouse tomatoes. Tomatoes should be aromatic; tomatoes with no aroma will have no taste. Avoid tomatoes with leathery, dark patches—this is a sign of blossom-end rot.

Caesar Salad

For "authentic" Caesar salad, use only romaine lettuce. But if you prefer, you may use another green or mix several different types.

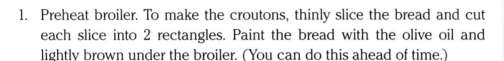

1. Preheat broiler. To make the croutons, thinly slice the bread and cut each slice into 2 rectangles. Paint the bread with the olive oil and lightly brown under the broiler. (You can do this ahead of time.)

2. To make the salad, thoroughly clean and dry the romaine. Roughly chop the leaves, and keep chilled. Clean and gently chop the parsley.

3. Whisk together the extra-virgin olive oil, eggs, vinegar, anchovy, cheese, pepper, and parsley.

4. Toss the romaine with the dressing, top with croutons, and serve.

Pasteurization Is Important

When using raw egg in a dish, such as the dressing in Caesar Salad, it is very important that you use pasteurized eggs. Pasteurization is not as important when cooking eggs in recipes, as any harmful bacteria will be killed during the cooking process. Raw eggs can carry salmonella and E. coli, *which can make you very ill.*

Serves 10

Croutons:
Crusty Italian bread
⅓ tablespoon olive oil

Salad:
3 heads romaine lettuce
¼ bunch fresh parsley
1 tablespoon extra-virgin olive oil
2 tablespoons pasteurized eggs
2 tablespoons balsamic vinegar
4 anchovy fillets
½ cup fresh-grated Parmesan cheese
Fresh-cracked black pepper

2 cups fresh mesclun greens
5 tomatoes
1 red onion
2 hard-boiled eggs
6 pepperoncini
½ pound capicola or
*   prosciutto*
½ pound Genoa salami or
*   soppressata*
½ pound provolone cheese,
*   sliced*
¼ pound pepperoni, sliced
¼ pound black olives
¼ pound green olives
3 anchovy fillets (optional)
½ cup salad dressing of
*   choice*

Antipasto Salad

Antipasto literally translates as "before the meal." In an authentic Italian restaurant, a whole section of the menu will be devoted to antipasto selections.

1. Gently clean and dry the greens. Clean and medium-dice the tomatoes. Peel and finely slice the onion.

2. Peel and slice the eggs. Leave the pepperoncini whole. Cut the capicola, salami, provolone, and pepperoni into thin strips.

3. Mound the greens in the center of a serving plate or platter. Arrange the other ingredients on top, and serve the salad dressing on the side at the table.

Antipasti

The Italian word for appetizer is antipasto. Although an antipasto course is not commonly found in Italian homes, it is a necessary element to all holiday meals and formal dinners. You will also find an antipasto section on the menu at most authentic Italian restaurants.

Fresh Mozzarella and Tomato Salad

Sliced fresh basil leaves sprinkled on top make a wonderful garnish for this popular salad. This addition will also make the salad more fragrant.

Serves 10

*1 pound fresh mozzarella
(in water)
2 pounds plum tomatoes
½ bunch fresh parsley
½ cup extra-virgin olive oil
½ cup roasted pine nuts
Fresh-cracked black pepper*

1. Remove the mozzarella from the water and pat dry. Slice thinly.

2. Clean and wedge the tomatoes. Clean and gently chop the parsley.

3. Arrange the cheese on a serving dish and top with the tomato slices. Drizzle with the oil and sprinkle with the pine nuts, parsley, and pepper.

Buying and Storing Leafy Greens
When buying greens such as escarole, kale, lettuce, and spinach, look for leafy parts that are tender but crisp. Store greens unwashed in sealed plastic bags. Rinse greens in cold water and pat dry with a paper towel right before use.

Serves 10

1 shallot
3 sprigs fresh thyme
1 lemon
3 cups cooked cannellini
    beans
⅓ cup extra-virgin olive oil
Fresh-cracked black pepper

Cannellini Bean Salad

If you use canned beans for this recipe, be sure to drain the beans, rinse them, and dry them thoroughly before mixing with the other ingredients.

1. Peel and mince the shallot. Clean the thyme and remove the leaves (discard the stems). Zest and juice the lemon. Thoroughly drain and dry the beans.

2. Mix together the shallot, thyme, oil, lemon juice, lemon zest, and black pepper.

3. Add the beans to the oil mixture, and combine thoroughly. Serve immediately.

Oil on Salads
When using olive oil for salads, it is best to use extra-virgin olive oil. Since it comes from the first pressing of the olives, it is more expensive but also more flavorful. Do not use extra-virgin olive oil for regular cooking, as it burns easily.

Aunt Gloria's Italian Green Bean Salad

*This simple dish is great to take on picnics.
It can be served chilled, slightly warm, or at room temperature.*

Serves 10

*2 pounds of chef or red
      potatoes
5 cups Italian flat green beans
2 red onions
⅔ cup extra-virgin olive oil
⅓ cup red wine vinegar
1 tablespoon dried oregano
Fresh-cracked black pepper*

1. Place the potatoes in a large pot and add enough water to cover. Simmer the potatoes until just fork-tender (do not overcook them). Drain well and dry in hot (400°F) oven for 2 minutes and let cool.

2. Fill a large pot with about 1 inch of water and bring to a simmer. Add the beans, and cook until just tender but still crisp. Drain well, shock in ice-cold water to stop cooking process, drain again, and let cool.

3. Peel and large-dice the potatoes. Peel and finely slice the onions.

4. Toss together all the ingredients in a large bowl, mixing well to distribute the spices and oil evenly.

Red Onions

Red onions are sweeter than white or yellow, but the taste is still very strong. If you are eating them raw, on sandwiches for example, the taste will be mellower if you soak the slices in cold water for 10 minutes, then drain and pat dry before using.

Serves 10

3 large bunches kale
10 cups shallots
⅓ cup olive oil
2 tablespoons balsamic
 vinegar
Coarse salt
Fresh-cracked black pepper

Wilted Kale Salad with Roasted Shallots

If you don't have kale, or you'd just like to try something different,
you can substitute escarole or even spinach.

1. Preheat oven to 375°F. Clean and dry the kale. Peel the shallots and leave whole.

2. Toss the shallots in the oil and place in a roasting pan and roast in the oven until fork-tender, about 20 minutes. Remove from oven and slice the shallots in half.

3. While shallots roast, quickly wilt the kale in 2 gallons of boiling water for 1 minute. Remove from heat, drain, and set aside to cool.

4. Serve by mounding the cooked kale in the center of a plate or platter. Top with the shallots, drizzle with the vinegar, and sprinkle with salt and pepper.

Lobster Salad

*Everyone loves the classic steamed lobster with
melted butter, but this salad gives lobster a whole new twist.
The herbs and spices create a fresh flavor.*

Serves 10

2 (2½-pound) live lobsters
2 bunches fresh parsley
3 leeks
3 gallons water
*2 cups white wine (such as
  pinot grigio)*
2 bay leaves
Juice of ½ lemon
1 tablespoon fresh lemon zest
⅓ cup extra-virgin olive oil
Kosher or coarse salt
Fresh-cracked black pepper

1. Rinse the lobsters in ice-cold water. Clean the parsley and leave whole. Thoroughly clean and finely slice the leeks (use green and white parts).

2. In a large stockpot, bring the water, wine, bay leaves, lemon juice, lemon zest, parsley, and leeks to a boil. Add the lobsters and cook for approximately 10 minutes, until the shells are red and the lobsters are thoroughly cooked. Remove the lobsters from the liquid with a slotted spoon. Allow the lobsters to cool, remove the meat from the shells, and cut into bite-sized chunks. Remove and discard the bay leaves and strain leek and parsley mixture.

3. Toss together the lobster and the wilted leek and parsley mixture. Drizzle with the oil and sprinkle with salt and pepper.

Bread Salad

Serves 10

2 large loaves crusty Italian
    bread
¼ bunch fresh parsley
¼ bunch fresh basil
⅔ cup extra-virgin olive oil
⅓ cup balsamic vinegar
2 tablespoons Roasted Garlic
    Paste (page 70)
⅓ cup fresh-grated Locatelli
    Romano cheese
Fresh-cracked black pepper

*This is one of those recipes that will really benefit from top-shelf extra-virgin
olive oil. Reserve inexpensive olive oil for other dishes.*

1. Slice and toast the bread. Cut into large dice. Clean and chop the parsley and basil.

2. Mix together the oil, vinegar, garlic paste, herbs, cheese, and pepper.

3. Toss with the bread and serve.

Grilled Tuna Salad

Serves 10

¼ cup olive oil
2 pounds fresh tuna steaks
Coarse salt
Fresh-cracked black pepper
20 tangerines
2 pomegranates
¼ bunch fresh parsley
½ teaspoon capers, rinsed

*Most grilled tuna salad recipes call for lemon or orange zest,
but other citrus fruits work just as well. This recipe calls for tangerines,
but you can use lime or grapefruit, too.*

1. Preheat grill. Lightly oil the fish and season with salt and pepper. Zest five of the tangerines using a citrus zester or vegetable peeler. Peel and section all of the tangerines. Remove the seeds from the pomegranates. Clean and chop the parsley.

2. Grill the tuna to desired doneness. Let cool, then thinly slice on the bias (at an angle).

3. Arrange the tuna and tangerines on a serving platter or plates. Drizzle with the remaining oil and sprinkle with the tangerine test, pomegranate seeds, parsley, and capers.

Savoy Cabbage Salad

*Fennel and anise seed can be used interchangeably.
Make this dish at least 8 hours ahead of time. You can prepare it
the night before and refrigerate until time to serve.*

Serves 10

1 head Savoy cabbage
3 bulbs fennel
3 Vidalia onions
3 cloves garlic
½ cup extra-virgin olive oil
⅓ cup white wine vinegar
3 anchovy fillets (optional)
Fresh-cracked black pepper
1 teaspoon fennel seeds

1. Clean and finely shred the cabbage and fennel bulbs. Peel and finely shred the onions. Peel and mince the garlic.

2. In a blender, mix together the oil, vinegar, and anchovy.

3. Toss the cabbage, fennel, and garlic with the oil mixture, the pepper, and fennel seeds.

4. Chill for at least 8 hours before serving.

Try Savoy

A head of Savoy cabbage is softer and more compact than the cabbage you are used to seeing in the market. The leaves are curlier, more wrinkled, and darker green in color. You can eat it raw by cutting it into very thin strips and seasoning it with balsamic vinegar, virgin olive oil, salt, and pepper.

1 lemon
3 celeriac (celery root)
2 large leeks
½ cup walnuts
½ cup Gorgonzola
¾ cup apple juice
½ cup extra-virgin olive oil
½ cup dried currants
Fresh-cracked black pepper

Celeriac Misto

Celeriac has a pretty mild flavor, but the extras in this salad really give it a tangy flavor. You can add more or fewer walnuts and currants according to your taste.

1. Zest and juice the lemon. Peel and shred the celeriac. In a bowl, soak the celeriac in cold water with 1 tablespoon of the fresh lemon juice for 2 minutes. Thoroughly clean and finely slice the leeks. Finely chop the walnuts.

2. Drain the celeriac and mix together all the ingredients. Serve.

Fennel
Available in winter, fennel (finocchio in Italian) has a delicate anise flavor and can be eaten raw—sliced and seasoned with virgin olive oil, lemon juice, pepper, and salt—or cooked in various ways. You can boil, broil, or fry fennel. It makes a great side dish to meat and can be the main ingredient in a salad.

Fresh Crab with Arugula Salad

*You can buy lump crabmeat in containers in the fresh fish
section of the market. Just be sure you don't pick up artificial crabmeat—
it is processed whitefish that is pressed and colored red.*

1. If shelling the crab, make sure all bits of shell are removed from the meat. If not precut, cut the crabmeat into bite-sized cubes.

2. Clean and dry the arugula. Clean and cut the plums in half (discard the pits).

3. To serve, mound the arugula on a serving platter and top with the crab and plums. Drizzle with the oil and vinegar, and sprinkle with salt and pepper.

Serves 10

2½ pounds fresh cooked
   crabmeat
2 bunches arugula
5 plums
½ cup extra-virgin olive oil
¼ cup white wine vinegar
Coarse salt
Fresh-cracked black pepper

Baby Greens with Apple and Mascarpone

*Sunflower seeds are good on this salad, but you may substitute
any other seed or nut (walnuts and slivered almonds work well),
or omit entirely if that is your preference.*

1. Thoroughly clean the greens. Zest and juice the lemon. Clean and thinly slice the apples.

2. Mix together the apples, lemon juice and zest, oil, and pepper.

3. Mound the greens on serving plates and top with the apple mixture, sunflower seeds, and dollops of the cheese.

Serves 10

5 cups baby salad greens
1 lemon
5 tart apples
2 tablespoons extra-virgin
   olive oil
Fresh-cracked black pepper
¼ cup shelled sunflower seeds
½ cup mascarpone cheese

2 toasted flatbreads of any flavor (see Chapter 6)
10 fresh figs
5 cups baby salad greens or mesclun
¼ bunch fresh parsley
¾ cup extra-virgin olive oil
½ cup orange juice
Fresh-cracked black pepper
½ cup crumbled Gorgonzola cheese

Fig and Gorgonzola Salad

Do not use dried figs for this recipe.
If you cannot find fresh figs, make another salad.
Figs come in white and black, and you can use either for this recipe.

1. Tear the toasted flatbread into bite-size pieces. Clean and wedge the figs. Clean and dry the greens. Clean and chop the parsley.

2. Whisk together the oil, orange juice, parsley, and pepper in large bowl.

3. Toss the figs, greens, parsley, and cheese with the oil mixture. Cover and refrigerate for 1 hour. Serve with the toasted flatbread pieces.

Figs

Fresh figs are a wonderful addition to salads. They are expensive, but a few go a long way. White figs, if you can find them, are pretty additions to any salad plate but there is virtually no difference in taste between the black and the white varieties.

Cheese Tortellini Salad

To prepare the tortellini for this salad, rinse with cold water after cooking, and lay out the tortellini in a single layer on wax paper to dry.

1. Peel and mince the shallots.

2. Clean and gently chop the marjoram leaves.

3. Mix together all the ingredients, and serve.

Serves 10

2 shallots
4 sprigs marjoram
½ recipe cooked Cheese
    Tortellini (page 136)
1 cup Roasted Eggplant Purée
    (page 72)
2 tablespoons extra-virgin
    olive oil
4 tablespoons red wine
    vinegar
Fresh-cracked black pepper

Christmas Eve Salad

*Cook the shrimp ahead of time to enable thorough chilling.
The eggplant can be prepared a few days early as well.*

1. Peel the shrimp and slice in half lengthwise. Cook quickly in boiling water. Drain and chill completely in the refrigerator or in ice-cold water (drain again if water is used).

2. Thoroughly clean and dry the greens. Peel and finely slice the onions. Mix together the ketchup, zest, and horseradish. Coat the shrimp with the ketchup mixture. Use a vegetable peeler to cut the Parmesan into fine curls. Remove the peel and pit from grapefruit with a sharp knife and cut the fruit into sections.

3. Mound the greens on a serving platter. Top with the onions, and place the pepperoni on one side and the eggplant on the other. Fan the grapefruit sections over the onion, then top with the shrimp and Parmesan curls. Drizzle with the oil and sprinkle with black pepper.

Serves 10

10 fresh extra-large shrimp,
    peeled and deveined
5 cups mixed baby greens
2 red onions
2 tablespoons ketchup
1 teaspoon lemon zest
1 teaspoon (or more to taste)
    prepared horseradish
¼ pound Parmesan cheese
2 grapefruit or oranges
1 cup thickly sliced pepperoni
1 cup Melanzane Marinate
    (Pickled Eggplants)
    (page 51)
¼ cup extra-virgin olive oil
Fresh-cracked black pepper

¼ cup pasteurized egg, or
   Egg Beaters
2 tablespoons Roasted Garlic
   Paste (page 70)
½ cup extra-virgin olive oil
¼ cup balsamic vinegar
3 anchovy fillets
Fresh-cracked black pepper
1 head romaine lettuce
2 red onions
2 hard-boiled eggs
12 Roasted Red Peppers
   (page 287)
¼ pound capicola,
   thinly sliced
¼ pound Genoa salami,
   thinly sliced
½ cup thinly sliced pepperoni
¼ cup black olives

Hearty Cold Antipasto Salad

*This is the perfect salad to serve at a picnic. It's full of delicious
ingredients and makes a colorful addition to your picnic table.
Just be sure it can rest in a cool, shaded spot.*

1. Prepare the Caesar dressing by emulsifying the egg, garlic paste, oil, vinegar, anchovy, and black pepper in a food processor or blender.

2. Clean the lettuce and remove the outer leaves and heart. Discard the heart and set aside the outer leaves. Gently chop the remainder into bite-sized pieces. Peel and slice the onions and hard-boiled eggs. Thickly dice the red peppers. Cut each slice of meat into quarters.

3. Lay out the large romaine leaves on a platter. Mix the chopped lettuce with the dressing and mound on top of the base leaves. Arrange the onion, egg, red pepper, meats, and olives decoratively on top. Serve.

Tired of Romaine?

*To add variety to your salads, experiment with the many types of greens
that are available in most markets. Oak leaf, frisée, arugula, spinach,
and dandelion are just a few. You can use one type or mix a few different varieties together for more color and texture.*

Eggplant Arugula Salad

*Don't use a highly flavored dressing on this salad—it will overpower
the delicate mix of flavors. A simple vinaigrette of extra-virgin olive oil
and a good balsamic vinegar, like the one here, is perfect.*

Serves 10

3 eggplants
3 shallots
½ bulb garlic
2 bunches arugula
3 ripe peaches or nectarines
5 ounces Parmesan cheese
2 tablespoons olive oil
⅓ cup pine nuts
½ cup extra-virgin olive oil
¼ cup balsamic vinegar
Fresh-cracked black pepper

1. Preheat oven to 375°F. Slice the eggplants in half lengthwise. Peel and finely dice the shallots. Peel and mince the garlic. Clean and dry the arugula. Cut the peaches into small wedges. Shave the Parmesan into thin curls using a vegetable peeler.

2. Rub the eggplant with the 2 tablespoons olive oil. Place the eggplant halves face down-in a baking pan and roast for approximately 45 minutes, until soft. Toast the pine nuts in the oven on a baking sheet until lightly brown. Allow the eggplant and pine nuts to cool.

3. To prepare the vinaigrette, blend the extra-virgin olive oil and vinegar.

4. Scoop out the eggplant flesh and toss with the shallots and garlic. Mound on serving plates. Arrange the arugula and cheese on one side and the peaches on the other. Drizzle with the vinaigrette and sprinkle with the toasted pine nuts and black pepper.

Serves 10

2 red onions
6 lemons
6 sprigs fresh oregano
6 plum tomatoes
3½ pounds fresh cod,
    flounder, or other light
    whitefish
¼ cup extra-virgin olive oil
Kosher salt
Fresh-cracked black pepper

Chilled Marinated Whitefish

No, this recipe isn't missing a step.
The fish is cooked by marinating it in the acidic lemon juice.

1. Peel and roughly slice the onions. Zest and juice the lemons. Clean and chop the oregano leaves. Clean and slice the tomatoes.

2. Mix together all the ingredients *except* the tomatoes and let marinate in the refrigerator for at least 4 hours but no longer than 8 hours.

3. Sprinkle with salt and pepper and serve with the tomatoes.

Serves 10

5 cups fresh green beans
½ cup hazelnuts
½ bunch fresh chives or
    scallions
½ cup fresh-grated Asiago
    cheese
½ cup extra-virgin olive oil
¾ cup orange juice
Fresh-cracked black pepper

Citrus Green-Bean Salad

The Italian cooking term al dente, which normally refers
to pasta, can also be used when cooking vegetables for salads.
The green beans in this recipe should be cooked until just al dente, or
until there is a bit of a crunch when you bite into them.

1. Clean and cut off the ends of the green beans. Crush the hazelnuts. Clean and slice the chives.

2. Blanch the green beans and shock in ice water.

3. Mix together all the ingredients, and serve.

Chapter 4

Appetizers

Clam-Stuffed Portobellos 50

Fresh Vegetable Dip with Crusty Italian Bread 51

Melanzane Marinate (Pickled Eggplants) 51

Melon and Prosciutto 52

Creamy Crab Appetizers 52

Baked Mixed Cheese Hors d'oeuvres 53

Garlic and Olive Bruschetta 54

Spicy Chicken Wings 55

Marinated Beef Skewers 55

Oregano Pork Ribs 56

Orange Shrimp 56

Pomodori Ripieni (Stuffed Roma Tomatoes) 57

Seafood Sausage Bread 58

Artichoke Leaves 58

Gorgonzola Browned Pears 59

Sausage-Filled Shallots 59

Frittura di Paranza (Pan-Fried Smelts) 60

Lobster Capicola 61

Grilled Pork Cubes 62

Cheese-Filled Prunes 62

Serves 10

1 tablespoon olive oil
5 fresh portobello
    mushrooms
1 cup dry white wine
2 dozen littleneck clams
4 large slices crusty Italian
    bread
6 fresh chives
1 cup Easy Alfredo Sauce
    (page 69)
Fresh-cracked black pepper

Clam-Stuffed Portobellos

*Portobello mushrooms are not a native Italian variety, but they are
used frequently in Italian-American cuisine. Portobellos can be found in most
large supermarkets, either loose, packaged whole, or cleaned and sliced.*

1. Preheat oven to 375°F. Lightly grease a large baking dish with the oil.
    Clean the mushrooms and remove the stems. Finely dice the mush-
    room stems.

2. Place the mushroom caps, stemmed-side up, in a baking dish along
    with the wine. Cover, and bake for 8 minutes.

3. Remove the clams from the shells, discard the shells, and clean the
    clams well. Chop the clam meat. Toast and finely dice the bread. Clean
    and slice the chives. Mix together the mushroom stems, clams, bread,
    chives, and Alfredo sauce.

4. Mound the clam mixture on top of the mushroom caps in the baking
    dish, and sprinkle with the pepper. Cover, and bake for approximately
    10 minutes.

Cleaning Mushrooms
*Mushrooms should not be washed in water since they absorb liquid like
a sponge. Instead, use a soft brush or damp paper towel and scrub the
mushrooms thoroughly. You simply want to remove any dirt or pebbles
that might remain from when the mushrooms were picked.*

Fresh Vegetable Dip
with Crusty Italian Bread

This is not a "classic" Italian dish, but it is a great recipe to use for entertaining. This dip can be served as an appetizer before a meal or as a snack.

1. Cut the bread into an oval bowl by hollowing out the center piece. Cut the center piece into bite-sized chunks.

2. Peel and finely grate the carrots. Clean and chop the arugula. Peel and mince the onions and garlic.

3. Mix together the carrots, arugula, onions, garlic, pepper flakes, mayonnaise, and sour cream.

4. Fill the bread bowl with the dip mixture and serve with the bread chunks for dipping.

Serves 10

1 loaf fresh crusty Italian bread
2 carrots
2 bunches arugula
2 red onions
½ bulb garlic
1 teaspoon red pepper flakes
1½ cups mayonnaise
1½ cups sour cream

Melanzane Marinate
(Pickled Eggplants)

This preparation is also great for marinating other vegetables, such as baby onions, carrots, cauliflower, peppers, celery, string beans, or cucumbers.

1. Clean and cut the eggplants into long strips. Peel and thinly slice the onion. Peel and mince the garlic.

2. Simmer all the ingredients in a large stockpot for 20 minutes.

3. Chill before serving. This dish can keep in the refrigerator for 1 month.

Serves 10

2 eggplants
1 yellow onion
½ bulb garlic
1 cup granulated sugar
2 cups white wine vinegar
2 bay leaves
5 sprigs fresh thyme

*1 large fresh honeydew or
    cantaloupe*
*½ pound fresh prosciutto,
    very thinly sliced*

Melon and Prosciutto

*Similar to the pairing of figs and Gorgonzola, the sweetness of melon
and the saltiness of prosciutto are a perfect combination.*

1. Peel the melon and cut the fruit into 10 wedges.

2. Wrap or drape each wedge with 1 slice of prosciutto, and serve.

Appetizer Advice
*Appetizers should complement the meal to come, not overpower it.
Serve items that have milder but similar flavors to the main dish. Also,
don't offer so many appetizers that your guests are full by the time the
main meal arrives. Keep appetizers simple and subtle.*

Serves 10

3 sprigs fresh basil
1 pound fresh lump crabmeat
1 cup sour cream
Fresh-cracked black pepper
*½ recipe Basic Pasta Dough
    (page 100), uncooked
    and unrolled*
1 cup vegetable oil

Creamy Crab Appetizers

*Similar to Chinese fried dumplings, these delicious appetizers
make great finger food for entertaining.*

1. Clean and gently slice the basil leaves. Mix together the basil, crab, sour cream, and fresh pepper.

2. Roll out the pasta dough to ¼ inch thickness and cut into 3-inch squares. Place 1 tablespoon of the crab mixture in the center of each square. Fold each square in half and seal tightly. Use a little water to help seal the ends if needed.

3. Heat the oil to medium-high temperature in a deep skillet. Fry the pouches until golden brown.

4. Drain on paper towels, and serve.

Baked Mixed Cheese Hors d'oeuvres

Serve these appetizers warm out of the oven and top with Fruit Chutney (page 77) for a hint of sweetness.

Serves 10

2 tablespoons olive oil
¼ cup Gorgonzola cheese
1½ cups mascarpone (or substitute cream)
¼ cup shredded fontina cheese
½ pasta recipe of choice (see Chapter 7, page 99)

1. Preheat oven to 350°F. Grease a baking sheet with 1 tablespoon of the oil.

2. Mix together all the cheeses thoroughly.

3. Roll out the dough to ½-inch thickness in a large rectangle. Paint the top of the dough with the remaining oil. Spread the cheese on top of the oiled dough. Carefully roll up the dough like a jellyroll and cut the log into slices.

4. Place the rolled pasta on the prepared baking sheet. Bake for 5 to 8 minutes or until golden brown. Serve.

Dessert "Cheese"
Mascarpone cheese is not really a cheese. It is actually a very rich cream that has been soured with fermenting bacteria. It is made in the Lombardy region, usually in the winter. It is commonly used as a filling in Italian desserts.

¼ bunch fresh parsley
1 cup black olives, pitted
½ bulb roasted garlic (see
    Roasted Garlic Paste,
    page 70, for garlic
    roasting instructions)
Kosher salt
Fresh-cracked black pepper
2 tablespoons virgin olive oil
1 loaf Italian bread

Garlic and Olive Bruschetta

*For more color and flavor you can add
tomatoes to the purée in this recipe.*

1. Preheat oven to 400°F. Clean and chop the parsley.

2. Purée the olives and garlic in a food processor. Add the parsley, salt, pepper, and oil, and blend thoroughly.

3. Slice the bread thinly and lay it out on a baking sheet.

4. Toast bread in the oven for 10 minutes. Spread the olive purée on the bread, and serve.

Keeping Herbs Fresh
It's easy to prolong the life of your fresh herbs. Simply wrap the stems in plastic wrap and stand them up in a tall glass that is filled halfway with cold water. Store in the refrigerator and use when needed.

Spicy Chicken Wings

*This Italian version of Buffalo chicken wings makes great party food.
Just be sure to put out plenty of napkins for your guests!*

Serves 10

3 sprigs fresh oregano
½ teaspoon red pepper flakes
2 tablespoons olive oil
2 tablespoons unsalted butter
Fresh-cracked black pepper
4 pounds chicken wings

1. Clean and gently chop the oregano leaves.

2. Mix together the oregano, red pepper flakes, oil, butter, and black pepper in a deep dish. Add the chicken wings and coat completely in the marinade. Let marinate in the refrigerator for at least 1 hour.

3. Preheat oven to 400°F.

4. Roast the marinated chicken for 15 to 20 minutes, until thoroughly cooked.

Marinated Beef Skewers

*The garlicky, nutty flavor of the marinade lends
a unique taste to these beef appetizers.*

Serves 10

2½ pounds sirloin beef
½ cup walnuts
*½ bulb roasted garlic (see
   Roasted Garlic Paste
   recipe for roasting
   instructions, page 70)*
¼ cup olive oil
½ cup dry red wine
Fresh-cracked black pepper

1. Thinly slice and skewer the beef. Place the skewers in a single layer in a baking dish large enough for the skewers to lie flat.

2. In a blender, finely grind the walnuts, then add the roasted (peeled) garlic cloves, oil, wine, and black pepper. Blend completely, and pour over the beef skewers in the dish, making sure to coat all the beef completely. Marinate the beef in the refrigerator no longer than 2 hours (the acid in the wine will "cook" the meat if left in too long).

3. Preheat oven to 400°F. Roast the skewers for 10 to 15 minutes. Serve hot.

Serves 10

4 cloves garlic
4 sprigs fresh oregano
3 tablespoons olive oil
1 tablespoon balsamic
    vinegar
Kosher salt
Fresh-cracked black pepper
3 pounds bone-in pork ribs

Oregano Pork Ribs

These spicy, finger-licking good ribs are an interesting variation
of the traditional barbecue sauce version.

1. Peel and mince the garlic. Clean and gently chop the oregano leaves. Blend together the garlic, oregano, oil, vinegar, salt, and pepper.

2. Place the ribs in a baking dish and completely coat all the meat in the oil mixture. Let marinate in the refrigerator for 8 to 12 hours.

3. Preheat oven to 400°F. Roast the ribs, uncovered, for 45 to 60 minutes. Serve.

Serves 10

2 pounds large shrimp
3 oranges
2 shallots
Fresh-cracked black pepper
1 teaspoon capers, rinsed
2 tablespoons olive oil

Orange Shrimp

The extra citrus-flavored sauce used in this recipe can be poured
into a small bowl and set aside for dipping.

1. Peel and devein the shrimp, but leave the tails on. Zest and juice the oranges. Peel and mince the shallots.

2. Mix together the orange juice, zest, shallots, pepper, capers, and oil.

3. Heat the oil mixture in a pan over medium-high temperature.

4. Quickly cook the shrimp in the oil mixture for about 2 or 3 minutes, until opaque in the center.

5. Remove the shrimp from the oil mixture and serve on a platter with a toothpick in each.

Pomodori Ripieni
(Stuffed Roma Tomatoes)

Roma tomatoes are also known as "plum" tomatoes and are smaller and more oblong in shape than beefsteak tomatoes. They are good for use in stuffing recipes because they generally have firmer meat, less juice, and fewer seeds.

Serves 10

20 Roma tomatoes
4 sprigs fresh basil
3 thick slices Italian bread
½ cup shredded provolone
*   cheese*
Fresh-cracked black pepper
1 tablespoon olive oil

1. Preheat oven to 400°F. Slice the tomatoes in half and scoop out and reserve the insides. Clean and gently slice the basil. Medium-dice the bread.

2. Mix together the tomato insides, basil, bread, cheese, and pepper in a medium-sized bowl.

3. Stuff each tomato half with the mixture. Place on baking sheet, drizzle with oil, and sprinkle with pepper. Roast for 8 minutes. Serve immediately.

Basil
Basil is an herb in the mint family and goes particularly well with tomato. Basil is also the main ingredient in pesto sauce. Basil is a good choice if you are picking one or two herbs to grow in a small kitchen garden. Most Italian dishes call for at least bit of fresh basil.

Seafood Sausage Bread

Serves 10

1 recipe Basic Flatbread (page 80)
¼ pound fontina cheese
1 recipe Seafood Sausage (page 215), unformed and uncooked

If you do not have time to make the flatbread recipe, you can substitute any kind of bread. A thinly sliced Italian loaf works well.

1. Preheat oven to 400°F. Lightly toast the flatbread and cut into small triangles. Shred the cheese.

2. Spread the toast with the sausage and top with the cheese.

3. Bake for 10 to 15 minutes, and serve hot.

Artichoke Leaves

Serves 10

1 tablespoon olive oil
3 whole artichokes
½ recipe Three-Meat Meatballs (page 201), unformed and uncooked

The most popular way to eat artichokes is to stuff them and then braise or bake them. The heart can be boiled, fried, or baked.

1. Preheat oven to 425°F. Lightly grease a baking sheet with the oil. Remove the outer leaves from the artichokes and snip off the prickly triangular end of each leaf.

2. Quickly blanch the leaves in boiling water, and shock in ice water to stop the cooking process.

3. Mound a spoonful of the meatball mixture on top of each leaf and place on the greased baking sheet. Roast for 8 minutes, and serve.

Gorgonzola Browned Pears

You can substitute apples for pears or substitute any citrus fruit for the oranges in this recipe. This is a great appetizer to experiment with.

1. Preheat broiler. Lightly grease a baking sheet with 1 teaspoon of the oil. Clean, zest, and juice the oranges. Clean and wedge the pears, leaving the skin intact.

2. Toss the pears in the remaining oil and the orange juice. Place the pears skin-side down on the prepared baking sheet. Sprinkle the cheese over the pears; then drizzle with the honey. Sprinkle with the zest and black pepper.

3. Quickly broil until browned, and serve immediately.

Serves 10

2½ teaspoons olive oil
2 large oranges
5 large pears (any variety)
½ cup crumbled Gorgonzola
    cheese
1 teaspoon honey
Fresh-cracked black pepper

Sausage-Filled Shallots

This recipe is just as wonderful made with Vidalia onions, especially if you find the smaller shallots difficult to work with.

1. Preheat oven to 375°F. Lightly grease a baking sheet with the oil. Carefully peel and slice the shallots in half lengthwise so you can remove the centers of the shallots. Mince the centers.

2. Mix the shallot centers with the sausage.

3. Place the shallot halves in a microwave-safe dish with the wine, bay leaf, and black pepper. Cook for 3 minutes or until the shallots are al dente. Let cool.

4. Stuff the hollowed shallots with the sausage mixture. Place on the prepared baking sheet. Bake for 20 minutes, and serve hot.

Serves 10

1 teaspoon olive oil
4 fresh shallots
½ recipe Rosemary Lamb
    Sausage (page 221),
    unformed and uncooked
2 cups white table wine
1 bay leaf
Fresh-cracked black pepper

Serves 10

¾ pound fresh smelts
1 cup all-purpose flour
1 tablespoon baking powder
1 tablespoon garlic powder
½ cup milk
2 tablespoons olive oil
Kosher salt
Fresh-cracked black pepper
½ cup balsamic vinegar
(optional)

Frittura di Paranza (Pan-Fried Smelts)

*Eat fried smelts like you eat corn on the cob—
nibble the flesh off the bone. Serve with green salad.*

1. Clean the smelts in ice-cold water and pat dry. Sift together the flour, baking powder, and garlic powder onto a plate. Pour the milk into a shallow bowl.

2. Heat the oil on medium temperature in a large sauté pan. Dust the smelts with the flour mixture, dip in the milk, and then dust with the flour again. Gently place in the oil.

3. Fry the smelts on each side for approximately 3 to 5 minutes or until browned and thoroughly cooked. Drain on a rack with paper towel beneath to catch the drippings.

4. Sprinkle with salt and pepper. Drizzle with balsamic vinegar, if desired, and serve hot.

Balsamic Vinegar
There are various types of Italian vinegar, but perhaps the most famous is balsamic vinegar. Balsamic vinegar is made from reduced wine and aged in special wood barrels for years. Each year's barrels are made of a different type of wood—the vinegar absorbs the flavor of the wood. Authentic balsamic vinegar ages for a minimum of 10 and up to 30 years.

Lobster Capicola

Soaking the skewers in water before threading the food onto them prevents them from burning when placed on the heat.

Serves 10

1 teaspoon olive oil
5 large lobster tails
10 thin slices capicola

1. Soak 10 wood skewers in water for about 15 minutes. Preheat oven to 400°F. Lightly grease a baking sheet with the olive oil.

2. Remove the shells from the lobster tails and slice the tails in half, lengthwise. Carefully wrap each tail half in 1 slice of the capicola, and thread each onto a skewer.

3. Place the skewers on the prepared baking sheet. Roast for 5 to 8 minutes, until heated through and the capicola is crispy.

Capicola
Capicola is an Italian ham "cold cut" purchased in the deli section of the supermarket. It is spicier than regular ham and also comes in a "hot" spicy variety. Commonly known as "cappy," ham capicola can be used in sandwiches, salads, and cooking, or eaten cold.

Serves 10

2 pounds thick boneless pork
    loin
1 teaspoon olive oil
Fresh-cracked black pepper
2 cups apple juice
Kosher salt

Grilled Pork Cubes

*The complementary flavors of pork and apple work perfectly
together in this simple but delicious recipe.*

1. Preheat grill to high heat. Rub the pork with the oil and season with the pepper.

2. In a small saucepan over high heat, reduce the juice by half the volume (about 1 cup).

3. Grill the pork to desired doneness. Transfer to a plate and tent with foil to keep warm. Let rest for about 5 minutes. Cut the pork into large cubes.

4. Serve on small skewers, drizzled with the reduced apple juice and sprinkled with salt.

Serves 10

2 cups prunes
½ cup pecans or walnuts
¾ cup mascarpone cheese
½ cup ricotta cheese

Cheese-Filled Prunes

*The softness of the prunes and cheese paired with the crunchiness
of the nuts in this recipe creates a fun texture.*

1. Cut the prunes into hollow halves. Finely chop the pecans.

2. Mix together the cheeses. Stir half the chopped pecans into the cheese mixture.

3. Stuff each prune with the cheese mixture and sprinkle with the remaining pecans. Serve.

Chapter 5

Sauces

Old World Gravy (Long-Cooking Tomato Sauce) 64

Fra Diavolo (Spicy Old World Gravy) 65

New World Fresh Sauce 66

Salsa Besciamella (Béchamel Sauce) 67

Mozzarella and Ricotta Cheese Sauce 68

Mascarpone Cheese Sauce 69

Easy Alfredo Sauce 69

Roasted Garlic Paste 70

Cannellini Bean Purée 70

Traditional Pesto 71

Roasted Eggplant Purée 72

Walnut Pesto 73

Oregano-Almond Pesto 73

Rosemary Pesto 74

Sage Pesto 74

Brown Sauce 75

Italian Pepperoncini Gremolata 76

Minty Fruit Chutney 76

Fruit Chutney 77

Makes 1 gallon

3 Vidalia onions
1 bulb garlic
6 pounds plum tomatoes
1 bunch fresh basil
½ bunch fresh oregano or
    marjoram
½ bunch fresh parsley
1 tablespoon olive oil
2½ pounds pork spare ribs
    (or any pork meat with
    bones)
1 pound Italian sausage
    (casings removed)
8 cups stock of choice (see
    Chapter 2, page 13)
Kosher salt
Fresh-cracked black pepper

Old World Gravy
(Long-Cooking Tomato Sauce)

*You can customize this sauce by adding different meats or poultry.
Poultry makes a thinner sauce. Always brown or thoroughly cook
your meat before adding it to the sauce.*

1. Peel and dice the onions. Peel and mince the garlic. Clean and roughly chop the tomatoes. Clean and gently chop the herbs.

2. Heat the oil to medium-high temperature in a large stockpot. Add the ribs and sausage, and brown for 10 minutes. Add the onions and garlic. Sauté for 5 minutes, then add the tomatoes and stock. Reduce heat to low and simmer for 3 hours, uncovered, stirring occasionally.

3. Add the herbs and spices, and simmer for a minimum of 3 more hours, uncovered and stirring occasionally.

4. Adjust seasonings to taste, and serve or store as desired. Store in sealed containers and refrigerate for up to 5 days or freeze for up to 3 months.

Gravy or Sauce?
When most Americans hear the word gravy, they think of thick brown sauce that is ladled over turkey, pork, or beef. However, in Italian cooking, "gravy" is the term used for red sauce to be served with meatballs over pasta.

Fra Diavolo
(Spicy Old World Gravy)

You will likely see Fra Diavolo sauce offered over lobster or seafood and pasta in restaurants; however, you can use this spicy version of Old World Gravy just like regular marinara— over pasta or pasta and meatballs.

Makes 1 gallon

4 yellow onions
1 bulb garlic
7 pounds plum tomatoes
½ bunch fresh parsley
1 tablespoon olive oil
1 pound pork bones
1 pound hot Italian pepperoni
1½ pounds Italian sausage (casings removed)
1 cup hearty red drinking wine
8 cups Beef Stock (page 15)
½ tablespoon red pepper flakes
Fresh-cracked black pepper
1 teaspoon garlic powder

1. Peel and dice the onions. Peel and mince the garlic. Clean and roughly chop the tomatoes. Clean and gently chop the parsley.

2. Heat the oil to medium-high temperature in a large stockpot. Add the pork bones, pepperoni, and sausage, and brown for 10 minutes. Add the onions and garlic, and sauté for 5 minutes. Add the tomatoes, wine, and stock. Reduce heat to low and simmer for 3 hours, uncovered and stirring occasionally.

3. Add the herbs and spices, and simmer for 2 more hours, uncovered and stirring occasionally.

4. Adjust seasoning to taste, and serve or store as desired. Store in sealed containers and refrigerate for up to 5 days or freeze for up to 3 months.

New World Fresh Sauce

Makes 1 gallon

7 pounds plum tomatoes
1 bulb garlic
2 shallots
½ bunch fresh basil
1 tablespoon olive oil
¼ cup pine nuts
Fresh-cracked black pepper

This sauce is called "fresh" because it has no meat and only needs to simmer for 1 hour—as opposed to the long-cooking traditional gravies.

1. Clean and chop the tomatoes. Peel and mince the garlic and shallots. Clean and chop the basil.

2. Heat the oil to medium temperature in a large stockpot.

3. Add all the remaining ingredients. Reduce temperature to low and simmer for 1 hour, uncovered. Serve. (Do not store. This sauce should be prepared fresh every time.)

Herb Arithmetic
Dried herbs are stronger than fresh, and powdered herbs are stronger than dried herbs. Here's a rule of thumb: ½ teaspoon of powered herb equals ¾ to 1 teaspoon of crumbled herb equals 2 teaspoons of fresh herb. If a recipe calls for fresh but you only have dried, go ahead and substitute—just be sure you adjust the amount accordingly.

Salsa Besciamella
(Béchamel Sauce)

Various flavorings can be stirred in at the end of the cooking process, just before serving. Some examples are tomato paste, cooked shrimp, parsley, capers, or egg (if the sauce will be an ingredient in a baked dish).

Makes 1 gallon

½ cup (1 stick) unsalted butter
¼ cup olive oil
¾ cup all-purpose flour
1½ gallons whole milk
½ gallon Chicken or
    Vegetable Stock (pages
    14 and 16)
¾ cup fresh-grated pecorino
    Romano cheese

1. Melt the butter in large saucepan over medium temperature, then add the oil. Sprinkle in the flour, and stir with a wooden spoon.

2. Whisk in the milk and stock, and increase temperature to medium-high. Simmer until the sauce thickens, about 10 minutes.

3. Remove from heat and stir in the cheese. This is best fresh, but it could be stored in the refrigerator in a sealed container for a couple of days.

Aged Cheese
Pecorino Romano is a type of aged cheese sometimes used in recipes that call for Parmesan cheese because it is a less expensive variety. Romano is aged under 1 year, while Parmesan is aged from 18 months to 5 years. Another feature that makes Parmesan more expensive is that it is made only from whole milk that comes from cows, which are fed only fresh grass.

Makes 1 gallon

¼ cup olive oil
¾ cup all-purpose flour
1 gallon Chicken or Vegetable
   Stock (pages 14 and 16)
1 cup whole milk
1 tablespoon fresh chopped
   oregano
1 pound mozzarella cheese,
   shredded (preferably
   fresh mozzarella in the
   water)
32 ounces ricotta cheese

Mozzarella and Ricotta Cheese Sauce

Both of these cheeses have a high salt content. So, when you are using this sauce over pasta, do not add salt to the boiling water.

1. Heat the oil to medium temperature in a large saucepan. Sprinkle in the flour, and stir with a wooden spoon.

2. Whisk in the stock, milk, and oregano. Simmer until the sauce thickens, about 10 minutes.

3. Remove from heat and stir in both cheeses. This is best fresh, but it can be stored in a sealed container for 2 days in the refrigerator.

Cutting Down on Salt

Cheese sauces can be used on many kinds of dishes. But when using a cheese sauce over pasta, it is a good idea to omit the salt that is usually put in the water to boil the pasta. Although it is a matter of personal taste, the saltiness of the cheese combined with the extra salt in the water might make the dish too salty.

Mascarpone Cheese Sauce

Mascarpone is made from soured cream. It has a creamy, soft texture and is often used as a filling for sweets and cakes, the most famous being tiramisu.

Makes 4 cups

½ cup (1 stick) unsalted butter
½ cup all-purpose flour
4 cups whole milk
2 cups light cream
8 ounces mascarpone

1. Melt the butter in a large saucepan over medium temperature. Sprinkle in the flour, and stir with a wooden spoon.

2. Whisk in the milk and cream (be careful not to scorch the sauce). Simmer until the sauce thickens, about 10 minutes.

3. Remove from heat and stir in the cheese. (Do not store. This is best made fresh for each use.)

Easy Alfredo Sauce

This rich sauce can be served over pasta or as a dip for focaccia bread or raw vegetables.

Makes 4 cups

6 cups heavy cream
1 cup fresh-grated Parmesan
Fresh-cracked black pepper

1. In a large saucepan, bring the cream to a simmer over medium heat. Reduce the cream to 4 cups.

2. Remove from heat, sprinkle in the cheese and pepper, and stir until smooth. This is best fresh, but it can be stored in a sealed container for 2 days in the refrigerator.

Makes 2 cups

8 large bulbs garlic
½ cup olive oil

Roasted Garlic Paste

This simple paste has many uses.
The most popular is for making bruschetta.

1. Preheat oven to 400°F. Slice the unpeeled bulbs in half crosswise. Pour the oil into a roasting pan. Place the garlic cut-side down in the pan, and cover tightly with a lid or foil.

2. Roast for 10 minutes, until the cloves are completely softened.

3. Let cool, and peel each clove. Mash the garlic cloves into a paste.

Makes 2 cups

2 cups dry cannellini beans
1½ gallons Vegetable Stock
  (page 16)
¼ bunch fresh parsley, stems
  only
1 bulb garlic
2 bay leaves
½ cup extra-virgin olive oil
Fresh-cracked black pepper

Cannellini Bean Purée

For variety, you can use other beans in this recipe, such as
kidney beans, chickpeas, navy beans, or black beans. Just remember that the
dried beans must be soaked in stock overnight before using.

1. Soak the beans overnight in ¾ gallon of the stock.

2. Drain the beans and discard the stock. Clean and chop the parsley stems. Peel and mince the garlic.

3. Place the beans in a large stockpot with the remaining stock, the parsley, garlic, and bay leaves. Set lid ajar and simmer over medium heat, until the beans are thoroughly cooked, about 1½ hours.

4. Drain, and remove the bay leaves. Purée beans in a food processor until smooth. Use as desired, drizzled with the oil and sprinkled with pepper.

Traditional Pesto

*Pesto can stand on its own as a sauce, or you can use just
a spoonful to add extra flavor to a number of other dishes—
especially stews, soups, and sauces.*

Makes 2 cups

2 bunches fresh basil
½ bulb garlic
½ cup toasted pine nuts
1 cup extra-virgin olive oil

1. Clean and roughly chop the basil. Peel and roughly chop the garlic.

2. In a food processor, pulse the basil, garlic, and nuts until well chopped and blended. Pour in the oil and blend until relatively smooth. Do not store—pesto should be made fresh for each use.

Freshness Is Essential

Do not even attempt to make pesto unless you have fresh herbs available. While dried herbs can be substituted in some recipes, only the freshest herbs will suffice in a pesto. Additionally, fresh herbs are the most aromatic, and a plate of steaming pasta with pesto should fill your house with a savory aroma.

Makes 2 cups

1 tablespoon olive oil
2 medium eggplants
8 cloves garlic
¼ bunch fresh oregano
Fresh-cracked black pepper

Roasted Eggplant Purée

You don't need to peel the eggplant before preparing this recipe.
The peel softens during cooking.

1. Preheat the oven to 375°F. Lightly grease a large baking sheet with ½ tablespoon of the oil. Slice the eggplants in half lengthwise. Peel and mince the garlic. Clean and gently chop the oregano.

2. Rub the eggplant with the remaining oil and sprinkle with the garlic, oregano, and pepper. Roast for 45 minutes, until fork-tender.

3. Let cool, then purée in a food processor. Store in a sealed container and refrigerate for up to 5 days or freeze for up to 3 months.

Fresh-Cracked Black Pepper
Like many seeds, a peppercorn's best flavor remains locked inside until it is smashed. If you don't have a pepper mill, take 10 peppercorns and fold them inside wax paper. Place on a flat, hard surface. Use a small skillet or saucepan to apply pressure, pushing with the heel of your hand to break the seeds a few at a time.

Walnut Pesto

With any pesto recipe, you can stir ½ cup grated Romano or Parmesan cheese into the sauce just before using for an extra kick of flavor.

1. Clean and roughly chop parsley. Peel and roughly chop garlic. Use a citrus zester or vegetable peeler to zest the lemon.

2. In a food processor, pulse the parsley, garlic, and walnuts until well chopped and blended. Pour in the oil, and blend until fairly smooth.

3. Stir in the lemon zest before serving. Do not store—pesto should be made fresh for each use.

Makes 2 cups

2 bunches fresh parsley
½ bulb garlic
1 lemon
½ cup walnuts
1 cup extra-virgin olive oil

Oregano-Almond Pesto

If your pesto is too thick, take a tablespoon of the boiling water from your pasta pot and stir it into the pesto to thin it out. This is also a good trick to warm pesto that has been refrigerated.

1. Clean the oregano. Remove the leaves from the stems and roughly chop the leaves (discard the stems). Peel and roughly chop the garlic.

2. In a food processor, pulse the oregano, garlic, and almonds until well chopped and blended. Pour in the oil, and blend until fairly smooth. Do not store—pesto should be made fresh for each use.

Makes 2 cups

2 bunches fresh oregano
½ bulb garlic
½ cup almonds
1 cup extra-virgin olive oil

Makes 2 cups

1 cup chestnuts in shells
1 bunch fresh rosemary
½ bulb garlic
1 fresh shallot
1 cup extra-virgin olive oil
Fresh-cracked black pepper

Rosemary Pesto

An important rule with pesto is to make it only when fresh herbs are available.
Dried herbs won't give the same flavor or texture.

1. Preheat the oven to 375°F. Slit the chestnuts with a sharp knife. Place the chestnuts on a baking sheet, and roast for 10 minutes. Once the chestnuts are cool enough to handle, shell and roughly chop the nuts.

2. Thoroughly clean and dry the rosemary. Remove the needles from the stems (discard the stems). Peel and roughly chop the garlic and shallot.

3. Combine all the ingredients in food processor and blend until smooth. Do not store—pesto should be made fresh for each use.

Makes 2 cups

2 bunches fresh sage
1 Vidalia onion
½ cup shelled sunflower seeds
1 cup white wine vinegar
Fresh-cracked black pepper

Sage Pesto

While pesto is generally used as a sauce over pasta or added to soups or stews
for an extra kick, you can also use it to flavor meat. Try rubbing a little pesto
on pork chops or chicken breasts before cooking.

1. Thoroughly clean and dry the sage. Peel and roughly chop the onion.

2. Combine all the ingredients in a food processor and blend until smooth.

Brown Sauce

*You can add chunks of veal or beef to this sauce
for more flavor and texture.*

Makes 4 cups

3 yellow onions
2 carrots
2 stalks celery
2 tomatoes
½ bulb garlic
¼ bunch fresh parsley
4 sprigs fresh thyme
1 teaspoon olive oil
1 cup dry red wine
1 gallon Beef Stock (page 15)
1 bay leaf
Fresh-cracked black pepper

1. Peel and roughly chop the onions and carrots. Clean and roughly chop the celery. Roughly chop the tomatoes. Peel the garlic, and leave whole. Clean the parsley and thyme.

2. Heat the oil to medium-high temperature in a large stockpot. Add the onions, carrots, celery, tomatoes, and garlic. Sauté for about 10 minutes, stirring frequently. Pour in the wine, and reduce by half the volume.

3. Add the stock, bay leaf, and pepper. Reduce heat, and simmer for 2 hours, uncovered. Strain through a fine-meshed sieve, and discard the solids. Return the liquid to the pan.

4. Increase heat to high and cook until thickened, about 45 to 60 minutes, stirring occasionally.

Thickening Agents
Some soups, stews, sauces, and gravies will thicken naturally throughout the cooking process. Lengthy cooking time and starchy ingredients like potatoes can do the trick. However, with certain recipes, you may want to use thickening agents such as roux, cornstarch, or other pure starch (such as potato starch), or tapioca to thicken it up.

Makes 2 cups

1 lemon
1 shallot
2 cups pepperoncini
Fresh-cracked black pepper

Italian Pepperoncini Gremolata

*Classic gremolata is used to flavor certain dishes
and helps offset the "fatty" flavor of hearty dishes.
The most popular dish made with gremolata is osso buco.*

1. Zest the lemon using a citrus zester or vegetable peeler. Peel and mince the shallot. Finely dice the pepperoncini.

2. Mix together all the ingredients, and use as desired. Do not store—this should be made fresh for each use.

Makes 4 cups

5 peaches
2 sprigs mint
1 shallot
Fresh-cracked black pepper
½ cup peach nectar (or
    substitute peach juice)

Minty Fruit Chutney

*Only make this chutney with fresh peaches and mint "in season."
Use local produce when possible.*

1. Clean and medium-dice the peaches. Clean and gently chop the mint leaves. Peel and mince the shallot.

2. Mix together all the ingredients, and use as desired.

Fruit Chutney

A spoonful of fruit chutney placed on top of a high-fat stewed or braised dish just before serving will ease the "fatty" flavor.

Makes 2 cups

5 sprigs fresh rosemary
5 sprigs fresh mint
1 cup shelled walnuts
2 oranges
1 yellow onion

1. Clean and chop the herbs. Chop the walnuts. Zest and juice the oranges, then remove the peel and dice the fruit. Peel and finely dice the onion.

2. Mix together all the ingredients, and use as desired.

Chapter 6

Flatbreads, Pizza, and Focaccia

Basic Flatbread 80

Whole-Wheat Flatbread 81

Chickpea Flatbread 82

Onion Flatbread 83

Roasted Garlic Flatbread 84

Herbed Flatbread 85

Spelt Flatbread 86

Saffron Flatbread 87

Cornmeal Flatbread 88

Barley Flatbread 89

Fried Dough 90

Easter Egg Bread 91

Crusty Egg Bread 92

Garlic and Herb Focaccia 93

Whole-Wheat Focaccia 94

Basic Cheese Pizza 95

Sicilian Pizza 95

Frisedda 96

Bread Sticks 96

Garlic Knots 97

4 cups all-purpose flour
½ teaspoon iodized salt
  (optional)
1–1⅓ cups cold water
1 teaspoon olive oil

Basic Flatbread

Iodized salt is better to use in baking recipes. It dissolves faster,
so you won't end up with gritty dough.

1. Sift together the flour and salt. Mix the flour and water in a mixer using a large dough hook for 3 minutes or until the ingredients are incorporated and the dough is formed. Let the dough rest for 1 hour in the refrigerator.

2. Form the dough into small balls. On a floured surface, use a floured rolling pin to roll out each ball into a circle about ½ inch thick.

3. For stovetop preparation, lightly grease a skillet with the oil and heat on medium. For oven preparation, preheat oven to 400°F and lightly grease a baking sheet with the oil.

4. Lightly brown the bread until thoroughly cooked, about 5 minutes per side.

Whole-Wheat Flatbread

You can use all whole-wheat flour for more nutritious dough, but using some all-purpose white flour makes for easier handling.

Serves 10

3 cups whole-wheat flour
1 cup all-purpose flour
½ teaspoon iodized salt
1–1¼ cups cold water
1 teaspoon olive oil

1. Sift together the flours and salt. Mix the flour and water in a mixer using a large dough hook for 3 minutes or until the ingredients are incorporated and the dough is formed. Let the dough rest for 1 hour in the refrigerator.

2. Form the dough into small balls. On a floured surface, use a floured rolling pin to roll out each ball into a circle about ½ inch thick.

3. For stovetop preparation, lightly grease a skillet with the oil and heat on medium. For oven preparation, preheat oven to 400°F and lightly grease a baking sheet with the oil.

4. Lightly brown the bread until thoroughly cooked, about 5 minutes per side.

Knife Know-How
Serrated-edge "bread" knives are great for cutting crumbly things that would crush under the pressure of a smooth blade. But for clean slices, especially when carving cooked meats, there's no substitute for a razor-sharp slicing knife.

2 cups chickpea flour
2 cups all-purpose flour
½ teaspoon iodized salt
1–1¼ cups cold water
1 teaspoon olive oil

Chickpea Flatbread

Chickpea flour can be found in the international or Middle Eastern section of most grocery stores and specialty markets.

1. Sift together the flours and salt. Mix the flour and water in a mixer using a large dough hook for 3 minutes or until the ingredients are incorporated and the dough is formed. Let the dough rest for 1 hour in the refrigerator.

2. Form the dough into small balls. On a floured surface, use a floured rolling pin to roll out each ball into a circle about ½ inch thick.

3. For stovetop preparation, lightly grease a skillet with the oil and heat on medium. For oven preparation, preheat oven to 400°F and lightly grease a baking sheet with the oil.

4. Lightly brown the bread until thoroughly cooked, about 5 minutes per side.

Onion Flatbread

This onion-flavored bread is great for dipping in soups or eating as a snack. For a snack, it doesn't need more than a light toasting and a bit of butter.

Serves 10

1 large yellow onion
3½ cups all-purpose flour
½ teaspoon iodized salt
1–1¼ cups cold water
1 teaspoon olive oil

1. Peel and finely mince the onion.

2. Sift together the flour and salt. Mix the flour and water in a mixer using a large dough hook for 3 minutes or until the ingredients are incorporated and the dough is formed. Add the onion and incorporate into the dough. Let the dough rest for 1 hour in the refrigerator.

3. Form the dough into small balls. On a floured surface, use a floured rolling pin to roll out each ball into a circle about ½ inch thick.

4. For stovetop preparation, lightly grease a skillet with the oil and heat on medium. For oven preparation, preheat oven to 400°F and lightly grease a baking sheet with the oil.

5. Lightly brown the bread until thoroughly cooked, about 5 minutes per side.

How Long Do You Need to Knead?
Developing a feel for how much to knead your dough comes with time and experience. If you overwork it, you overdevelop the gluten in the dough, making it tough. This causes the bread to have a chewy, unpleasant texture. A few quick motions should be all the kneading your dough needs.

Serves 10

2¾ cups whole-wheat flour
1 cup all-purpose flour
½ teaspoon iodized salt
½ cup Roasted Garlic Paste
    (page 70)
1–1¼ cups cold water
1 teaspoon olive oil

Roasted Garlic Flatbread

*Flatbread is often served with soup, cheese, or salad.
You could get a little more creative and use this or the other
flatbread recipes as a crust for pizza toppings.*

1. Sift together both flours and the salt. Mix the garlic paste with the sifted flour. Mix the flour and water in a mixer using a large dough hook for 3 minutes or until the ingredients are incorporated and the dough is formed. Let the dough rest for 1 hour in the refrigerator.

2. Form the dough into small balls. On a floured surface, use a floured rolling pin to roll out each ball into a circle about ½ inch thick.

3. For stovetop preparation, lightly grease a skillet with the oil and heat on medium. For oven preparation, preheat oven to 400°F and lightly grease a baking sheet with the oil.

4. Lightly brown the bread until thoroughly cooked, about 5 minutes per side.

Herbed Flatbread

Only use fresh herbs in this recipe. Dried herbs will not give the flavor needed to season this bread.

Serves 10

¼ bunch fresh herb of choice
3 cups whole-wheat flour
1 cup all-purpose flour
½ teaspoon iodized salt
1–1¼ cups cold water
1 teaspoon olive oil

1. Clean and finely chop the herb. Sift together the flours and salt. Mix the flour and water in a mixer using a large dough hook for 3 minutes or until the ingredients are incorporated and the dough is formed. Add the herb and incorporate into the dough. Let the dough rest for 1 hour in the refrigerator.

2. Form the dough into small balls. On a floured surface, use a floured rolling pin to roll out each ball into a circle about ½ inch thick.

3. For stovetop preparation, lightly grease a skillet with the oil and heat on medium. For oven preparation, preheat oven to 400°F and lightly grease a baking sheet with the oil.

4. Lightly brown the bread until thoroughly cooked, about 5 minutes per side.

Serves 10

2 cups spelt flour
2 cups all-purpose flour
½ teaspoon iodized salt
1–1¼ cups cold water
1 teaspoon olive oil

Spelt Flatbread

You can substitute another flour such as chickpea flour for spelt
if you cannot find it in your local market.

1. Sift together the flours and salt. Mix the flour and water in a mixer using a large dough hook for 3 minutes or until the ingredients are incorporated and the dough is formed. Let the dough rest for 1 hour in the refrigerator.

2. Form the dough into small balls. On a floured surface, use a floured rolling pin to roll out each ball into a circle about ½ inch thick.

3. For stovetop preparation, lightly grease a skillet with the oil and heat on medium. For oven preparation, preheat oven to 400°F and lightly grease a baking sheet with the oil.

4. Lightly brown the bread until thoroughly cooked, about 5 minutes per side.

Salt

When baking, choose iodized salt—as opposed to coarse or kosher—because it dissolves better than other types of salt. Also, iodized salt blends better with flour and baking powder when sifting the ingredients together. You don't want grains of undissolved salt showing up in your baked goods.

Saffron Flatbread

Powdered saffron dissolves better than saffron threads.
But if you are using the threads, chop them well and increase the amount
of powdered saffron called for by at least ⅛ teaspoon.

Serves 10

4 cups all-purpose flour
½ teaspoon saffron threads
½ teaspoon iodized salt
1–1¼ cups cold water
1 teaspoon olive oil

1. Sift together the flour, saffron, and salt. Mix the flour and water in a mixer using a large dough hook for 3 minutes or until the ingredients are incorporated and the dough is formed. Let the dough rest for 1 hour in the refrigerator.

2. Form the dough into small balls. On a floured surface, use a floured rolling pin to roll out each ball into a circle about ½ inch thick.

3. For stovetop preparation, lightly grease a skillet with the oil and heat on medium. For oven preparation, preheat oven to 400°F and lightly grease a baking sheet with the oil.

4. Lightly brown the bread until thoroughly cooked, about 5 minutes per side.

2 cups cornmeal (or corn
   flour)
2 cups all-purpose flour
½ teaspoon iodized salt
1–1¼ cups cold water
1 teaspoon olive oil

Cornmeal Flatbread

*Each culture has its own version of flatbread.
This one, made with cornmeal, is similar to a Mexican tortilla.*

1. Sift together the cornmeal, flour, and salt. Mix the flour and water in a mixer using a large dough hook for 3 minutes or until the ingredients are incorporated and the dough is formed. Let the dough rest for 1 hour in the refrigerator.

2. Form the dough into small balls. On a floured surface, use a floured rolling pin to roll out each ball into a circle about ½ inch thick.

3. For stovetop preparation, lightly grease a skillet with the oil and heat on medium. For oven preparation, preheat oven to 400°F and lightly grease a baking sheet with the oil.

4. Lightly brown the bread until thoroughly cooked, about 5 minutes per side.

Barley Flatbread

Barley flour is made from ground barley, which is a whole grain.
Barley is a common ingredient in soups, and this bread is great for dipping!

Serves 10

3 cups barley flour
1 cup all-purpose flour
½ teaspoon iodized salt
1–1¼ cups cold water
1 teaspoon olive oil

1. Sift together the flours and salt. Mix the flour and water in a mixer using a large dough hook for 3 minutes or until the ingredients are incorporated and the dough is formed. Let the dough rest for 1 hour in the refrigerator.

2. Form the dough into small balls. On a floured surface, use a floured rolling pin to roll out each ball into a circle about ½ inch thick.

3. For stovetop preparation, lightly grease a skillet with the oil and heat on medium. For oven preparation, preheat oven to 400°F and lightly grease a baking sheet with the oil.

4. Lightly brown the bread until thoroughly cooked, about 5 minutes per side.

Serves 10

1 (¼-ounce) packet dry active
   yeast
¼ cup warm water (should
   not exceed 120°F)
4 eggs
¼ cup melted unsalted butter
1 pound all-purpose flour
1 teaspoon granulated sugar
¼ teaspoon iodized salt
2 cups vegetable oil
Confectioners' sugar

Fried Dough

*This is a classic Italian street vendor's treat. Fried dough is delicious with any of
a number of sweet toppings, including powdered sugar, honey, and jam.*

1. In a small bowl, stir together the yeast and the water, and let stand for about 5 minutes, until foamy. In a medium-sized bowl, beat the eggs and stir in the slightly cooled melted butter. Sift together the flour, sugar, and salt in a large bowl.

2. Combine the egg mixture with the dissolved yeast mixture.

3. Combine the wet and dry ingredients in a mixer with a dough hook until fully incorporated and the dough forms into a ball.

4. Cover and let rise for 1 hour in a warm place. Punch down the dough and knead it. Form the dough into flat 4-inch circular pieces (½ inch thick), cover, and let rise in a warm place again for 30 minutes.

5. Heat the oil on medium-high in a skillet. Fry the dough pieces one at a time until browned and cooked through. Transfer the fried dough to paper towels to drain. Let cool slightly, then sprinkle with confectioners' sugar and serve.

Yeast

When dissolving yeast in warm water to use in a baking recipe, you must take care that the water is not too hot. If the water is over 115°F, it will kill the yeast and the bread will not rise. The same result will occur if the yeast you use is not fresh. Always check the package for freshness dates and storing instructions.

Easter Egg Bread

This tasty bread is a tradition for Easter Sunday dinner, and the colored eggs make it a visual treat as well.

Serves 10

1 (¼-ounce) dry active packet yeast
¼ cup warm water (should not exceed 120°F)
1½ cups scalded milk (100 to 115°F)
¼ cup unsalted butter
5 cups all-purpose flour
½ cup granulated sugar
½ teaspoon iodized salt
3 colored hard-boiled eggs

1. In a small bowl, combine the yeast and the water, and let stand for about 5 minutes, until foamy. Once the scalded milk has cooled, stir in the butter. In a large bowl, sift together the flour, sugar, and salt (you may need to add more or less flour depending on the level of humidity).

2. Mix together all the ingredients *except* the eggs in mixer at medium speed with a dough hook for about 5 minutes, until the dough forms into a ball. Let the dough rest in a warm place for about 1 hour, until it rises.

3. Preheat oven to 375°F. Punch down the dough and form into desired shape (loaf or braid). Press the eggs into the top of the dough, allowing no more than ⅓ of each egg to show. (If too much of each egg is showing, it could crack or explode from the heat of the oven.)

4. Bake for about 1 hour, until the bread is golden brown.

Crusty Egg Bread

This is a great bread to serve as part of a brunch buffet,
or with a pot of soup and a crisp salad.

1. Preheat oven to 350°F. Lightly grease a baking sheet with the olive oil. Slice the bread into 10 thick (1½- to 2-inch) slices, then hollow out part of the center of each (leaving approximately 1 inch in diameter, including crust) to form a shallow bread cup. Reserve the centers.

2. Beat the eggs. Cut the prosciutto into thin ⅛- to ¼-inch strips. Peel and mince the shallot. Clean and gently chop the chervil.

3. Lay out the bread cups on the prepared baking sheet. Place 1½ to 2 tablespoons mascarpone in each, then add the shallot. Pour in the eggs, filling the cups to the top but being careful not to let them overflow. Top with the prosciutto.

4. Bake for about 10 to 15 minutes, until the eggs are set and lightly brown.

5. Sprinkle with the chervil and pepper, and serve.

Garlic and Herb Focaccia

This focaccia is great with soup or salad for a light lunch.
Serve warm with fresh-grated Parmesan cheese.

Serves 10

2 teaspoons olive oil, divided
1 (¼-ounce) dry active packet yeast
½ cup warm water (should not exceed 120°F)
6 cups all-purpose flour
¼ teaspoon salt
2 cups water
½ bunch fresh basil
3 cloves garlic

1. Lightly grease a 13" × 9" baking pan with 1 teaspoon of the olive oil. In a small bowl, stir together the yeast and warm water, and let stand for about 5 minutes, until foamy. Sift together the flour and salt (you may need more or less flour depending on level of humidity).

2. Mix together the flour, dissolved yeast mixture, and the water by hand or in a mixer with a dough hook at slow speed for 3 to 5 minutes, until the dough forms into a ball. Remove from the bowl, cover with a clean kitchen towel, and let rest on a floured surface for 1 hour.

3. While the dough rests, clean and gently chop the basil. Peel and mince the garlic. Toss the basil and garlic in the remaining oil.

4. Place the dough in the prepared pan, either leaving it as a ball or forming as desired. Use your fingers to gently push the garlic and basil into the bread, evenly distributing them over the entire surface. Cover with a kitchen towel and let rise in a warm place for about 1 hour.

5. Preheat oven to 425°F. Bake the bread for 1 hour, until lightly brown.

Focaccia Dough
There is a quick trick you can use to customize your focaccia dough. To make it crispier, drizzle a little olive oil on the crust before baking. To make the bread softer, brush the crust with oil immediately after it comes out of the oven.

1 teaspoon olive oil
*1 (¼-ounce) packet dry active
    yeast*
*2½ cups warm water (should
    not exceed 120°F)*
5 cups whole-wheat flour
2 cups all-purpose flour
1 pinch salt
1 cup water

Whole-Wheat Focaccia

*This focaccia dough can be used for deep-dish and Sicilian pizza recipes.
Just add various pizza toppings and bake until lightly brown.*

1. Lightly grease a 13" × 9" baking pan with the olive oil. In a bowl, stir together the yeast and warm water, and let stand for about 5 minutes, until foamy. Sift together the flours and salt.

2. Mix together the flour, dissolved yeast mixture, and water by hand or in a mixer with a dough hook until the dough forms into a ball. Remove from the mixing bowl and cover with a clean kitchen towel. Let rise in a warm place for about 45 minutes.

3. Knead the dough for 3 minutes, place in the prepared pan, and cover with a towel. Let rise again for about 30 minutes. Either leave dough as a ball or form as desired.

4. Preheat oven to 425°F. Bake for 45 minutes, until lightly brown.

Focaccia Variations
Cooked vegetables or herbs can be added to the focaccia recipe to make different flavored breads. Also, you can shape focaccia dough into any shape you like. Create long rolls for sub sandwiches or tight balls for bread to serve with dinner.

Basic Cheese Pizza

This recipe has as many variations as your imagination allows.
Experiment with different toppings and combinations.

∼

1. Preheat oven to 425°F. Lightly grease 2 pizza pans with ½ tablespoon of the oil. Peel and mince the garlic.

2. Roll out the dough on a floured surface into 2 large circles. Place the rolled dough on the pizza pans. Ladle the sauce over the dough, spreading it out evenly over the surface. Top with the cheeses, and sprinkle with the garlic, herbs, and pepper. Drizzle with the remaining oil.

3. Bake for 15 to 20 minutes, until the cheese is melted and the dough is cooked through.

Serves 10

1 tablespoon olive oil, divided
½ bulb garlic
1 recipe Basic Flatbread (page 80), unformed and uncooked
1 cup Old World Gravy (Long-Cooking Tomato Sauce) (page 64)
1 cup shredded provolone cheese
1 cup shredded mozzarella cheese
½ teaspoon dried oregano
½ teaspoon dried basil
½ teaspoon dried marjoram
Fresh-cracked black pepper

Sicilian Pizza

The oblong shape makes this traditional Sicilian Pizza.
Try topping this with sliced olives and fresh sage or rosemary.

∼

1. Preheat oven to 425°F. Lightly grease an oblong pan with ½ tablespoon of the oil. Clean and gently chop the basil and oregano leaves.

2. Roll out the dough on a floured surface into a 2-inch-thick rectangle, and place in the prepared pan. Allow to rise again for 30 minutes.

3. Ladle the sauce over the dough, spreading it out evenly over the entire surface. Top with cheese, and sprinkle with the herbs and pepper. Drizzle with the remaining oil.

4. Bake for 20 to 25 minutes.

Serves 10

1 tablespoon olive oil, divided
4 sprigs fresh basil
4 sprigs fresh oregano
1 recipe Whole-Wheat Focaccia dough (page 94), uncooked
1½ cups Old World Gravy (Long-Cooking Tomato Sauce) (page 64)
1½ cups shredded mozzarella cheese
¼ cup fresh-grated Romano cheese
Fresh-cracked black pepper

Serves 10

1 tablespoon olive oil
1 recipe Whole-Wheat
   Focaccia dough (page
   94), uncooked

Frisedda

*Frisedda originates in the Puglia section of Italy.
This twice-baked bread can be served as is, or soaked in water and
seasoned with oil, fresh tomato, oregano, and salt.*

1. Preheat oven to 400°F. Lightly grease a baking sheet with ½ tablespoon of the oil. Roll out the dough on a floured surface, separate it into 3-inch balls, and roll out the balls slightly. Poke a hole in the center of each to form a bagel shape. Allow to rise for 30 minutes.

2. Place the bread on the prepared pan. Bake for 15 minutes.

3. Slice in half crosswise. Drizzle with the remaining oil. Return to the oven for 10 minutes, until toasted golden.

Serves 10

1 tablespoon olive oil
1 recipe Basic Flatbread
   (page 80), unformed and
   uncooked

Bread Sticks

*This Italian classic is great for dipping in tomato sauce, Alfredo sauce,
or just extra-virgin olive oil with pepper.*

1. Preheat oven to 400°F. Lightly grease a baking sheet with half of the oil.

2. Roll out the dough on a floured surface until about 1 inch thick and cut into 6-inch-long strips.

3. Place strips on the prepared baking sheet, and bake for 15 to 20 minutes.

Garlic Knots

Serve these in a linen-lined basket at dinner.
They are especially great for sopping up sauce after a hearty pasta meal.

Serves 10

1 tablespoon olive oil, divided
1 recipe Whole-Wheat
Focaccia dough (page
94), uncooked
1 bulb garlic
Fresh-cracked black pepper
¼ cup fresh-grated Parmesan
cheese (optional)

1. Lightly grease a baking sheet with ½ tablespoon of the oil. Roll out the dough on a floured surface to 1 inch thick and cut into 12-inch strands. Form into four 4-inch knots. Place the knots on the prepared pan, cover with a clean kitchen towel, and let rise in a warm place.

2. While the dough rises, peel and mince the garlic.

3. Preheat oven to 425°F. Sprinkle the dough knots with the remaining oil, then sprinkle with the garlic and pepper.

4. Bake for 15 to 20 minutes. Sprinkle with the cheese, and serve.

Garlic

Aglio is the Italian word for "garlic." It is a staple that appears extensively—both cooked and raw—in Italian cuisine. It is one of the oldest known cultivated plants and is closely related to the onion. The bulb, or head, is a cluster of cloves connected at the root end and held together by papery skin. Store in an open container, in a cool, dark, dry place ,and unpeeled garlic will stay fresh for 3 to 4 weeks.

Chapter 7

Homemade Pasta

Basic Pasta 100

Spelt Pasta 101

Whole-Wheat Pasta 102

Eggless Pasta 103

Egg White Pasta 104

Spinach Pasta 105

Fresh Basil Pasta 106

Fagioli Pasta (Bean Pasta) 107

Roasted Garlic Pasta 108

Acini di Pepe 109

Cornmeal Pasta 110

Tomato Pasta 111

Eggplant Pasta 112

Saffron and Shallot Pasta 113

Strawberry Pasta 114

Chicken Pasta 115

Salmon Pasta 116

Scallop Pasta 117

Walnut Pasta 118

Gnocchi 119

Roasted Potato and Garlic
   Gnocchi 120

Stuffed Rigatoni 121

Traditional Lasagna 122

Vegetarian Lasagna 123

Lobster Ravioli 124

Pasta-Wrapped Shrimp with Pesto 125

Baccalà with Pasta and Fresh Peas 126

Pork-Filled Pasta Shells 127

Pasta Stuffed with Fresh Cod in Saffron
   Broth 128

Classic Fettuccine Alfredo 129

Fettuccine Alfredo con Capesante 130

Stuffed Shells 131

Baked Spaghetti Tart 132

Pasta Dumplings 132

Pasta con Ragu Bolognese 133

Bowtie Pasta with Braised Beans and
   Greens 134

Deep-Fried Pasta 135

Cheese Tortellini 136

Meat Ravioli 137

3 cups durum wheat
(semolina) flour
⅛ teaspoon iodized salt
3 eggs
¼ cup olive oil
¼ cup water (room
temperature)

Basic Pasta

*When making pasta dough, use your judgment about
how much flour to add. You may need to add more or less flour
depending on the level of humidity.*

1. Sift together the flour and salt into a large mixing bowl. Whisk the eggs in a small bowl. Mix the olive oil and water into the eggs.

2. Make a well in the center of the flour and pour in the egg mixture. Mix together the wet and dry ingredients by hand or in a mixer with a dough hook until the dough forms into a ball. Wrap the dough in plastic wrap and let rest in the refrigerator for at least 1 hour, or up to 1 day. Allow dough to return to room temperature if it has rested in the refrigerator for more than an hour.

3. Roll out the dough on a floured surface, then form or shape pasta as desired.

4. To cook, bring a large pot of water to a slow boil. Add the pasta, and stir to prevent sticking. Cook until al dente. (Cooking times will vary depending on the size of the pasta formed.) Drain, and serve as desired.

Semolina
Semolina flour is the basis of most types of pasta and Italian breads. It is made from hard durum wheat and has a fine texture. It contains more protein and vitamins than regular white flour and many essential amino acids. Semolina also has a low calorie count and a very low fat content.

Spelt Pasta

*Chickpea flour may be substituted for spelt flour if you
prefer or if it is what you have on hand.*

Serves 10

*2 cups spelt flour
1 cup all-purpose flour
⅛ teaspoon iodized salt
3 eggs
1 egg white
¼ cup olive oil
1 tablespoon water*

1. Sift together the spelt flour, all-purpose flour, and salt into a large mixing bowl. Whisk the eggs and the egg white in a small bowl. Mix the olive oil and water into the eggs.

2. Make a well in the center of the flour and pour in the egg mixture. Mix together the wet and dry ingredients by hand or in a mixer with a dough hook until the dough forms into a ball. Wrap the dough in plastic wrap and let rest in the refrigerator for at least 1 hour, or up to 1 day. Allow dough to return to room temperature if it has rested in the refrigerator for more than an hour.

3. Roll out the dough on a floured surface, then form or shape pasta as desired.

4. To cook, bring a large pot of water to a slow boil. Add the pasta, and stir to prevent sticking. Cook until al dente. (Cooking times will vary depending on the size of the pasta formed.) Drain, and serve as desired.

Separating Eggs

If you don't have an egg separator in your kitchen, break the egg neatly in half and transfer the yolk back and forth from one side of the shell to the other, catching the whites in a small bowl underneath. In some recipes even the smallest amount of yolk in an egg white can cause the recipe to fail. So, don't break that yolk!

Serves 10

2½ cups whole-wheat flour
½ cup all-purpose flour
⅛ teaspoon iodized salt
2 eggs
2 egg whites
¼ cup olive oil
2 tablespoons water

Whole-Wheat Pasta

You can use any grain flour in this recipe. Different flours will impart different flavors and textures to the pasta.

1. Sift together the wheat flour, all-purpose flour, and salt into a large bowl. Whisk the eggs and egg whites. Mix the olive oil and water into the egg mixture.

2. Make a well in the center of the flour and pour in the egg mixture. Mix together the wet and dry ingredients by hand or in a mixer with a dough hook until the dough forms into a ball. Wrap the dough in plastic wrap and let rest in the refrigerator for at least 1 hour, or up to 1 day. Allow the dough to return to room temperature if it has rested in the refrigerator for more than an hour.

3. Roll out the dough on a floured surface, then form or shape pasta as desired.

4. To cook, bring a large pot of water to a slow boil. Add the pasta, and stir to prevent sticking. Cook until al dente. (Cooking times will vary depending on the size of the pasta formed.) Drain, and serve as desired.

Eggless Pasta

This is the perfect pasta for those who need to watch their cholesterol intake. The olive oil adds flavor so you won't miss the eggs.

Serves 10

2 cups durum wheat (semolina) flour
2 cups all-purpose flour
⅛ teaspoon iodized salt
⅓ cup virgin olive oil
⅓ cup water

1. Sift together the dry ingredients into a large mixing bowl. Whisk together the oil and water in a separate bowl.

2. Make a well in the center of the flour, and pour in the egg mixture. Mix together the wet and dry ingredients by hand or in a mixer with a dough hook until the dough forms into a ball. Wrap the dough in plastic wrap and let rest in the refrigerator for at least 1 hour, or up to 1 day. Allow dough to return to room temperature if it has rested in the refrigerator for more than an hour.

3. Roll out the dough on a floured surface, then form or shape pasta as desired.

4. To cook, bring a large pot of water to a slow boil. Add the pasta, and stir to prevent sticking. Cook until al dente. (Cooking times will vary depending on the size of the pasta formed.) Drain, and serve as desired.

2½ cups grain flour
½ cup all-purpose flour
⅛ teaspoon iodized salt
6 egg whites
½ cup olive oil
¼ cup water

Egg White Pasta

Like Eggless Pasta (page 103), this recipe without the egg yolk is an excellent choice for those who need to cut back on cholesterol.

1. Sift together the grain flour, all-purpose flour, and salt into a large mixing bowl. Whisk together the egg whites, olive oil, and water in a separate bowl.

2. Make a well in the center of the flour and pour in the egg mixture. Mix together the wet and dry ingredients by hand or in a mixer with a dough hook until the dough forms into a ball. Wrap the dough in plastic wrap and let rest in the refrigerator for at least 1 hour, or up to 1 day. Allow dough to return to room temperature if it has rested in the refrigerator for more than an hour.

3. Roll out the dough on a floured surface, then form or shape pasta as desired.

4. To cook, bring a pot of water to a slow boil. Add the pasta, and stir to prevent sticking. Cook until al dente. (Cooking times will vary depending on the size of the pasta formed.) Drain, and serve as desired.

Testing Egg Freshness
To test whether or not an egg is fresh, immerse it in a pan of cool, salted water. If it sinks to the bottom, it is fresh. If it rises to the surface, it is spoiled. If the eggs in your refrigerator are approaching or have passed their freshness date, always perform this test before using the eggs.

Spinach Pasta

If you don't like spinach, any cooked vegetable can be substituted here.
Try carrots, beets, or red peppers for a different color and flavor.

Serves 10

*2 cups durum wheat
     (semolina) flour
2 cups all-purpose flour
⅛ teaspoon iodized salt
½ cup spinach
2 eggs
¼ cup olive oil
1 tablespoon water*

1. Sift together the flours and salt into a large mixing bowl. Cook and purée spinach. In a separate bowl, whisk the eggs, then thoroughly blend the eggs with the spinach, olive oil, and water.

2. Make a well in the center of the flour and pour in the egg mixture. Mix together the wet and dry ingredients by hand or in a mixer with a dough hook until the dough forms into a ball. Wrap the dough in plastic wrap and let rest in the refrigerator for at least 1 hour, or up to 1 day. Allow dough to return to room temperature if it has rested in the refrigerator for more than an hour.

3. Roll out the dough on a floured surface, then form or shape pasta as desired.

4. To cook, bring a large pot of water to a slow boil. Add the pasta, and stir to prevent sticking. Cook until al dente. (Cooking times will vary depending on the size of the pasta formed.) Drain, and serve as desired.

1 large bunch basil
1½ cups durum wheat
  (semolina) flour
2½ cups all-purpose flour
⅛ teaspoon iodized salt
2 eggs
2 egg whites
¼ cup olive oil
1 tablespoon olive oil

Fresh Basil Pasta

If you like, you can try another fresh herb in this recipe. Also, you can use the leaves of the herb, as this recipe calls for, or you can purée the herb.

1. Thoroughly clean and dry the basil. Remove the leaves (reserve stems for another recipe, if desired).

2. Sift together the flours and salt into a large mixing bowl. Whisk the eggs, egg whites, and ¼ cup oil in a separate bowl.

3. Make a well in the center of the flour and pour in the egg mixture. Mix together the wet and dry ingredients by hand or in a mixer with a dough hook until the dough forms into a ball. Wrap the dough in plastic wrap and let rest in the refrigerator for at least 1 hour, or up to 1 day. Allow dough to return to room temperature if it has rested in the refrigerator for more than an hour.

4. Separate the dough into 2 balls. Roll out 1 ball on a floured surface into a sheet about ⅛ to ¼ inch thick. Brush very lightly with 1 tablespoon oil, and spread the basil leaves evenly over the dough. Roll out the other ball into a sheet the same size as the first, and place on top of the first sheet. Roll to ensure the 2 sheets are stuck together. Cut the pasta into desired shapes.

5. To cook, bring a large pot of water to a slow boil. Add the pasta, and stir to prevent sticking. Cook until al dente. (Cooking times will vary depending on the size of the pasta formed.) Drain, and serve as desired.

Don't Drown Your Pasta
The correct way to eat pasta, according to Italians, is to have it "alla macchiato," or with just enough sauce on it to "stain it." Avoid lots of heavy sauces—instead, use just enough sauce to complement the delicate flavor of the pasta, without drowning it.

Fagioli Pasta (Bean Pasta)

Serve this as you would regular pasta—with butter and cheese, red sauce, or garlic and oil. If you use canned beans, make sure to rinse and drain them well before using.

Serves 10

½ cup cooked cannellini beans (or substitute another legume of your choice)

2 cups whole-grain flour

1 cup all-purpose flour

⅛ teaspoon salt

3 eggs

¼ cup olive oil

¼ cup water or Vegetable Stock (page 16)

1. Purée the cooked beans. Sift the flours and salt into a large bowl. In a separate bowl, whisk the eggs. Mix the beans, oil, and water (or stock) into the eggs.

2. Make a well in the center of the flour, and pour in the egg mixture. Mix together all the ingredients by hand or in a mixer with a dough hook for about 3 minutes, until the dough forms into a ball. Wrap the dough in plastic wrap and let rest in the refrigerator for at least 1 hour, or up to 1 day. Allow dough to return to room temperature if it has rested in the refrigerator for more than an hour.

3. Knead the dough for a few minutes before rolling it out on a floured surface. Form or shape pasta as desired.

4. To cook, bring a large pot of water to a slow boil. Add the pasta, and stir to prevent sticking. Cook until al dente. (Cooking times will vary depending on the size of the pasta formed.) Drain, and serve as desired.

1 cup durum wheat
    (semolina) flour
1 cup whole-wheat flour
2 cups all-purpose flour
⅛ teaspoon iodized salt
2 eggs
¼ cup virgin olive oil
¼ cup water
1 tablespoon olive oil
¼ cup Roasted Garlic Paste
    (page 70)

Roasted Garlic Pasta

*To help balance the strong flavor of the garlic, serve this pasta
with thick slices of plain warm Italian bread.*

1. Sift together the flours and salt into a large bowl. Whisk the eggs in a small bowl. Whisk the ¼ cup virgin olive oil, and water into the eggs. Make a well in the center of the flour and pour in the egg mixture. Mix together the wet and dry ingredients by hand or in a mixer with a dough hook until fully incorporated and the dough forms into a ball. Wrap the dough in plastic wrap and let rest in the refrigerator for at least 1 hour, or up to 1 day. Allow dough to return to room temperature if it has rested in the refrigerator for more than an hour.

2. Separate the dough into 2 balls. Roll out 1 ball on a floured surface into a sheet about ⅛ to ¼ inch thick. Brush very lightly with 1 tablespoon oil, and spread the garlic paste on the dough. Roll out the other ball into a sheet the same size as the first, and place on top of the first sheet of dough. Roll to ensure the sheets are stuck together. Cut or form the pasta into desired shapes.

3. To cook, bring a large pot of water to a slow boil. Add the pasta, and stir to prevent sticking. Cook until al dente. (Cooking times will vary depending on the size of the pasta formed.) Drain, and serve as desired.

Testing for Doneness

Different types of pasta cook at different rates, so there is no set length of time for cooking. The only way to be sure your pasta is cooked enough is to taste and feel it. Pasta should be "al dente," or just firm to the bite. Also, pasta continues to cook a bit as you take it off the heat and drain it, so take this into account when testing for doneness.

Acini di Pepe

This tiny pasta is perfect for use in soups,
such as Pork Soup with Acini di Pepe (page 30).

Serves 10

1½ cups durum wheat
   (semolina) flour
¼ cup fresh-grated Parmesan
   cheese
2 eggs
2 tablespoons olive oil
1 tablespoon water

1. Mix together the flour and cheese. In a separate bowl, whisk the eggs, then whisk in the oil and water.

2. Make a well in the center of the flour and pour in the egg mixture. Mix together the wet and dry ingredients by hand or in a mixer with a dough hook until fully incorporated and the dough forms into a ball. Wrap the dough in plastic wrap and let rest in the refrigerator for at least 1 hour, or up to 1 day. Allow dough to return to room temperature if it has rested in the refrigerator for more than an hour.

3. Cut the dough into tiny pieces and roll into tiny pea-sized balls.

4. To cook, bring a large pot of water to a boil. Add the pasta, and stir to prevent sticking. Cook until al dente, approximately 3 to 5 minutes. Drain, and serve as desired.

1½ cups cornmeal flour
2½ cups all-purpose flour
⅛ teaspoon iodized salt
3 eggs
¼ cup olive oil
2 tablespoons water

Cornmeal Pasta

Serve this pasta with a hearty, spicy meat dish.
It will hold up well with heavy gravies, too.

1. Sift together the cornmeal, all-purpose flour, and salt into a large mixing bowl. Whisk the eggs in a separate bowl. Whisk the olive oil and water into the eggs.

2. Make a well in the center of the flour and pour in the egg mixture. Mix together the wet and dry ingredients by hand or in a mixer with a dough hook until fully incorporated and the dough forms into a ball. Wrap the dough in plastic wrap and let rest in the refrigerator for at least 1 hour, or up to 1 day. Allow dough to return to room temperature if it has rested in the refrigerator for more than an hour.

3. Roll out the dough on a floured surface, then form or shape pasta as desired.

4. To cook, bring a large pot of water to a slow boil. Add the pasta, and stir to prevent sticking. Cook until al dente. (Cooking times will vary depending on the size of the pasta formed.) Drain, and serve as desired.

Tip for Cooking Pasta

After putting the pasta in the boiling water, put a tablespoon of olive oil into the water to prevent the pasta from sticking together. You can also add a pinch of salt to the water to help speed up the cooking, but don't do this when you're making an already salty dish.

Tomato Pasta

It is okay to use canned puréed tomatoes in this recipe instead of fresh.
Try to find the imported ones from San Marzano.

Serves 10

2 cups durum wheat
  (semolina) flour
1½ cups all-purpose flour
⅛ teaspoon iodized salt
3 eggs
½ cup puréed fresh tomatoes
  (or substitute canned
  tomato purée)
¼ cup olive oil
2 tablespoons water

1. Sift together the flours and salt into a large mixing bowl. Whisk together the eggs and tomato purée in a separate bowl. Whisk the olive oil and water into the egg mixture.

2. Make a well in the center of the flour and pour in the egg mixture. Mix together the wet and dry ingredients by hand or in a mixer with a dough hook until fully incorporated and the dough forms into a ball. Wrap the dough in plastic wrap and let rest in the refrigerator for at least 1 hour, or up to 1 day. Allow dough to return to room temperature if it has rested in the refrigerator for more than an hour.

3. Roll out the dough on a floured surface, then form or shape pasta as desired.

4. To cook, bring a large pot of water to a slow boil. Add the pasta, and stir to prevent sticking. Cook until al dente. (Cooking times will vary depending on the size of the pasta formed.) Drain, and serve as desired.

1 cup durum wheat
  (semolina) flour
1 cup whole-wheat flour
1½ cups all-purpose flour
⅛ teaspoon iodized salt
3 eggs
½ cup eggplant purée
¼ cup olive
2 tablespoons water

Eggplant Pasta

To make the eggplant purée called for in this recipe:
Slice an eggplant lengthwise, lightly brush with olive oil,
roast in a 375°F oven for 20 minutes, and purée.

1. Sift together the flours and salt into a large mixing bowl. Whisk together the eggs and eggplant purée in a separate bowl. Whisk the olive oil and water into the egg mixture.

2. Make a well in the center of the flour and pour in the egg mixture. Mix together the wet and dry ingredients by hand or in a mixer with a dough hook until fully incorporated and the dough forms into a ball. Wrap the dough in plastic wrap and let rest in the refrigerator for at least 1 hour, or up to 1 day. Allow dough to return to room temperature if it has rested in the refrigerator for more than an hour.

3. Roll out the dough on a floured surface, then form or shape pasta as desired.

4. To cook, bring a large pot of water to a slow boil. Add the pasta, and stir to prevent sticking. Cook until al dente. (Cooking times will vary depending on the size of the pasta formed.) Drain, and serve as desired.

Saffron and Shallot Pasta

Roast the shallots by tossing them in olive oil and placing in a 375°F oven for approximately 15 minutes before puréeing them.

Serves 10

1 cup durum wheat
    (semolina) flour
2 cups all-purpose flour
⅛ teaspoon iodized salt
2 eggs
2 egg whites
3 roasted shallots, puréed
½ teaspoon saffron threads
¼ cup olive oil
2 tablespoons water

1. Sift together the flours and salt into a large mixing bowl. Whisk together the eggs, egg whites, puréed shallots, and saffron in a separate bowl. Whisk the olive oil and water into the egg mixture.

2. Make a well in the center of the flour and pour in the egg mixture. Mix together the wet and dry ingredients by hand or in a mixer with a dough hook until fully incorporated and the dough forms into a ball. Wrap the dough in plastic wrap and let rest in the refrigerator for at least 1 hour, or up to 1 day. Allow dough to return to room temperature if it has rested in the refrigerator for more than an hour.

3. Roll out the dough on a floured surface, then form or shape pasta as desired.

4. To cook, bring a large pot of water to a slow boil. Add the pasta, and stir to prevent sticking. Cook until al dente. (Cooking times will vary depending on the size of the pasta formed.) Drain, and serve as desired.

Dried Pasta: The Good and the Bad

Not all pasta is created equal. If your pasta comes out gummy or has a sour, bitter, or floury taste, try switching brands. There can be a significant difference between the quality of pasta brands and only a slight difference in price. If you like the brand a friend uses, try it out in your own kitchen.

2 eggs
2 egg whites
½ cup puréed fresh
    strawberries
¼ cup melted unsalted butter
1 tablespoon water
3 cups all-purpose flour

Strawberry Pasta

*This unusual but tasty pasta can be used as a dessert
by serving it with puréed fresh fruit, or you can deep-fry it
and coat it with confectioners' sugar or honey.*

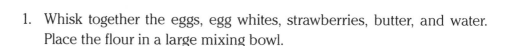

1. Whisk together the eggs, egg whites, strawberries, butter, and water. Place the flour in a large mixing bowl.

2. Make a well in the center of the flour and pour in the egg mixture. Mix together the wet and dry ingredients by hand or in a mixer with a dough hook until fully incorporated and the dough forms into a ball. Wrap the dough in plastic wrap and let rest in the refrigerator for at least 1 hour, or up to 1 day. Allow dough to return to room temperature if it has rested in the refrigerator for more than an hour.

3. Roll out the dough on a floured surface, then form or shape pasta as desired.

4. To cook, bring a large pot of water to a slow boil. Add the pasta, and stir to prevent sticking. Cook until al dente. (Cooking times will vary depending on the size of the pasta formed.) Drain, and serve as desired.

Chicken Pasta

Make sure to finely purée the meat in this recipe.
You need smooth dough to make smooth pasta.

Serves 10

1½ cups all-purpose flour
1½ cups whole-wheat flour
Fresh-cracked black pepper
¼ teaspoon iodized salt
3 eggs
¾ cup puréed cooked chicken
¼ cup olive oil
1 tablespoon water

1. Sift together the flours, black pepper, and salt into a large mixing bowl. Whisk together the eggs, chicken, oil, and water in another bowl.

2. Make a well in the center of the flour and pour in the egg mixture. Mix together the wet and dry ingredients by hand or in a mixer with a dough hook until fully incorporated and the dough forms into a ball. Wrap the dough in plastic wrap and let rest in the refrigerator for at least 1 hour, or up to 1 day. Allow dough to return to room temperature if it has rested in the refrigerator for more than an hour.

3. Roll out the dough on a floured surface, then form or shape pasta as desired.

4. To cook, bring a large pot of water to a slow boil. Add the pasta, and stir to prevent sticking. Cook until al dente. (Cooking times will vary depending on the size of the pasta formed.) Drain, and serve as desired.

2 cups all-purpose flour
¾ cups whole-wheat flour
¼ teaspoon iodized salt
4 egg whites
¾ cup puréed cooked salmon
¼ cup olive oil
1 tablespoon water

Salmon Pasta

*This pasta is excellent with a cheesy béchamel sauce
and some crusty Italian bread for dipping.*

1. Sift together the flours and salt into a large mixing bowl. Whisk together the egg whites, salmon, oil, and water in a separate bowl.

2. Make a well in the center of the flour and pour in the egg mixture. Mix together the wet and dry ingredients by hand or in a mixer with a dough hook until fully incorporated and the dough forms into a ball. Wrap the dough in plastic wrap and let rest in the refrigerator for at least 1 hour, or up to 1 day. Allow dough to return to room temperature if it has rested in the refrigerator for more than an hour.

3. Roll out the dough on a floured surface, then form or shape pasta as desired.

4. To cook, bring a large pot of water to a slow boil. Add the pasta, and stir to prevent sticking. Cook until al dente. (Cooking times will vary depending on the size of the pasta formed.) Drain, and serve as desired.

Scallop Pasta

This pasta is best served with a cream sauce, such as Alfredo.
Stir cooked peas into the Alfredo sauce to give the dish some nice color.

Serves 10

2 cups all-purpose flour
1 cup whole-wheat flour
Fresh-cracked black pepper
¼ teaspoon iodized salt
3 eggs
¾ cup puréed cooked scallops
2 tablespoons heavy cream
1 tablespoon olive oil

1. Sift together the flours, black pepper, and salt into a large mixing bowl. Whisk together the eggs, scallops, cream, and oil in a separate bowl.

2. Make a well in the center of the flour and pour in the egg mixture. Mix together the wet and dry ingredients by hand or in a mixer with a dough hook until fully incorporated and the dough forms into a ball. Wrap the dough in plastic wrap and let rest in the refrigerator for at least 1 hour, or up to 1 day. Allow dough to return to room temperature if it has rested in the refrigerator for more than an hour.

3. Roll out the dough on a floured surface, then form or shape pasta as desired.

4. To cook, bring a large pot of water to a slow boil. Add the pasta, and stir to prevent sticking. Cook until al dente. (Cooking times will vary depending on the size of the pasta formed.) Drain, and serve as desired.

Serves 10

½ cup walnuts
2 eggs
2 egg whites
2 tablespoons heavy cream
¼ cup melted unsalted butter
3 cups all-purpose flour

Walnut Pasta

*This is great served with a pesto sauce, as a side
with a main dish or all on its own.*

1. Finely chop the walnuts. Whisk together the eggs, egg whites, cream, butter, and walnuts in a bowl. Sift the flour into a large mixing bowl.

2. Make a well in the center of the flour and pour in the egg mixture. Mix together the wet and dry ingredients by hand or in a mixer with a dough hook until fully incorporated and the dough forms into a ball. Wrap the dough in plastic wrap and let rest in the refrigerator for at least 1 hour, or up to 1 day. Allow dough to return to room temperature if it has rested in the refrigerator for more than an hour.

3. Roll out the dough on a floured surface, then form or shape pasta as desired.

4. To cook, bring a large pot of water to a slow boil. Add the pasta, and stir to prevent sticking. Cook until al dente. (Cooking times will vary depending on the size of the pasta formed.) Drain, and serve as desired.

Gnocchi

The word gnocchi literally translates as "lumps."
These are potato dumplings that are served in the same method as pasta.

Serves 10

2 cups durum wheat
 (semolina) flour
1 teaspoon iodized salt
3 eggs
1 cup cooked mashed potato
¼ cup olive oil
2 tablespoons water

1. Sift together the flour and salt into a large bowl. Whisk the eggs in a separate bowl. Add the potato, oil, and water, and stir to mix.

2. Make a well in the center of the flour and pour in the egg mixture. Mix together the wet and dry ingredients by hand or in a mixer with a dough hook until fully incorporated and the dough forms into a ball.

3. Use 2 spoons to form the dough into ovals about ½ teaspoon in size.

4. To cook, bring a large pot of water to a slow boil. Add the pasta, and stir to prevent sticking. Boil for 10 to 15 minutes, until al dente. Drain, and serve.

Gnocchi

A tip for making your gnocchi come out perfectly is to cook the mashed potato at least 1 or 2 hours ahead of time. Set it aside in a glass bowl and cover with a cloth. Letting the potatoes stand like this for a few hours helps them lose some of their moisture, thereby producing the perfect texture.

*3 baking potatoes, baked
    until fork-tender*
*½ bulb fresh roasted garlic
    (see Roasted Garlic Paste
    recipe for garlic roasting
    instructions, page 70)*
*2 cups durum wheat
    (semolina) flour*
⅛ teaspoon iodized salt
2 eggs
2 tablespoons olive oil
1 tablespoon water

Roasted Potato and Garlic Gnocchi

*When cooking gnocchi—or any fresh pasta—you should use a slower boil, as
opposed to the strong rolling boil you use when cooking dry pasta.*

1. Thoroughly purée the potato and garlic together in a food processor
    or blender. Sift together the flour and salt into a large bowl. Whisk the
    eggs in a small bowl. Whisk the oil into the eggs, and stir in the potato
    and garlic purée.

2. Make a well in the center of the flour and pour in the egg mixture.
    Mix together the wet and dry ingredients by hand or in a mixer with a
    dough hook until fully incorporated and the dough forms into a ball.
    Wrap the dough in plastic wrap and let rest in the refrigerator for 1
    hour, or up to 1 day. Allow dough to return to room temperature if it has
    rested in the refrigerator for more than an hour.

3. Use 2 spoons to form the dough into ovals about ½ teaspoon in size.

4. To cook, bring a large pot of salted (optional) water to a slow boil. Add
    the pasta, and stir to prevent sticking. Boil for 10 to 15 minutes, until al
    dente. Drain, and serve.

Stuffed Rigatoni

Make extra and freeze it in a sealed container for later use. Just put parchment or wax paper between the layers, and don't place rigatoni too close to each other. Sprinkle a little flour over each layer to help prevent sticking before placing the paper on the pasta.

Serves 10

1 shallot
¼ bunch fresh marjoram
2 thick slices Italian bread, toasted
2 pounds ground chicken
1 egg white
¼ cup chopped toasted walnuts
1 recipe Basic Pasta (page 100), unformed and uncooked
1½ cups Brown Sauce (page 75)
½ cup raisins (optional)

1. Peel and mince the shallot. Remove the marjoram leaves from the stems, and clean and chop the leaves. Soak the toasted bread in water, then squeeze out excess water. Mix together the chicken, egg white, walnuts, shallot, marjoram, and bread.

2. Roll out the pasta dough on a floured surface and cut into 1-inch by 2-inch rectangles. Place 1 teaspoon meat mixture on each rectangle and roll into small rigatoni.

3. In a shallow pan, reduce the Brown Sauce by half the volume over medium-high heat.

4. Bring a large pot of water to a slow boil. Add the rigatoni, and stir to separate. Boil for 15 to 20 minutes, until the chicken is thoroughly cooked. Drain.

5. Serve drizzled with the reduced sauce and sprinkled with the raisins.

Parchment Paper
Keep a roll of parchment paper in your kitchen. It comes in handy for a number of kitchen tasks. Roll it into a funnel for pouring dry ingredients into containers; line your counter with it when working with lasagna to separate the noodles to dry; use it to line baking sheets and cake pans for nonstick cooking and easy cleanup; and more.

1 recipe Basic Pasta (page
100), unformed and
uncooked
3 sprigs fresh basil
3 sprigs fresh oregano
8 cups tomato sauce of
choice (see Chapter 5,
page 63)
1 meatball recipe of choice
(see Chapter 11, page
199), 1 to 2 inches in
diameter and cooked
1 pound sweet Italian
sausage, cooked
¾ cup ricotta
1 cup shredded mozzarella
cheese
¼ cup fresh-grated Parmesan
cheese
Fresh-cracked black pepper

Traditional Lasagna

Be creative with lasagna—almost anything can be stuffed between the flat noodles. Layers of seafood, different vegetables, or meats can be used.

1. Preheat oven to 350°F. Roll out the pasta dough into long lasagna sheets about ¼ inch thick. Clean and chop the basil and oregano leaves. Bring a large pot of water to a slow boil, add pasta and partially cook for approximately 4 minutes, and then shock in ice water.

2. Spoon a thin layer of the tomato sauce into the bottom of a large baking pan. Layer pasta sheets over with sauce, then top with a layer of the meatballs, sausage, cheeses, basil, oregano, and pepper. Ladle sauce over the top. Repeat layering until the pan is almost full, finishing with a top layer of pasta, cheese, and sauce.

3. Cover, and bake for 45 minutes. Uncover, and bake for 15 minutes or until lightly browned and bubbling.

4. Remove from oven, and let stand for 5 to 10 minutes before serving.

Vegetarian Lasagna

If you prefer, you can substitute other greens for the kale in this recipe, such as spinach or escarole.

Serves 10

½ recipe Whole-Wheat Pasta (page 102), unformed and uncooked
½ recipe Spelt Pasta (page 101), unformed and uncooked
1 large yellow bell pepper
2 shallots
½ small bunch fresh parsley
1 tablespoon olive oil
4 cups Old World Gravy (Long-Cooking Tomato Sauce) (page 64)
1 cup Roasted Garlic Paste (page 70)
1 cup cooked red lentils
1 cup steamed kale
1 cup shredded fontina cheese
Fresh-cracked black pepper

1. Preheat oven to 350°F. Bring a large pot of water to a slow boil. While the water heats, combine the 2 types of pasta dough and roll out into lasagna sheets ¼ inch thick. Partially cook pasta in boiling water for approximately 4 minutes, then shock in ice water.

2. Dice the bell pepper, and peel and finely slice the shallots. Clean and gently chop the parsley.

3. Sauté the bell pepper and shallots in the oil until soft.

4. Ladle enough sauce into a large baking pan to coat the bottom. Layer pasta sheets over the sauce, then top with layers of the garlic paste, lentils, kale, peppers, cheese, shallots, parsley, and black pepper. Ladle sauce over the top. Repeat layering until the pan is almost full, finishing with a top layer of pasta, cheese, and sauce.

5. Cover, and bake for 30 to 45 minutes until heated through and the cheese is melted. Uncover and bake for another 10 to 15 minutes. Remove from oven and let stand for 5 to 10 minutes before serving.

Serves 10

2 pounds fresh uncooked lobster meat
2 bunches leeks
½ bunch fresh parsley
Fresh-cracked black pepper
1 recipe Roasted Garlic Pasta (page 108), uncut and uncooked
4 cups Mascarpone Cheese Sauce (page 69)

Lobster Ravioli

When making homemade dough for ravioli, the dough should be a bit thicker than for regular pasta shapes because it must endure more manipulation.

1. Roughly chop the lobster meat into bite-sized pieces. Thoroughly wash and dry the leeks. Thinly slice both the white and green parts. Clean and chop the parsley.

2. In a large bowl, mix together the lobster, leeks, parsley, and black pepper.

3. Roll out the pasta dough on a floured surface into sheets about ½ inch thick. Cut into circles 3 inches in diameter.

4. Spoon teaspoonfuls of the lobster mixture onto the centers of the circles. Lightly paint the outer edge of the pasta with a tiny amount of water, fold in half, and seal by pressing closed with your fingers.

5. Bring 2 gallons of water to a slow boil. Add the ravioli and cook until al dente, approximately 10 minutes. While the ravioli cooks, heat the cheese sauce.

6. Serve the ravioli with the cheese sauce and sprinkle with black pepper.

Cooking Ravioli

To prevent ravioli from sticking, stir them gently after dropping them into the boiling water. If you remove them with a slotted spoon as soon as they rise to the surface of the water, they will not overcook. Spooning them out instead of draining into a colander helps keep the delicate ravioli intact.

Pasta-Wrapped Shrimp with Pesto

This pasta-wrapped shrimp makes an impressive presentation.
And the taste is equally fantastic.

Serves 10

3 shallots
½ bulb garlic
Fresh-cracked black pepper
2 pounds large fresh shrimp
1 recipe Basic Pasta (page
    100), unformed and
    uncooked
1 recipe Walnut Pesto (page
    73)

1. Peel and mince the shallots and garlic, and combine in a bowl with the black pepper. Peel, devein, and clean the shrimp (remove the tails, too).

2. Roll out the pasta dough into a sheet as thin as possible, taking care not to tear the dough. Cut into 3-inch squares.

3. Place 1 shrimp in the center of each square. Add approximately ¼ to ½ teaspoon of the garlic and shallot mixture. Wrap and seal the shrimp in pasta.

4. Bring a large pot of water to a boil. Add the pasta, and cook for 3 to 5 minutes, until the pasta is al dente and the shrimp are cooked through. Drain, and serve with the pesto. (Do not heat the pesto.)

Serves 10

1 pound baccalà (dried,
    salted cod)
1 recipe Basic Pasta (page
    100), unformed and
    uncooked
1 pound fresh peas
1 teaspoon olive oil
4 cups heavy cream
Fresh-cracked black pepper

Baccalà with Pasta and Fresh Peas

*Baccalà is whole, small cod that is cured in brine and air-dried.
Dried cod is commonly used in Italian cuisine and is usually
cooked in sauces with tomato and milk or cream.*

1. Pound on the dried cod with a wooden spoon or pestle and then soak
    in cool water in the refrigerator for 4 to 5 days (2 days at the very least)
    prior to preparation. Change the water at least 2 to 3 times a day, and
    gently rinse the fish each time. After soaking, drain the fish and cut it
    into large squares. Set aside.

2. Roll out the pasta dough on a floured surface into a sheet about ¼ inch
    thick, and cut into desired shape.

3. Shuck the peas, and steam until al dente.

4. Heat the olive oil on medium in a large sauté pan. Add the baccalà, and
    sauté for 8 minutes. Add the cream, and reduce by half the volume over
    medium to medium-high heat.

5. Bring a large pot of water to a slow boil, and add the pasta. Cook until
    al dente, and drain. Add the pasta and peas to the pan with the bac-
    calà, and remove from heat. Stir to combine, and serve.

Pork-Filled Pasta Shells

Many Italian recipes call for bread to be soaked in wine or water.
Use day-old Italian bread slices.

Serves 10

1 tablespoon olive oil
3 yellow onions
6 fresh plum tomatoes
½ bunch fresh oregano
4 slices toasted Italian bread
¼ cup robust red wine, mixed
*   with ½ cup water*
2 pounds lean ground pork
1 egg
⅓ cup fresh-grated Parmesan
*   cheese*
1 recipe Basic Pasta (page
*   100), unformed and*
*   uncooked*
8 cups New World Fresh
*   Sauce (page 66)*
Fresh-cracked black pepper

1. Preheat oven to 375°F. Grease a large Dutch oven or heavy ovenproof pan (with a lid) with the oil. Peel and finely dice the onions. Clean and finely dice the tomatoes. Clean and gently mince the oregano leaves. Soak the toast in the wine mixture, then squeeze out excess liquid.

2. In a large mixing bowl, combine, the pork, egg, ½ of the cheese, the onion, tomato, oregano, and bread. Roll into ¼-inch ovals.

3. Roll out the pasta dough on a floured surface into a sheet about ¼ inch thick. Cut into 4-inch circles. Place a meat ovals into the center of each pasta circle. Gently fold up 2 sides and pinch the ends together to form a shell.

4. Ladle sauce into the prepared pan to coat the bottom. Place the stuffed shells in the pan, and ladle more sauce on top. Sprinkle with the remaining cheese and the black pepper.

5. Cover, and bake for 45 to 60 minutes, until the pork is thoroughly cooked.

Serves 10

1½ pounds fresh cod
1 bunch green onions
6 cloves garlic
¼ cup black olives
1 recipe Basic Pasta (page
    100), unformed and
    uncooked
1 bunch leeks
1 teaspoon olive oil
½ cup dry white wine (not
    cooking wine)
8 cups Fish Stock (page 16)
1 teaspoon saffron

Pasta Stuffed with Fresh Cod in Saffron Broth

You can make the cod-filled pasta a day ahead and refrigerate.

1. Cut the fish into medium dice. Clean and finely slice the green onions. Peel and mince the garlic. Finely slice the black olives.

2. In a large bowl, mix together the fish, green onions, garlic, and olives.

3. Roll out the pasta dough on a floured surface into 3-inch by 6-inch rectangles. Place 1½ to 2 tablespoons of the fish mixture on each rectangle. Dampen the edges of the pasta with water, fold in half, and press closed. Seal by pressing the edges with fork tines.

4. Thoroughly clean and thinly slice the white and green parts of the leeks. Heat the oil on medium in a large stockpot. Add the leeks, and sauté for about 5 minutes. Add the wine and reduce by half. Add the stock and saffron, and simmer for 45 minutes, uncovered.

5. Bring a large pot of water to a slow boil. Add the pasta, and cook for about 6 minutes, until al dente (the pasta will float to the top).

6. Ladle the leek broth into serving bowls, add the cod pasta, and serve.

Classic Fettuccine Alfredo

This butter, cream, and cheese sauce was made famous by a restaurateur named Alfredo in Rome in the 1920s when he served it with fettuccini.

Serves 10

1 recipe Basic Pasta (page
   100), unformed and
   uncooked
1 bunch fresh parsley
8 cups heavy cream
½ cup (1 stick) unsalted
   butter, chilled
¼ cup fresh-grated Romano
   cheese
¼ cup fresh-grated Parmesan
   cheese
Fresh-cracked black pepper

1. Roll out the pasta on a floured surface into a sheet about ¼ inch thick. Cut into fettuccini about ¼ inch wide and 12 to 18 inches long. Bring a large pot of water to a slow boil. Add the pasta, and cook until al dente, approximately 6 minutes. Drain, shock in cold water, and drain again.

2. Clean and finely chop the parsley. In a saucepan, reduce the heavy cream to ¾ quart over medium to medium-high temperature. Add the cold butter a little at a time, stirring after each addition until melted and incorporated into the cream. Remove from heat.

3. Add the pasta and both cheeses to the reduced cream, and gently toss for 1 to 2 minutes to mix and reheat the pasta.

4. Serve on a heated platter, sprinkled with the parsley and pepper.

1½ pounds sea scallops
3 shallots
4 red bell peppers
½ bunch fresh parsley
1 recipe Basic Pasta (page 100), unformed and uncooked
1 teaspoon olive oil
½ cup dry white wine
2 quarts heavy cream
3 tablespoons cold unsalted butter
½ cup fresh-grated Asiago cheese
Fresh-cracked black pepper

Fettuccine Alfredo con Capesante

Although scallops are usually sold already cleaned and shelled, they can be served in their shell, heated in a sauté pan with oil, garlic, salt and pepper, lemon juice, and parsley until they are steamed open.

1. Remove the muscles from the scallops (the small, tough piece). Peel and finely dice the shallots. Clean and finely slice the red peppers. Clean and chop the parsley.

2. Roll out the pasta on a floured surface into a sheet about ¼ inch thick. Cut into fettuccini about ¼ inch wide and 12 to 18 inches long. Bring a large pot of water to a slow boil. Add the pasta, and cook until al dente, approximately 6 to 8 minutes. Drain, shock in cold water, and drain again. Set aside.

3. Heat the oil in a large saucepan to medium temperature. Add the shallots and red peppers, and toss until the onions just begin to wilt, about 2 minutes. Add the scallops, and cook for about 2 minutes. Add the wine, cover, and simmer for 3 minutes.

4. In a separate large saucepan, reduce the cream to about 1¾ quarts over medium heat. Add the butter and cheese, and immediately remove from heat.

5. Add the cream mixture to the scallop mixture, which should still be on the heat. Add the pasta into the scallop mixture, and stir for a minute to reheat. Remove the final mixture from heat. Serve on a heated platter, sprinkled with the parsley and black pepper.

Stuffed Shells

Most people think of stuffing these pasta shells with ricotta and mozzarella cheese, but try this version with mascarpone and Gorgonzola.

Serves 10

½ bunch fresh basil
1 cup mascarpone
½ cup Gorgonzola
3 eggs
1 teaspoon red pepper flakes
1 recipe Spelt Pasta (page 101), unformed and uncooked
4 cups New World Fresh Sauce (page 66)

1. Preheat oven to 350°F. Clean and gently chop the basil. Mix together the mascarpone, Gorgonzola, eggs, red pepper flakes, and basil. Ladle ½ cup of the sauce into a large baking pan to coat the bottom of the pan.

2. Roll out the pasta dough on a floured surface into a sheet about ½ inch thick. Cut into 4-inch ovals. Place 2 heaping tablespoons of the cheese mixture in the center of each oval. Fold up 2 edges and pinch the ends together to form shells. Place in the pan. Ladle the remaining sauce over the top of the shells.

3. Cover, and bake for 20 minutes. Uncover, and bake for 5 more minutes, until lightly browned and bubbling.

Serves 10

4 tablespoons olive oil,
    divided
½ recipe Roasted Garlic Pasta
    (page 108), uncut and
    uncooked
2 Vidalia onions
1 bunch fresh arugula
2 slices crusty Italian bread
1 cup Chicken or Vegetable
    Stock (pages 14 or 16)
¼ cup melted unsalted butter
½ cup fresh-grated Romano
    cheese
Fresh-cracked black pepper

Baked Spaghetti Tart

*Though this is an unusual way to prepare spaghetti,
you will find it to be very delicious.*

1. Preheat oven to 375°F. Lightly grease a large round casserole pan with 1 tablespoon of the oil. Roll out and cut the pasta into spaghetti. Peel and finely slice the onions. Clean the arugula. Toast and finely chop the bread.

2. Mix together the pasta, the remaining oil, the onions, arugula, and stock, and place in the prepared casserole dish. Cover, and bake for 30 minutes.

3. Meanwhile, mix together the butter, cheese, pepper, and bread.

4. Top the tart with the bread mixture. Bake for 5 more minutes, uncovered.

Serves 10

1 gallon stock of choice (see
    Chapter 2, page 13)
1 recipe Basic Pasta (page
    100), unformed and
    uncooked

Pasta Dumplings

*This is an easy way to make gnocchi without the potatoes.
These drop dumplings can be eaten the same way,
with tomato or Alfredo sauce.*

Bring the stock to a slow boil and drop in teaspoonfuls of the pasta dough. Boil until al dente or fully cooked, about 15 to 20 minutes. Drain, and serve as desired.

Pasta con Ragu Bolognese

Oregano and marjoram can be used interchangeably—the flavors are similar. Commonly believed food lore is that Bolognese sauce originated from someone using a leftover meatloaf to fortify a sauce.

Serves 10

3 bell peppers (any color)
6 plum tomatoes
3 shallots
½ bulb garlic
¼ bunch fresh marjoram or oregano
¼ bunch fresh parsley
4 slices toasted Italian bread
½ pound lean ground beef
½ pound ground veal
½ pound lean ground pork
1 egg
¼ cup fresh-grated Romano cheese
1 recipe Basic Pasta (page 100), unformed and uncooked
2 cups heavy cream
Fresh-cracked black pepper

1. Preheat oven to 350°F. Clean and medium-dice the bell peppers. Clean and dice the tomatoes. Peel and mince the shallots and garlic. Clean and chop the marjoram and parsley. Soak the bread in water and immediately squeeze out liquid.

2. In a large loaf pan, mix together the ground meats, egg, cheese, shallots, garlic, marjoram, bread, and peppers. Bake for 45 minutes.

3. Finely break up the meat in a large saucepan, add the tomatoes and peppers, and simmer for 1 hour, uncovered.

4. While the sauce simmers, roll out the pasta on a floured surface and cut into desired shape. Bring a large pot of water to a boil. Add the pasta, and cook until al dente. Drain, and set aside.

5. In a small saucepan, reduce the cream by half the volume, then whisk it into the tomato-meat mixture.

6. Add the pasta to the sauce and toss to mix. Serve on a heated platter, sprinkled with the parsley and black pepper.

1 cup dried garbanzo or
 cannellini beans
2 large yellow onions
2 carrots
2 stalks celery
½ bulb garlic
2 bunches kale
4 sprigs thyme
¼ cup olive oil
8 cups Chicken Stock (page
 14)
2 bay leaves
½ recipe Basic Pasta (page
 100), unformed and
 uncooked
Fresh-cracked black pepper

Bowtie Pasta with Braised Beans and Greens

Escarole or spinach can be substituted for the kale in this recipe.

1. Soak the beans overnight in 8 cups water. Drain. Peel and dice the onions and carrots. Clean and the dice celery. Peel and mince the garlic. Clean and roughly chop the kale, including the stems. Clean the thyme, remove the leaves, and discard the stems.

2. Heat the oil to medium temperature in a large stockpot. Add the onions, carrots, celery, and garlic. Cover, and let sweat for about 8 minutes, stirring occasionally.

3. Add the beans, bay leaves, stock, and thyme, and reduce heat. Simmer for 3 to 4 hours, with lid ajar, until the beans are thoroughly cooked.

4. Meanwhile, roll out the pasta dough on a floured surface into a sheet about ¼ inch thick. Cut into 1-inch by 3-inch rectangles. Pinch each rectangle in the center to form a bowtie. Bring a large pot of water to a slow boil. Add the pasta, and cook until al dente. Drain.

5. Add the kale to the bean sauce, stir, and cover. Let braise for 5 minutes. Add the pasta to the sauce, and toss to mix.

6. Remove the bay leaves. Serve in soup bowls, and sprinkle with the pepper.

Deep-Fried Pasta

*Deep-fried is a scary term, but that shouldn't stop you from enjoying this.
Using olive oil will reduce the cholesterol in this dish.*

Serves 10

¼ recipe Basic Pasta (page
100), unformed and
uncooked
4 cups cooking oil

1. Roll out the dough on a floured surface, and form as desired. (A spaghetti noodle works well and makes interesting garnish.) The pasta doesn't need to be cooked unless it has dried. If it has dried, it should be cooked al dente and then drained.

2. Heat the oil to medium-high temperature in a large, deep pan.

3. Fry the pasta until lightly golden brown.

Great Garnish

Deep-fried pasta is not intended to be eaten as a main dish. However, it makes a fantastic garnish for many different foods. Try sprinkling some deep-fried pasta on soups, stews, or salads for a crunchy, fun twist.

1 bunch fresh parsley

4 cloves garlic

¾ cup ricotta

¼ cup mascarpone (optional)

¼ cup shredded mozzarella cheese

¼ cup fresh-grated Romano cheese

1 egg

Fresh-cracked black pepper

1 recipe Basic Pasta (page 100), unformed and uncooked

Cheese Tortellini

Tortellini literally translates as "stuffed straight hat with a hole." In Italy, stuffed pastas originated from the necessity to use good leftovers.

1. Clean and dry the parsley, and finely chop the leaves and stems. Peel and mince the garlic.

2. Mix together the cheeses, egg, parsley, garlic, and pepper.

3. Roll out the pasta dough on a floured surface into a sheet about ⅛ to ¼ inch thick. Cut into 2-inch squares.

4. Place ¼ to ½ teaspoon of the cheese mixture on each pasta square. Dampen the edges, and fold up opposite corners to form a triangle, then seal together the edges. Gently pull down the base ends of the triangle and bring them together until they overlap, forming a ringlike shape. Press the ends together to secure them. (The top of the triangle will stand up a bit, like a hat.)

5. Bring a large pot of salted (optional) water to a slow boil. Add the pasta, and cook for about 10 minutes. Drain, and serve as desired.

Meat Ravioli

These can be made larger and called tortelli. Ravioli or tortelli can be stuffed with numerous different ingredients.

Serves 10

6 cloves fresh garlic
1 fresh shallot
¼ bunch fresh oregano
4 thick slices crusty Italian
 bread (either stale or
 toasted)
¾ pound lean ground beef
¾ pound lean ground pork
¼ cup fresh-grated Asiago,
 Parmesan, or Romano
 cheese
Fresh-cracked black pepper
1 recipe Basic Pasta (page
 100), unformed and
 uncooked

1. Peel and mince the garlic and shallot. Clean and dry the oregano, and chop the leaves (discard the stems). Soak the bread in water, then squeeze out all excess water.

2. In a large mixing bowl, mix together the beef, pork, cheese, pepper, garlic, shallot, oregano, and bread.

3. Roll out the pasta dough on a floured surface into a sheet about ⅛ to ¼ inch thick. Cut into 3-inch squares.

4. Place 1 to 1½ teaspoons of the meat mixture in the center of each square. Lightly wet the edges with water using a small pastry brush or your finger. Fold over 1 corner to form a triangle, and seal together the edges.

5. Bring a large pot of water to a slow boil. Add the pasta, and cook for about 20 minutes. Drain, and serve as desired.

Chapter 8

Risotto

Basic Risotto 140

Roasted Carrot Risotto 141

Grilled Broccoli Raab and Alfredo Risotto 142

Browned Risotto Patties 143

Carciofi Ripieni con Risotto

   (Artichokes Stuffed with Risotto) 144

Tomato and Parmesan Risotto 145

Spicy Risotto 146

Risotto-Encased Meatballs 146

Seared Filet Mignon Risotto 147

Stewed Veal Risotto 148

Braised Veal and Pepper Risotto 149

Lamb Risotto 150

Seasoned Beef Risotto 151

Chicken Saltimbocca Risotto 152

Chicken and Oregano Risotto 153

Braised Duck Risotto 154

Creamy Clam Risotto 154

Turkey and Walnut Risotto 155

Red Snapper and Pepper Risotto 156

Seafood Risotto 157

Lemon Scampi Cod Risotto 158

Lobster Risotto 159

Risotto Seafood Pepper Cakes 160

Basic Risotto

*Riso is the Italian word for "rice." Risotto refers more to a
cooking method in which rice is first "toasted" with oil and onions
and then liquid is added a little at a time.*

1. Peel and mince the garlic and shallots. Heat the oil in a large saucepan over medium heat. Add the garlic and shallots. Sauté for about 3 minutes, then add the rice. Stir constantly.

2. Add the wine and stir until fully absorbed. Add the stock ½ cup at a time, stirring frequently and allowing each addition to be completely absorbed before adding the next. Continue until all the stock is absorbed and the rice is tender.

3. Remove from heat and add the cheese and pepper. Stir, and serve.

The Perfect Pan
Risotto should always be cooked in a heavy saucepan with a large, flat bottom so that the flame underneath can be evenly distributed. If the heat is not evenly distributed throughout the risotto, the grains of rice will cook at different rates, leaving you with the occasional crunchy grain.

Roasted Carrot Risotto

*When entertaining, to save time, the carrots can be prepared
the day before and refrigerated until ready to use.*

Serves 10

1 pound fresh carrots
3 large yellow onions
4 large sprigs rosemary
3 tablespoon olive oil, divided
2 cups arborio rice
½ cup dry white wine (not
   cooking wine)
5½ cups Vegetable Stock
   (page 16)
Fresh-cracked black pepper

1. Preheat oven to 375°F. Peel and thickly dice the carrots and onions. Clean and remove the leaves from the rosemary.

2. Toss the carrots and onions with 2 tablespoons of the oil and ½ of the rosemary. Spread out in an even layer on a baking sheet and roast for about 15 minutes. Set aside.

3. Heat the remaining oil to medium temperature in a large saucepan. Add the rice and stir for 1 minute. Add the wine and stir until fully absorbed.

4. Add the stock ½ cup at a time, stirring frequently and allowing each addition to be completely absorbed before adding the next. Continue until all the stock is absorbed and the rice is tender.

5. Remove from heat. Add the roasted carrots and the remaining rosemary, and season with pepper. Serve in a heated bowl.

2 pounds broccoli raab

5 tablespoons olive oil, divided

Fresh-cracked black pepper

2 shallots

2 cloves garlic

2½ cups arborio rice

½ cup dry white wine (not cooking wine)

6 cups stock of choice (see Chapter 2, page 13)

1½ cups cream

¼ cup cold unsalted butter

¼ cup shredded fontina cheese

Grilled Broccoli Raab and Alfredo Risotto

The classic Alfredo sauce gives this risotto a rich and creamy taste. The bright green of the broccoli raab mounded on the creamy rice contrasts nicely with the white sauce, making for a beautiful presentation.

1. Preheat grill. Clean and dry the broccoli raab, toss in 4 tablespoons of the olive oil, and sprinkle with black pepper. Grill for 2 minutes on each side.

2. Peel and mince the shallots and garlic. Heat the remaining oil to medium temperature in a large saucepan. Sauté the shallots and garlic for 5 minutes. Add the rice, and stir for 2 minutes.

3. Add the wine, and stir until completely absorbed. Add the stock ½ cup at a time, stirring frequently and allowing each addition to be completely absorbed before adding the next. Continue until all the stock is absorbed and the rice is tender.

4. Prepare the Alfredo sauce by heating the cream to medium-high temperature in small saucepan until reduced by half the volume. Add the cold butter a bit at a time, and stir to incorporate before adding more. Remove from heat and stir in the cheese.

5. To serve, mound the rice in a serving bowl, top with the broccoli raab, and drizzle with the sauce.

Rice for Risotto

The best variety of rice for making risotto is arborio rice—an imported Italian rice. Other types of rice cannot absorb as much liquid or hold their shape throughout the constant stirring required when making risotto.

Browned Risotto Patties

*The Italian version of "potato pancakes," these patties
are a great way to use up leftover risotto.*

Serves 10

*2 tablespoons olive oil,
    divided
1 large yellow onion
½ cup cold unsalted butter
2 cups arborio rice
6 cups stock of choice (see
    Chapter 2, page 13)
¼ cup shredded fontina
    cheese
Fresh-cracked black pepper*

1. Preheat broiler. Lightly grease a baking sheet with 1 tablespoon of the oil and finely chop the onion. Cut the butter into pats.

2. Heat the remaining oil to medium temperature in large saucepan. Sauté the onion for about 2 minutes. Add the rice, and stir for 2 minutes. Add the stock ½ cup at a time, stirring frequently and allowing each addition to be completely absorbed before adding the next. Continue until all the stock is absorbed and the rice is tender.

3. Remove from heat and stir in the cheese. Let cool, then form into ½-cup patties.

4. Place the patties on the prepared baking sheet, place a pat of butter on top of each patty, and brown lightly under the broiler. Serve.

Carciofi Ripieni con Risotto
(Artichokes Stuffed with Risotto)

Stuffed artichokes are a nice dish for special dinners,
such as holidays like Thanksgiving and Christmas Day.

Serves 10

5 artichokes
2 tablespoons olive oil, divided
2 large leeks
½ bulb garlic
2 cups arborio rice
½ cup dry white wine (not cooking wine)
5½ cups stock of choice (see Chapter 2, page 13)
½ cup ricotta cheese
1 tablespoon red pepper flakes (optional)
3 anchovy fillets, mashed (optional)

1. Prepare the artichokes by cutting each in half lengthwise, leaving the stem on. Snip off the pointy ends of each leaf. Peel the outer skin of the stem. Remove the "choke" (the purplish white center) and discard. Parboil the artichokes and shock in ice water.

2. Preheat oven to 375°F. Lightly grease a baking sheet with 1 tablespoon of the oil. Thoroughly clean and finely dice the leeks, using both the white and green parts. Peel and mince the garlic.

3. Heat the remaining oil to medium temperature in a large saucepan. Add the leeks, garlic, and rice. Stir for 2 minutes. Add the wine, and stir until completely absorbed. Add the stock ½ cup at a time, stirring frequently and allowing each addition to be completely absorbed before adding the next. Continue until all the stock is absorbed and the rice is tender.

4. Remove from heat, and stir in the ricotta. Stuff each artichoke leaf with the risotto, and place on the prepared baking sheet. Bake for 20 minutes.

5. Sprinkle with red pepper flakes and anchovy, if desired, and serve.

Tomato and Parmesan Risotto

This dish is like baked ziti but with risotto instead of pasta.

Serves 10

1 large yellow onion
½ bulb garlic
¼ bunch fresh basil
¼ bunch fresh oregano
¼ bunch fresh parsley
1 tablespoon olive oil
2 cups arborio rice
6 cups Chicken Stock (page 14)
4 cups Old World Gravy (Long-Cooking Tomato Sauce) (page 64)
½ cup fresh ricotta
½ cup shredded fresh mozzarella cheese
Fresh-cracked black pepper

1. Preheat oven to 350°F. Peel and dice the yellow onion. Peel and mince the garlic. Clean and chop the basil, oregano, and parsley leaves.

2. Heat the oil to medium temperature in a large saucepan. Sauté the onions and garlic for 3 minutes. Add the rice, and stir for 1 minute. Add the stock ½ cup at a time, stirring frequently and allowing each addition to be fully absorbed before adding the next. Continue until all the stock is absorbed and the rice is tender.

3. Pour 2 cups of the Old World Gravy into a large baking dish. Spoon the risotto on top in an even layer. Place dollops of the ricotta all over the risotto, and sprinkle with the shredded mozzarella and ½ of the fresh herbs. Ladle the remaining Old World Gravy over the top. Cover with foil, and bake for 10 minutes. Uncover, and bake for 5 more minutes.

4. Sprinkle with black pepper and the remaining herbs, and serve.

Plenty of Patience

Cooking risotto requires a watchful eye and lots of patience. It is important to let each ingredient be fully incorporated before adding the next one. Careful stirring will achieve the creamy consistency of a perfect risotto, while neglecting the cooking rice will leave you with a burned mess.

5 Italian peppers
2 fresh plum tomatoes
2 large yellow onions
½ bulb fresh garlic
4 sprigs fresh marjoram or
    oregano
1 tablespoon olive oil
2 cups arborio rice
½ cup pinot noir or other red
    drinking wine of choice
5½ cups Chicken Stock (page
    14)
1 cup Old World Gravy (Long-
    Cooking Tomato Sauce)
    (page 64)
⅓ cup Parmesan cheese
1 tablespoon red pepper
    flakes
Fresh-cracked black pepper

Serves 10

1 tablespoon olive oil
2 shallots
3 cloves garlic
¼ bunch fresh basil
1 slice toasted Italian bread
¾ pound lean ground pork
    and/or beef (you can
    substitute ground chicken
    or turkey)
1 egg
¼ cup shredded fontina
    cheese
2 cups Basic Risotto (page
    140)
Fresh-cracked black pepper

Spicy Risotto

This spicy risotto makes a great accompaniment to any roast or meatloaf.

1. Clean and finely dice the peppers and tomatoes. Peel and dice the onions. Peel and mince the garlic. Clean and gently chop the marjoram leaves.

2. Heat the oil to medium temperature in a large frying pan. Lightly sauté the peppers, onion, garlic, and rice for 2 minutes. Pour in the wine, and stir until absorbed. Add the stock ½ cup at a time, stirring frequently and allowing each addition to be completely absorbed before adding the next. Continue until all the stock is absorbed and the rice is tender.

3. Add the Old World Gravy, tomatoes, and marjoram. Remove from heat and sprinkle with cheese, red pepper flakes, and black pepper. Serve.

Risotto-Encased Meatballs

Your guests will be impressed by this original way to serve meatballs.

1. Preheat oven to 350°F. Lightly grease a baking pan with the oil.

2. Peel and mince the shallots and garlic. Clean and slice the basil leaves. Soak the bread in water and immediately squeeze out liquid.

3. Mix together the meat, egg, half the cheese, the shallots, garlic, half the basil, and bread. Form into balls, oval patties, or any desired shape.

4. Completely encase each meatball with risotto, and place in the prepared baking pan. Sprinkle with the remaining cheese. Cover the pan with foil, and bake for 30 minutes. Uncover, and bake for 20 minutes, until lightly browned.

5. Serve sprinkled with the remaining basil and the pepper.

Seared Filet Mignon Risotto

*Keeping the meat cold in the refrigerator until just ready to broil
or grill helps the meat to sear better.*

Serves 10

½ bulb garlic
3 tablespoons olive oil
Fresh-cracked black pepper
1¼ pounds filet mignon (or
    other tender beef)
2 cups arborio rice
½ cup robust red wine (not
    cooking wine)
5½ cups Beef Stock (page 15)
¼ cup fresh-grated Romano
    cheese
2 tablespoons cold unsalted
    butter

1. Preheat grill to medium-high heat. Peel and mince the garlic. Mix together half the oil, half the garlic, and some pepper. Rub the mixture onto the meat and place in the refrigerator until ready to cook.

2. Heat the remaining oil in a large saucepan to medium-high temperature. Add the remaining garlic and the rice, and stir for 1 minute. Pour in the wine, and stir until absorbed. Stir in the stock ½ cup at a time, stirring frequently and allowing each addition to be completely incorporated before adding the next. Continue until all the stock is absorbed and the rice is tender.

3. Stir in the cheese, butter, and pepper to taste. Keep covered and warm until ready to serve.

4. Approximately 10 minutes before the risotto is done, sear the meat on the hot grill to desired doneness. Slice thinly, and fan over the rice. Serve immediately.

Serves 10

3 large yellow onions
6 cloves fresh garlic
2 stalks celery
1 pound fresh plum tomatoes
2 large carrots
2 tablespoons olive oil
1 pound veal stew meat
1 tablespoon dried oregano
1 tablespoon dried thyme
1 bay leaf
1 cup hearty red wine
6 cups water
2 cups arborio rice
5½–6 cups Beef Stock (page 15)
¼ cup fresh-grated Parmesan cheese
¼ cup fresh-grated Romano cheese
Fresh-cracked black pepper

Stewed Veal Risotto

You can prepare the veal ahead of time and reheat when ready to serve.

1. Peel and slice the onions and garlic. Clean and chop the celery and tomatoes. Peel and chop the carrots.

2. Heat 1 tablespoon of the oil to medium temperature in a large Dutch oven. Brown the meat, onions, garlic, celery, and carrots for about 4 minutes. Reduce heat to medium-low. Add the tomatoes, oregano, thyme, bay leaf, ½ cup of the wine, and the water. Cover, and simmer for 3 to 4 hours, until the veal is fork-tender.

3. Heat the remaining oil to medium temperature in a large saucepan. Add the rice, and sauté for 1 minute. Add the remaining wine, and stir until absorbed. Stir in the stock ½ cup at a time, stirring frequently and allowing each addition to be completely absorbed before adding the next. Continue until the rice is fork-tender. Before adding the last ½ cup of stock, add the veal.

4. Remove from heat. Stir in the cheeses and black pepper. Keep warm.

5. Ladle the veal into serving bowls and top with the risotto.

Varieties of Rice
There are two main types of Italian rice: hard and soft grain; and four varieties: common, semifine, fine, and superfine. There is no difference in nutrition between the types, but there is a difference in price. Superfine is the most expensive. "Riso Fino," fine long-grain rice, is best suited for risotto.

Braised Veal and Pepper Risotto

Although a little more complex in preparation than most dishes, this fragrant and delicious veal and pepper mix is worth the extra effort and makes a great dish for a cold winter weekend.

Serves 10

Veal:
1½ pounds veal meat (keep chilled)
6 green bell peppers
3 large yellow onions
½ bulb garlic
½ pound fresh parsnips or carrots
½ bunch fresh parsley
1 tablespoon olive oil
1 cup hearty red wine
4 cups Beef Stock (page 15)
2 cups Brown Sauce (page 75)

Risotto:
½ bunch fresh parsley
1 tablespoon olive oil
1½ cups arborio rice
4½ cups Beef Stock (page 15)
½ cup fresh-grated Asiago cheese
Fresh-cracked black pepper

To prepare the veal:

1. Preheat oven to 350°F. Cut the veal into 2½ inch cubes. Clean and cut the peppers into large wedges. Peel and chop the onions. Peel and mince the garlic. Peel and chop the parsnips. Clean and chop the parsley.

2. Heat a Dutch oven (or other heavy-bottomed ovenproof pot with a lid) to medium-high temperature, then add the cold veal. Sear, until browned on all sides. Add the peppers, onions, garlic, oil, parsnips, and sauté for 3 to 4 minutes. Add the wine and reduce by half the volume. Add the stock and sauce. Bring to simmer, add the parsley, and cover.

3. Transfer the pot to the oven and cook for 2 hours.

To prepare the risotto:

1. Clean and mince the parsley. Heat the oil to medium temperature in a large saucepan. Add the rice, and toss in the oil for 1 minute.

2. Add the stock ½ cup at a time, stirring frequently and allowing each addition to be completely absorbed before adding the next. Continue until all the stock is absorbed and the rice is tender.

3. Remove from heat. Stir in the cheese and parsley.

4. Serve in bowls with the veal mixture.

Lamb:
½ bulb fresh garlic
¼ bunch fresh mint
2 tablespoons olive oil
1½ pounds boneless lamb

Risotto:
3 cloves garlic
¼ bunch fresh mint
1 tablespoon olive oil
1½ cups arborio rice
½ cup Merlot wine (or other
    dry red drinking wine of
    choice)
4½ cups Beef Stock (page 15)
½ cup mascarpone cheese
2 tablespoons cold unsalted
    butter
Fresh-cracked black pepper

Lamb Risotto

*Marinate the lamb for about 8 hours prior to making this dish.
The meat will need to be seared well; searing means to quickly
brown the meat on the outside on high heat.*

To prepare the lamb:

1. Peel and mince the garlic. Clean and chop the mint.

2. Mix together the garlic, mint, and oil. Coat the whole piece of lamb in the mixture, and let marinate for at least 8 hours and no longer than 16 hours in the refrigerator.

3. Preheat grill to medium-high to high (or heat a skillet to medium-high). Sear the lamb for 1 to 2 minutes, browning the outside but keeping the meat rare.

4. Cut the meat into small cubes.

To prepare the risotto:

1. Peel and mince the garlic. Clean and chop the mint, reserving several tops for garnish.

2. Heat the oil to medium temperature in large saucepan. Add the garlic and rice, and stir for 2 minutes. Add the wine, and stir until absorbed. Add the stock ½ cup at a time, stirring frequently and allowing each addition to be completely absorbed before adding the next. Continue until all the stock is absorbed and the rice is tender.

3. Remove from heat and add the lamb, mint, cheese, and butter. Stir thoroughly.

4. Serve in bowls, garnished with the reserved mint.

Seasoned Beef Risotto

True to their name, pine nuts, or pignoli in Italian, are the edible kernels of several varieties of pine. They are an essential ingredient in authentic pesto.

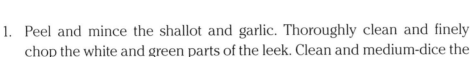

Serves 10

1 shallot
4 cloves garlic
1 large leek
4 fresh plum tomatoes
3 sprigs fresh thyme
4 sprigs fresh basil
1 tablespoon olive oil
1½ pounds lean ground beef
¼ cup pine nuts
1½ cups arborio rice
½ cup Merlot wine (or other
    dry red drinking wine of
    choice)
4½ cups Beef Stock (page 15)
⅓ cup fresh-grated Asiago
    cheese
Fresh-cracked black pepper

1. Peel and mince the shallot and garlic. Thoroughly clean and finely chop the white and green parts of the leek. Clean and medium-dice the tomatoes. Clean the thyme and remove the leaves (discard the stems). Clean and gently chop the basil.

2. Heat the oil to medium temperature in a large skillet. Add the beef, shallots, garlic, and pine nuts. Cook for about 15 minutes, until the beef is lightly browned. Drain excess fat from the pan. Add the leeks, tomatoes, and rice, and cook for 5 minutes, stirring frequently.

3. Pour in the wine, and stir until absorbed. Add the stock ½ cup at a time, stirring frequently and allowing each addition to be completely absorbed before adding the next. Continue until all the stock is absorbed and the rice is tender.

4. Remove from heat. Stir in the thyme, basil, cheese, and black pepper. Serve hot.

Cleaning Leeks
As leeks grow, sand and dirt accumulate between the layers, so it is important to clean them thoroughly. Before slicing them into rounds, trim off the ends, and make deep slits in each end. Soak in a bowl of water with ice cubes for 15 minutes. This will loosen any dirt, which can quickly be rinsed away after soaking.

2½ pounds skinless, boneless chicken breasts
¼–½ pound thinly sliced prosciutto
¼ bunch fresh Italian flat-leaf parsley
1 tablespoon olive oil
1½ cups arborio rice
1 cup Chardonnay (or other dry white wine of choice)
4 cups Chicken Stock (page 14)
⅓ cup shredded provolone cheese
Fresh-cracked black pepper

Chicken Saltimbocca Risotto

Do not add any salt to this dish, as the prosciutto and cheese have enough salt in them to flavor the risotto.

1. Preheat oven to 375°F. Wrap each piece of chicken with 1 slice of the prosciutto. Roast for 30 minutes on a well-oiled rack in a roasting pan in the oven.

2. While the chicken cooks, clean and chop the parsley. Heat the oil in a large saucepan to medium temperature. Add the rice, and stir for 2 minutes. Pour in the wine, and stir until absorbed.

3. Add the stock ½ cup at a time, stirring frequently and allowing each addition to be completely absorbed before adding the next. Continue until all the stock is absorbed and the rice is tender.

4. Remove from heat, and stir in the cheese.

5. To serve, mound spoonfuls of the risotto into serving bowls. Slice the prosciutto-wrapped chicken breasts on the bias, and fan over the top of the risotto. Sprinkle with the parsley and pepper.

Chicken and Oregano Risotto

Fresh oregano leaves are essential for this dish.
They are not as difficult to get as they used to be—most supermarkets
keep fresh herbs in the produce section.

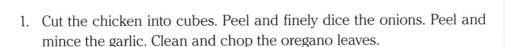

Serves 10

2½ pounds skinless, boneless
    chicken
2 large yellow onions
6 cloves garlic
½ bunch fresh oregano
2 tablespoons olive oil
1½ cups arborio rice
1 cup dry white wine (not
    cooking wine)
4½ cups Chicken Stock (page
    14)
½ cup fresh-grated Asiago
    cheese
Fresh-cracked black pepper

1. Cut the chicken into cubes. Peel and finely dice the onions. Peel and mince the garlic. Clean and chop the oregano leaves.

2. Heat the oil to medium-high temperature in a large saucepan. Add the chicken, and cook for 5 to 8 minutes, until lightly browned. Add the onions, and sauté for 2 minutes. Add the garlic, and sauté for 1 minute. Add the rice and cook for 1 minute longer, stirring to thoroughly combine the ingredients.

3. Pour in the wine, and stir until completely absorbed. Add the stock ½ cup at a time, stirring frequently and allowing each addition to be completely absorbed before adding the next. Continue until all the stock is absorbed and the rice is tender.

4. Remove from heat, and add the cheese, oregano, and pepper. Serve hot.

Serves 10

3 pounds duck, skin removed
1 teaspoon each dried thyme, parsley, and oregano
Kosher salt and fresh-cracked black pepper
2 large yellow onions
2 carrots
½ bulb garlic
2 stalks celery
2 bay leaves
1 cup hearty red wine (not cooking wine)
4 cups Brown Sauce (page 75)
½ recipe Basic Risotto (page 140)

Serves 10

2 dozen littleneck clams
4 cloves garlic
2 shallots
¼ bunch fresh marjoram or oregano
2 tablespoons olive oil
1½ cups arborio rice
½ cup dry white wine (not cooking wine)
2 cups clam juice
2 cups Fish Stock (page 16)
¼ cup fresh-grated Parmesan cheese
Fresh-cracked black pepper

Braised Duck Risotto

Starting preparation for this dish at least 12 hours in advance is suggested. A day ahead will work as well.

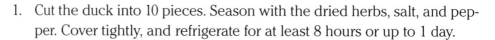

1. Cut the duck into 10 pieces. Season with the dried herbs, salt, and pepper. Cover tightly, and refrigerate for at least 8 hours or up to 1 day.

2. Preheat oven 350°F. Thoroughly rinse the duck in cold water. Peel and thickly dice the onions and carrots. Peel and mince the garlic. Clean and thickly dice the celery.

3. Place all the ingredients except the risotto in large baking pan. Cover, and bake for 1 hour. Uncover, and bake for 30 minutes.

4. Serve with the risotto.

Creamy Clam Risotto

Always use fresh clams for the best results.

1. Scrub the clams well. Peel and mince the garlic and shallots. Clean and gently chop the marjoram leaves.

2. Heat the oil to medium-high temperature in a large saucepan. Add the garlic, shallots, and rice. Sauté for 1 minute. Pour in the wine and clam juice, and stir until absorbed.

3. Stir in the stock ½ cup at a time, stirring frequently and allowing each addition to be fully absorbed before adding the next. Add the clams just before adding the last ½ cup stock, and stir until all the stock is absorbed and the rice is tender.

4. Remove from heat, and stir in the cheese, marjoram, and pepper. Serve hot.

Turkey and Walnut Risotto

*This is a great way to prepare turkey (which is not commonly
used in Italy) in a traditional Italian style.*

Serves 10

3 tablespoons olive oil,
   divided
2 pounds boneless turkey
   (breast, thigh, leg)
1 cup shelled walnuts
½ bulb fresh garlic
½ bunch fresh parsley
1 egg
Kosher salt and fresh-cracked
   black pepper
1½ cups arborio rice
¾ cup pinot grigio (or other
   white drinking wine of
   choice)
4 cups Chicken Stock (page
   14)
½ cup fresh-grated Romano
   cheese
1 tablespoon cold unsalted
   butter

1. Preheat oven to 375°F. Lightly grease a baking pan with 1 tablespoon of the oil. Clean and dry the turkey, and cut into medallions about ¾ to 1 inch thick. Finely chop or grind the walnuts. Peel and mince the garlic. Clean and gently chop the parsley. Lightly beat the egg.

2. Season the turkey with salt and pepper. Dip in the egg, and lightly coat with nuts. Heat 1 tablespoon of the oil in a large frying pan. Lightly brown the turkey on each side, about 3 minutes per side. Transfer the turkey to the prepared baking pan. Bake for about 8 to 12 minutes, until cooked through.

3. Add the remaining 1 tablespoon of oil to the frying pan and heat to medium temperature. Add the garlic and rice, and stir for 1 minute.

4. Pour in the wine, and stir until completely absorbed. Add the stock ½ cup at a time, stirring frequently and allowing each addition to be completely absorbed before adding the next. Continue until all the stock is absorbed and the rice is tender.

5. Remove from heat, and add the turkey, parsley, cheese, and butter. Serve hot.

Sweet or Salted?
Always use sweet unsalted butter in risottos to keep the salt content down. The stock you add will contribute plenty of salty flavor, and if you add cheese, this will also add salt to the final dish.

Serves 10

1 large yellow onion
2 red bell peppers
2 yellow bell peppers
¼ bunch fresh parsley
3 tablespoons olive oil
1½ cups arborio rice
½ cup white wine vinegar
2 tablespoons lemon juice
1 cup pinot grigio
5 cups Fish Stock (page 16)
¼ cup shredded fontina
    cheese
Fresh-cracked black pepper
1¼ pounds red snapper fillets
2 tablespoons all-purpose
    flour
2 tablespoons cold unsalted
    butter

Red Snapper and Pepper Risotto

*Preparing the rice and fish simultaneously to have both complete
at the same time is ideal, but you can make the rice first and set it
aside while prepping the snapper if you are entertaining.*

1. Peel and thinly slice the onion. Thinly slice the bell peppers. Clean and gently chop the parsley.

2. Heat 1 tablespoon of the oil to medium temperature in a large saucepan. Add half the onion and the rice, and stir for 3 minutes. Stir in ¼ cup of the vinegar and the lemon juice, and let absorb.

3. Pour in the wine, and stir until absorbed. Stir in the stock ½ cup at a time, stirring frequently and allowing each addition to be completely absorbed before adding the next. Continue until all the stock is absorbed and the rice is tender.

4. Remove from heat, and stir in the cheese, half the parsley, and the black pepper. Keep warm.

5. Heat the remaining oil to medium temperature in a large sauté pan. Dredge the fish in the flour. Cook for 3 minutes, then turn the fillets. Add the bell peppers and the remaining onion and vinegar. Cover, and cook for 3 to 5 minutes, until the fish is cooked through and the peppers and onion are tender. Uncover, and add the butter.

6. To serve, mound the risotto on a serving platter, top with the fish, and sprinkle with the remaining parsley and some black pepper.

Seafood Risotto

*Chock-full of juicy shrimp, lobster, and scallops,
this dish impresses guests and family alike.*

Serves 10

*1½ pounds cooked shrimp,
  scallops, and lobster (or
  any seafood combination
  of choice)*
2 leeks
1 bunch fresh parsley
1½ tablespoons olive oil
1½ cups arborio rice
*½ cup dry white wine (not
  cooking wine)*
4½ cups Fish Stock (page 16)
*½ cup fresh-grated Asiago
  cheese*
*2 tablespoons cold unsalted
  butter*
Fresh-cracked black pepper

1. Clean, shell, and cut the seafood into bite-sized chunks. Thoroughly clean the leeks and cut into small dice, using both the white and green parts. Clean and gently chop the parsley.

2. Heat the oil to medium temperature in a large saucepan. Add the leeks, and sauté for 2 minutes. Add the rice, and stir for 1 minute.

3. Pour in the wine, and stir until fully absorbed. Add the stock ½ cup at a time, stirring frequently and allowing each addition to be completely absorbed before adding the next. Continue until all the stock is absorbed and the rice is tender.

4. Remove from heat, and stir in the seafood, cheese, and butter. Serve on a heated platter, sprinkled with the parsley and pepper.

Risotto Patties

Don't throw away your leftover risotto. This can be mixed with eggs and grated Parmesan cheese, formed into patties, and fried for a quick and tasty side dish. Risotto patties make a great accompaniment to roasted meat dishes.

3 lemons
½ bunch fresh parsley
6 cloves garlic
3 tablespoons olive oil
Fresh-cracked black pepper
1¼ pounds fresh cod fillets
1½ cups arborio rice
¼ cup pinot grigio (or other
    light white drinking wine)
5 cups Fish Stock (page 16) or
    water
2 tablespoons fresh-grated
    Asiago cheese

Lemon Scampi Cod Risotto

*The addition of lemon and the classic "scampi" flavoring
(garlic, oil, parsley) to this risotto make it an interesting variation
on the traditional risotto combinations.*

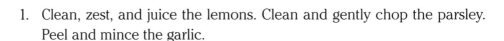

1. Clean, zest, and juice the lemons. Clean and gently chop the parsley. Peel and mince the garlic.

2. Mix together half the lemon zest, half the parsley, half the garlic, 2 tablespoons of the oil, and some black pepper. Gently rub the mixture into the fish fillets. Heat a large sauté pan to medium temperature and sauté the fish for 3 minutes on each side. Cut the fish into large chunks, and keep warm.

3. Heat the remaining oil to medium temperature in a large saucepan. Add the remaining garlic and the rice, and stir for 2 minutes. Add the lemon juice, and let stand until fully absorbed. Pour in the wine, and stir until completely absorbed.

4. Stir in the stock ½ cup at a time, stirring frequently and allowing each addition to be completely absorbed before adding the next. Before adding the last ½ cup stock, add the fish. Cook until all the stock is absorbed and the rice is tender.

5. Remove from heat, and add the remaining lemon zest and parsley, and the cheese and pepper. Stir to combine, and serve hot.

Lobster Risotto

It is extra work to buy whole lobsters and prep them to retrieve the chunks of meat, but everyone will love the taste and elegance of this creamy and fragrant dish.

~

Serves 10

5 (1-pound) whole lobsters, cooked
4 ½ cups Fish Stock (page 16)
10 sprigs fresh thyme
1 tablespoon olive oil
1½ cups arborio rice
1 cup pinot grigio (or other dry white drinking wine)
½ cup shredded fontina cheese
Fresh-cracked black pepper

1. Split the warm lobsters in half lengthwise. Remove the tail meat from the shell, and dice the meat. Reserve the lobster cavities. Place the lobster meat in a dish or pan with a tight-fitting lid. Pour in a bit of the Fish Stock to keep the meat moist, and cover securely to keep warm. (Use caution to just keep warm; you don't want to cook the lobster meat further.) Set aside.

2. Clean the thyme and remove the leaves (discard the stems). Heat the oil to medium temperature in a large saucepan.

3. Add the rice, and stir for 1 minute. Add the wine, and stir until fully absorbed. Add the stock ½ cup at a time, stirring frequently and allowing each addition to be completely absorbed before adding the next. Continue until all the stock is absorbed and the rice is tender.

4. Remove from heat, and stir in the cheese.

5. To serve, place each lobster half on a serving plate. Fill each tail cavity with a large scoop of risotto. Sprinkle with the lobster meat, thyme, and pepper.

Serves 10

2 tablespoons olive oil,
    divided
2 red bell peppers
2 yellow bell peppers
1 shallot
¼ bunch fresh parsley
1½ cups arborio rice
½ cup light white wine, such
    as pinot grigio
4¾ cups Fish Stock (page 16)
¾ pound par-cooked crab
¾ pound par-cooked shrimp
¼ cup shredded provolone
    cheese
Fresh-cracked black pepper

Risotto Seafood Pepper Cakes

*To par-cook seafood, drop it into boiling water for 30 seconds,
or bake in a 400°F oven for 5 minutes. This recipe is a good
use for leftover risotto—just start with step 4.*

1. Preheat oven to 375°F. Lightly grease a baking sheet with 1 tablespoon of the oil. Clean and finely dice the bell peppers. Peel and mince the shallot. Clean and chop the parsley.

2. Heat the remaining oil to medium temperature in a large saucepan. Sauté the peppers and shallots for 2 minutes. Add the rice, and stir for 1 minute.

3. Add the wine, and stir until fully absorbed. Add the broth ½ cup at a time, stirring frequently and allowing each addition to be completely absorbed before adding the next. Continue until all the stock is absorbed and the rice is tender.

4. Remove from heat, and stir in the crab, shrimp, and cheese. Form into cakes, and place on the prepared baking sheet. Bake for 8 minutes.

5. Sprinkle with the parsley and black pepper, and serve.

Bell Peppers
Bell peppers have different flavors depending on their color. Green is the most acidic and sour tasting. Red has the most peppery flavor. Yellow and orange have a gentle and slightly sweet flavor. A combination of all colors creates a balanced flavor and a beautiful appearance.

Chapter 9

Polenta

Basic Polenta 162

Polenta with Stock 163

Creamy Polenta 163

Polenta with Roasted Corn 164

Grilled Portobello Mozzarella Polenta 165

Fried Green Tomatoes and Mascarpone Polenta . . . 166

Garlic-Saffron Polenta Triangles 167

Gorgonzola Polenta Cakes with

    Braised Broccoli Raab 168

Stewed Fish with Polenta 169

Fontina and Parmesan Polenta with

    Sun-Dried Tomatoes 170

Savory Breakfast Egg Polenta 171

Sweet Breakfast Egg Polenta 171

Citrus Polenta 172

Polenta with Poached Eggs 172

Cinnamon-Nutmeg Polenta with Dried Fruit and Nuts 173

Braise Veal with Polenta Dumplings 174

Beef and Polenta Casserole 175

Minty Polenta-Encrusted Lamb Chops 176

Seafood Polenta 177

5 cups water
¼ cup unsalted butter
1¼ cups cornmeal
Fresh-cracked black pepper
(optional)
Kosher salt (optional)

Basic Polenta

By using ½ to 1 cup less liquid than is called for in polenta recipes, you can produce a semifirm loaf of polenta that can be cooled and cut into serving portions. Reheat in the oven before serving.

1. Heat the water and butter to a simmer over medium to medium-high temperature in a large saucepan.

2. Slowly whisk in the cornmeal, stirring constantly to avoid lumps.

3. Reduce heat to low. Cook for 20 to 25 minutes, uncovered and stirring frequently, until thick and creamy.

4. Season with pepper and salt as desired.

Keep It Simple

Polenta is delicious just served hot and dotted with butter and sprinkled with fresh-grated Parmesan cheese. Slice the polenta, arrange it in a baking dish, dot with butter and Parmesan, and bake for a hot, savory side. Leftover polenta can be sliced, fried in oil, or lightly grilled, and served as a side dish as well.

Polenta with Stock

To slightly vary the flavor of this polenta, you can substitute any type of stock. See Chapter 2 for other stock recipes.

$\sim$

1. Bring the stock and butter to a simmer over medium to medium-high heat in a large saucepan.

2. Slowly whisk in the cornmeal, stirring constantly to avoid lumps.

3. Reduce heat to low. Cook for 20 to 25 minutes, uncovered and stirring frequently, until thick and creamy.

4. Season with pepper and salt as desired.

Serves 10

5 cups Chicken Stock (page 14)
¼ cup unsalted butter
1¼ cups cornmeal
Fresh-cracked pepper (optional)
Kosher salt (optional)

Creamy Polenta

For a special treat, you can use heavy cream instead of whole milk in this recipe. This substitution will give you a "Decadently Creamy Polenta."

$\sim$

1. Bring the stock, milk, and butter to a simmer over medium to medium-high heat in a large saucepan.

2. Slowly whisk in the cornmeal, stirring constantly to avoid lumps.

3. Reduce heat to low. Cook for 20 to 25 minutes, uncovered and stirring frequently, until thick and creamy.

4. Sprinkle with the cheese, and season with pepper and salt as desired.

Serves 10

3 cups stock of choice (see Chapter 2, page 13)
2 cups whole milk
¼ cup unsalted butter
1½ cups cornmeal
½ cup fresh-grated Parmesan cheese
Fresh-cracked black pepper (optional)
Kosher salt (optional)

3 ears corn on the cob
*2 tablespoons olive oil,
    divided*
Fresh-cracked black pepper
*2½ cups Chicken Stock
    (page 14)*
2½ cups whole milk
1¼ cups cornmeal
*½ cup shredded fontina
    cheese*

Polenta with Roasted Corn

*The combination of fresh corn with the cornmeal
intensifies the flavor of the polenta. This dish is strong enough in
flavor to be served with any hearty stew or roast.*

1. Heat oven to 375°F. Remove the outer husks from the corn. Rub the corn with 1 tablespoon of the oil, and season with black pepper. Bake right on oven rack until tender, about 20 minutes. Let cool slightly; then cut the kernels off the cobs. Set aside.

2. Bring the remaining oil, the stock, and milk to a simmer over medium to medium-high heat in a large saucepan. Slowly whisk in the cornmeal, stirring constantly to avoid lumps.

3. Reduce heat to low. Cook for 20 to 25 minutes, uncovered and stirring frequently, until thick and creamy.

4. Remove from heat. Add the corn kernels, cheese, and black pepper.

Instead of Bread

In Italy, polenta is usually served as a starchy accompaniment to a meal, in place of bread. In this case, it is not sauced, but made into a loaf and cut with a string. This is a nice practice as it allows you to incorporate more ingredients into the polenta (herbs, vegetables, etc.), whereas bread usually only contains a few basic ingredients.

Grilled Portobello Mozzarella Polenta

Mushrooms should be cleaned without water because they absorb moisture. Wipe them with a paper towel or dust clean with a pastry brush.

1. Preheat grill to medium temperature. Separate the mushroom stems and caps. Clean the mushrooms. Brush the mushroom caps with 1 tablespoon of the oil, and season with pepper. Grill for 2 minutes on each side or until the mushrooms are tender. Keep warm.

2. Mince the mushroom stems. Peel and mince the shallots and garlic. Clean and chop the parsley.

3. Heat the remaining oil to medium temperature in a large saucepan. Add the mushroom stems, shallots, and garlic. Sauté for 5 minutes, stirring constantly. Add the stock, and bring to simmer. Slowly whisk in the cornmeal, stirring constantly to avoid lumps.

4. Reduce heat to low. Cook for 20 to 25 minutes, until thick and creamy.

5. Stir in the milk, and cook for 5 minutes. Remove from heat. Add the butter.

6. To serve, spoon the polenta onto serving plates. Slice the grilled mushrooms and fan them over the polenta. Sprinkle with the parsley and cheese.

Serves 10

10 whole portobello mushrooms
2 tablespoons olive oil, divided
Fresh-cracked black pepper
3 shallots
½ bulb garlic
½ bunch fresh parsley
5 cups Vegetable Stock (page 16)
1¼ cups cornmeal
1 cup whole milk or light cream
2 tablespoons unsalted butter
½ cup shredded mozzarella cheese

4 cups stock of choice (see Chapter 2, page 13)
2 tablespoons unsalted butter
¾ cup white cornmeal
½ cup mascarpone cheese
2 pounds green tomatoes
1 large yellow onion
½ bulb garlic
3 eggs
¼ cup milk
½ cup all-purpose flour
1 tablespoon baking powder
¼ cup olive oil
Kosher salt
Fresh-cracked black pepper

Fried Green Tomatoes and Mascarpone Polenta

Though they're a staple in today's Italian cuisine,
tomatoes were not used in Italy until the late seventeenth century.
They were introduced by travelers from Central and northern America.

1. Bring the stock and butter to a medium simmer in a large saucepan. Slowly whisk in the cornmeal, stirring constantly to avoid lumps. Reduce heat to low. Cook for 20 to 25 minutes, uncovered and stirring frequently, until thick and creamy. Remove from heat, and stir in the mascarpone. Keep warm.

2. Clean and cut the tomatoes into slices about 1 inch thick. Peel and finely chop the onion and garlic. In a small bowl, beat the eggs, and add the milk. Sift together the flour and baking powder into a shallow bowl.

3. Heat the oil to medium temperature in a large sauté pan. Dust the tomatoes with the flour. Dip the tomatoes in the egg mixture, then coat with flour again. Brown on each side for 3 to 5 minutes.

4. To serve spoon the polenta on serving plates and top with tomatoes. Sprinkle with salt and pepper.

Garlic-Saffron Polenta Triangles

These polenta triangles can actually take any shape you like.
You can make polenta squares, circles, or even stars.

Serves 10

1 bulb garlic
1 shallot
2 tablespoons olive oil
5½ cups Chicken Stock (page 14)
½ cup white wine (such as pinot grigio)
1 tablespoon saffron threads
1½ cups cornmeal
Fresh-cracked black pepper

1. Peel and mince the garlic and shallot. Lightly grease a large baking sheet with 1 tablespoon of the oil.

2. Heat the remaining oil to medium temperature in a large saucepan. Add the garlic and shallot, and sauté for 1 to 2 minutes. Add the stock, wine, and saffron. Bring to a simmer. Slowly whisk in the cornmeal, stirring constantly to avoid lumps. Reduce heat to low. Cook for 20 to 25 minutes, uncovered and stirring frequently, until thick and creamy.

3. Spread out the polenta 1 to 2 inches thick on lightly floured surface, and let cool completely.

4. Preheat broiler. Cut the polenta into triangles (or desired shape). Place on the prepared baking sheet.

5. Brown the polenta under the broiler for 5 to 10 minutes. Sprinkle with pepper, and serve.

Italian Polenta

In Italy, polenta is usually cooked in a paiolo, a copper pot with a convex bottom. The polenta is stirred with a special wooden spoon shaped like a paddle, called a tarello. Though these are the tools used to make authentic Italian polenta, your household kitchen utensils will work just fine.

Gorgonzola Polenta Cakes
with Braised Broccoli Raab

Serves 10

5 cups Vegetable Stock (page 16)

1 cup whole milk

1 tablespoon unsalted butter

1¼ cups cornmeal

1½ cups crumbled Gorgonzola

2 tablespoons olive oil, divided

2 pounds broccoli raab

2 shallots

¼ cup balsamic vinegar

Fresh-cracked black pepper

You can prepare the polenta one day early to save time. However, if you do this, leave out the Gorgonzola and sprinkle it on top the next day.

1. Bring the stock, milk, and butter to slow simmer over medium heat in a large saucepan. Slowly whisk in the cornmeal, stirring constantly to avoid lumps. Reduce heat to low. Cook for 20 to 25 minutes, uncovered and stirring frequently, until thick and creamy. Remove from heat, and stir in ½ cup of the Gorgonzola.

2. Allow the polenta to cool, then form into ½-cup cakes about 2 inches thick.

3. Preheat oven to 375°F. Grease a large baking sheet with 1 tablespoon of the oil. Clean the broccoli raab, and peel and mince the shallots. Heat the remaining oil in a large saucepan. Sauté the shallots and broccoli raab for 3 minutes. Add the vinegar and pepper. Cover, and simmer for 10 minutes.

4. Place the polenta cakes on the prepared pan. Sprinkle the remaining Gorgonzola on the polenta cakes. Bake for 8 to 10 minutes.

5. Serve the polenta cakes atop the braised broccoli raab.

Stewed Fish with Polenta

This polenta makes a great addition to any stew dish. It can also be served on its own or with a light salad or soup as an appetizer.

---

1. Clean the fish and cut into 10 serving pieces. Peel and mince the shallots and garlic. Clean and chop the tomatoes. Clean and thinly slice the celery. Clean and chop the parsley. Clean the thyme and remove the leaves (discard the stems).

2. Heat the oil to medium-high temperature in a skillet. Add the shallot, garlic, and fish. Lightly brown the fish for 2 minutes on each side. Add the tomatoes, celery, parsley, thyme, wine, bay leaves, salt, and pepper. Simmer for 45 to 60 minutes, with the lid ajar.

3. Meanwhile, bring the stock, water, and butter to a medium simmer in a large saucepan. Slowly whisk in the cornmeal, stirring constantly to avoid lumps. Reduce heat to low. Cook for 20 to 25 minutes, uncovered and stirring frequently, until thick and creamy.

4. Add the saffron to polenta just before serving. Serve the fish over the polenta.

Serves 10

2½ pounds halibut fillets
3 shallots
½ bulb garlic
10 fresh tomatoes
3 stalks celery
½ bunch fresh parsley
3 sprigs thyme
1 tablespoon olive oil
1 cup dry white wine (not cooking wine)
2 bay leaves
Kosher salt
Fresh-cracked black pepper
4 cups Fish Stock (page 16)
1 cup water
3 tablespoons unsalted butter
2 cups cornmeal
¾ teaspoon saffron threads

Fontina and Parmesan Polenta
with Sun-Dried Tomatoes

Serves 10

2 tablespoons olive oil,
    divided
2 cups dry red wine (such as
    Merlot or pinot noir)
1 cup sun-dried tomatoes
3 sprigs fresh basil
3 sprigs fresh oregano
1 recipe Creamy Polenta
    (page 163)
¼ cup Roasted Garlic Paste
    (page 70)
1 cup fontina cheese
Fresh-cracked black pepper

Fontina is a great cheese to use in many Italian dishes. It melts quickly and tastes great in combination with many other cheeses.

1. Preheat oven to 375°F. Lightly grease large baking sheet with 1 table-spoon of the oil. Bring the wine to a simmer over medium heat in a saucepan. Add the tomatoes, and simmer for 5 minutes. Remove from heat, and let stand 15 minutes. Clean and gently chop the basil and oregano.

2. Drain the wine from the tomatoes, and discard the wine. Spread out the polenta 1 to 2 inches thick in a baking pan.

3. Top the polenta with the tomatoes, herbs, garlic paste, fontina, and pepper. Drizzle with the remaining oil. Bake for 15 to 20 minutes, until lightly browned and the cheese is melted.

Savory Breakfast Egg Polenta

This is a great dish to serve in a brunch buffet alongside other Italian favorites, such as Breakfast Pork Sausage (page 215).

1. Bring the stock and butter to slow simmer over medium temperature. Slowly whisk in the cornmeal, stirring constantly to avoid lumps. Reduce heat to low. Cook for 20 minutes, uncovered and stirring frequently, until thick and creamy.

2. Beat the eggs, and stir them into the polenta. Cook for about 5 more minutes.

3. Remove from heat. Stir in the cheese and pepper. Serve hot.

Serves 10

4½ cups Chicken Stock (page 14)
3 tablespoons unsalted butter
1½ cups cornmeal
8 eggs
½ cup fresh-grated Parmesan or Romano cheese
Fresh-cracked black pepper

Sweet Breakfast Egg Polenta

You can top this polenta with dried or fresh fruit and nuts to add extra flavor, color, and texture.

1. Bring the water, milk, and butter to medium simmer in a large saucepan. Slowly whisk in the cornmeal, stirring constantly to avoid lumps. Reduce heat to low. Cook for 20 to 25 minutes, uncovered and stirring frequently, until thick and creamy.

2. Remove from heat, and stir in the honey. Serve hot.

Serves 10

5 cups water
1 cup milk
2 tablespoons unsalted butter
1¼ cups cornmeal
¾ cup honey

Citrus Polenta

*This dish can be served as a breakfast or dessert,
or it can accompany a hearty meat recipe.*

1. Zest and juice the oranges.

2. Bring the orange juice, ½ of the zest, the water, butter, and honey to a simmer over medium to medium-high heat in a large saucepan. Slowly whisk in the cornmeal, stirring constantly to avoid lumps.

3. Reduce heat to low. Cook for 20 to 25 minutes, uncovered and stirring frequently, until thick and creamy.

4. Serve sprinkled with the remaining zest, the sugar, and nuts.

Polenta with Poached Eggs

*When poaching eggs, adding a drop of
vinegar to the water helps keep the eggs intact.*

1. Bring the stock, 1 cup of the water, and the butter to a simmer over medium to medium-high heat. Slowly whisk in the cornmeal, stirring constantly to avoid lumps. Reduce heat to low. Cook for 20 to 25 minutes, uncovered and stirring frequently, until thick and creamy. Keep warm.

2. Heat the cheese sauce in a small saucepan. Keep warm.

3. Bring the remaining water and the vinegar to a boil in a large, shallow pan. Gently break the eggs into the boiling water one at a time, and poach for about 3 minutes, or to desired doneness.

4. Spoon the polenta on serving plates, and top with the egg, sauce, salt, and pepper.

Cinnamon-Nutmeg Polenta
with Dried Fruit and Nuts

To reduce heavy cream, heat it at a medium to medium-high temperature, making sure you don't scorch the cream or let it boil over.

Serves 10

1½ cups cornmeal
½ cup brown sugar (optional)
1 tablespoon cinnamon (preferably freshly ground)
½ teaspoon ground nutmeg
4 cups water
1 cup whole milk
2 tablespoons unsalted butter
1 cup heavy cream (or substitute plain yogurt)
½ cup honey
½ cup finely chopped pecans or walnuts
½ cup raisins or other dried fruit of choice

1. Sift together the cornmeal, brown sugar, cinnamon, and nutmeg.

2. Bring the water, milk, and butter to a simmer over medium to medium-high heat in a large saucepan. Slowly whisk in the cornmeal mixture, stirring constantly to avoid lumps. Reduce heat to low. Cook for 20 to 25 minutes, uncovered and stirring frequently, until thick and creamy.

3. If using heavy cream, reduce by half the volume in a large sauté pan.

4. Spoon out the polenta into individual servings and drizzle with the cream and honey. Sprinkle with the nuts and raisins, and serve.

Grind Fresh Herbs and Nuts
You can use a coffee bean grinder to grind fresh herbs and spices, or nuts. A tip for cleaning it out before and after using it for anything other than coffee is to grind 3 tablespoonfuls of uncooked rice kernels in it and then wipe it dry with a clean cloth or paper towel. The rice works as an abrasive and cleans the inside of the grinder while it absorbs the flavors and oils of previous ingredients.

5 cups Beef Stock (page 15)

2¼ cups dry red wine (not cooking wine)

1 tablespoon unsalted butter

¾ cup cornmeal

2½ pounds boneless veal

1½ pounds plum tomatoes (or substitute 2½ cups canned)

2 large yellow onions

3 carrots

3 stalks celery

½ bulb garlic

½ bunch fresh parsley

3 sprigs fresh thyme

3 sprigs fresh marjoram or oregano

2 tablespoons olive oil

2 bay leaves

Fresh-cracked black pepper

½ cup fresh-grated Asiago cheese

Braised Veal with Polenta Dumplings

The polenta in this recipe is made using the same method as dumplings in chicken soup. The mixture is spooned into simmering soup and poached.

1. Bring 3 cups of the stock, ¼ cup of the wine, and the butter to simmer in a large saucepan. Slowly whisk in the cornmeal, stirring constantly to avoid lumps. Reduce heat to low. Cook for 20 to 25 minutes, uncovered and stirring frequently, until thick and creamy. Remove from heat and let cool.

2. Cut the veal into large cubes. Clean and roughly chop the tomatoes. Peel and wedge the onions. Peel and slice the carrots. Clean and slice the celery. Peel and mince the garlic. Clean and gently chop the parsley, thyme, and marjoram.

3. Heat the oil to medium-high temperature in a stockpot. Add the veal, and brown for 8 minutes. Add the onions and carrots, and sauté for 3 minutes. Add the tomatoes, celery, and garlic, and sauté for 2 minutes. Pour in the remaining wine, and reduce by half the volume.

4. Add the remaining stock, all the herbs, and the pepper. Simmer on medium-low heat for 2 hours, uncovered.

5. Drop tablespoonfuls of the polenta into the simmering stew, cover, and cook for 5 to 10 minutes. Serve sprinkled with the cheese.

Beef and Polenta Casserole

*Similar to lasagna, the ingredients in this dish
are spread between layers of polenta.*

—◦—

1. Preheat oven to 350°F. Lightly grease a large casserole dish with 1 table-spoon of the oil. Peel and dice the onions. Peel and mince the shallot and garlic. Clean and slice the tomatoes. Clean and gently chop the basil leaves.

2. Heat the remaining oil to medium temperature in a skillet. Add the onions, shallots, garlic, and beef. Sauté for 10 to 15 minutes, until the beef is browned. Drain off excess grease.

3. Spread a thin layer of the polenta in the bottom of the prepared cas-serole dish. Spread layers of the beef, tomatoes, escarole, ricotta, basil, and pepper on top. Top with the remaining polenta. Sprinkle with the cheese. Drizzle with the butter.

4. Bake for 20 minutes, and serve.

When to Use a Slow Cooker
Slow cookers are excellent appliances if you want to make a meal while you aren't at home or if you want to keep an appetizer warm for several hours. Soups and stews work well, as does any dish that doesn't require the food to brown and doesn't need to be quick-cooked, such as fried foods.

Serves 10

2 tablespoons olive oil, divided
2 Vidalia onions
1 shallot
1 bulb garlic
4 tomatoes
3 sprigs basil
1½ pounds lean ground beef
½ recipe Basic Polenta (page 162)
1 bunch steamed escarole (or any bitter greens)
½ cup ricotta
Fresh-cracked black pepper (optional)
¼ cup fresh-grated Romano cheese
2 tablespoons melted unsalted butter

Serves 10

8 sprigs fresh mint
2½ cups stock of choice (see
    Chapter 2, page 13)
2 tablespoons unsalted butter
¾ cup cornmeal
1 tablespoon olive oil
20 lamb chops
Fresh-cracked black pepper
20 slices pancetta

Minty Polenta-Encrusted Lamb Chops

It is a good idea to make the polenta ahead of time for this dish.
Allowing the polenta to stand helps it to hold together better
and makes it easier to wrap around the lamb chops.

1. Clean and chop the mint.

2. Bring the stock and butter to a simmer in a large saucepan over medium heat. Slowly whisk in the cornmeal, stirring constantly to avoid lumps. Reduce heat. Simmer for 20 to 25 minutes, uncovered and stirring frequently, until thick and creamy. Remove from heat and stir in the mint. Let cool.

3. Preheat oven to 400°F. Lightly grease a baking pan with the oil. Season the lamb chops with pepper. Spread the polenta on the outside of the chops, then wrap each with 1 slice of the pancetta.

4. Place in the prepared baking pan, and bake for about 20 minutes. Serve hot.

Seafood Polenta

After cleaning and shelling the fish, put the shells in an airtight plastic freezer bag and store in the freezer for use in future stocks.

1. Prepare the polenta: Bring the stock, wine, and butter to a simmer over medium to medium-high heat in a large saucepan. Slowly whisk in the cornmeal, stirring constantly to avoid lumps. Reduce heat. Simmer for 20 to 25 minutes, uncovered and stirring frequently, until thick and creamy. Keep warm.

2. Prepare the seafood mixture: Peel and mince the garlic. Zest and juice the lemons, and reserve a few lemon slices for garnish. Mince the zest. Clean and chop the parsley, reserving a couple of parsley sprigs for garnish. Remove shellfish from the shells.

3. Heat the oil to medium-high temperature in a large sauté pan. Add the garlic and seafood, and sauté for about 2 minutes. Add the lemon juice, ½ of the zest, and the wine. Cover, and simmer for 3 to 5 minutes. Add the butter and ½ of the parsley, and stir to mix.

4. Serve the seafood mixture over the polenta. Sprinkle with the remaining zest and parsley, and the black pepper.

Serves 10

Polenta:
4½ cups Fish Stock (page 16)
½ cup dry white wine (not cooking wine)
1 tablespoon unsalted butter
1 cup cornmeal

Seafood Mixture:
½ bulb garlic
2 lemons
½ bunch fresh parsley
2 pounds fresh seafood (scallops, shrimp, and/or lobster)
2 tablespoons olive oil
½ cup dry white wine (not cooking wine)
¼ cup cold unsalted butter
Fresh-cracked black pepper

Chapter 10

Frittata

Basic Frittata 180

Bell Pepper Frittata 181

Four-Cheese Frittata 182

Grilled Vegetable Frittata 183

Sun-Dried Tomato and Fresh Basil Frittata 184

Asparagus–Egg White Frittata 185

Baked Potato and Mascarpone Frittata. 186

Pasta Frittata. 186

Cipolla Frittata (Onion Frittata) 187

Toasted Italian Bread Frittata 188

Chickpea and Escarole Frittata 189

Risotto Frittata 190

Smashed Potato and Capicola Frittata 190

Roasted Potato and Shallot Frittata 191

Frittata-Stuffed Baked Potatoes 192

Beef and Tomato Frittata 193

Sausage and Pepper Frittata 194

Stuffed Italian Pepper Frittata 195

Shrimp Frittata 196

Mushroom and Crab Frittata 197

5 chef potatoes
2 yellow onions
10 eggs
½ cup whole milk
¼ cup shredded mozzarella
*   cheese*
2 tablespoons olive oil
Fresh-cracked black pepper

Basic Frittata

All of the frittata recipes in this book call for potatoes.
Potatoes are a common ingredient in frittata, but they're not a necessity.
You can vary these recipes according to your tastes and moods.

1. Preheat oven to 375°F. Peel the potatoes if desired. Thinly slice the potatoes. Peel and slice the onions. Beat the eggs in a bowl, and whisk in the milk and cheese.

2. Heat the oil to medium temperature in a large ovenproof frying pan. Add the potatoes and onions. Cover, and cook for 3 minutes. Turn the potatoes, cover, and cook for 3 more minutes. Continue cooking and turning the potatoes every 3 to 5 minutes until tender and lightly browned.

3. Pour in the egg mixture, and mix thoroughly.

4. Place the pan in the oven and bake, uncovered, until the egg is thoroughly cooked and set, about 15 to 20 minutes. Serve sprinkled with black pepper.

Italian Omelet
Frittata is the Italian version of the omelet. Once you know how to make the basic frittata, there are many ways you can vary the recipe by adding ingredients. You can make frittata with almost any type of vegetable, cheese, meat, or fish.

Bell Pepper Frittata

This is the Italian version of the Western omelet.
You can use Idaho or red potatoes in this recipe.

Serves 10

4 large chef potatoes
2 Vidalia onions
2 red bell peppers
2 green bell peppers
1 yellow bell pepper
10 eggs
½ cup whole milk
¼ cup fresh-grated Parmesan
  cheese
3 tablespoons olive oil
Fresh-cracked black pepper

1. Preheat oven to 375°F. Peel the potatoes if desired. Thinly slice the potatoes. Peel and dice the onions. Clean and dice the bell peppers. Beat the eggs in a bowl, and whisk in the milk and cheese.

2. Heat the oil to medium temperature in a large ovenproof frying pan. Add the potatoes. Cover, and cook for 3 minutes. Turn the potatoes, cover, and cook for 3 more minutes. Add the peppers and onions, stir, and cover. Continue cooking and turning the potatoes every 3 to 5 minutes until tender and lightly browned.

3. Pour in the egg mixture, and mix thoroughly.

4. Place the pan in the oven and bake, uncovered, until the egg is set, about 15 to 20 minutes. Serve sprinkled with black pepper.

Serves 10

5 red potatoes
3 Vidalia onions
10 eggs
½ cup whole milk
½ cup shredded mozzarella
   cheese
½ cup part-skim ricotta
   cheese
¼ cup mascarpone cheese
¼ cup fresh-grated Parmesan
   cheese
¼ bunch fresh parsley
2 tablespoons olive oil
Fresh-cracked black pepper

Four-Cheese Frittata

*Serve this frittata warm with fresh crusty Italian bread
and a leafy green salad on the side.*

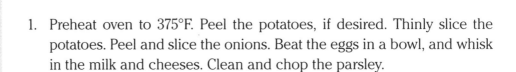

1. Preheat oven to 375°F. Peel the potatoes, if desired. Thinly slice the potatoes. Peel and slice the onions. Beat the eggs in a bowl, and whisk in the milk and cheeses. Clean and chop the parsley.

2. Heat the oil to medium temperature in a large ovenproof sauté pan. Add the potatoes and onions. Cover, and cook for 3 minutes. Turn the potatoes, cover, and cook for 3 more minutes. Continue cooking and turning the potatoes every 3 to 5 minutes until tender and lightly browned.

3. Pour in the egg and cheese mixture, and mix thoroughly.

4. Place the pan in the oven and bake, uncovered, until the egg is set, about 15 to 20 minutes. Serve sprinkled with the parsley and black pepper.

Grilled Vegetable Frittata

The vegetables can be grilled ahead of time and set aside until you're ready to prepare the rest of the dish.

Serves 10

¼ cup, plus 1 teaspoon olive oil
6 shallots
1 large eggplant
2 medium zucchini
2 red bell peppers
2 red onions
12 eggs
½ cup whole milk
¼ cup fresh-grated Asiago cheese
Fresh-cracked black pepper

1. Preheat oven to 350°F. Lightly grease a baking dish with 1 teaspoon oil. Preheat grill to medium temperature. Peel and mince the shallots. Clean and cut the eggplant and zucchini lengthwise into 1-inch-thick slices. Clean and cut the bell peppers in half and remove the seeds. Peel the onions and slice into 1-inch-thick slices. Separate the onion slices, but leave the rings intact for easier grilling.

2. Mix together the shallots and ¼ cup oil in a shallow bowl large enough to dip the vegetable slices in. Dip the vegetables in the oil mixture and shake off excess. Grill for 2 minutes on each side. Remove and drain on a rack with paper towels underneath to catch the drippings.

3. Layer the grilled vegetables in the prepared baking dish. Beat the eggs in a bowl, and whisk in the milk and cheese. Pour the egg mixture over the vegetables.

4. Bake for about 20 minutes, uncovered, until the egg is set. Serve sprinkled with black pepper.

Zucchini
Zucchini is a wonderfully versatile squash that can be grown in almost any climate. It is good when small and still has many uses as it grows large. Many cooks use it instead of eggplant because it adds a subtle flavor and a great deal of substance to a dish. It also works much like tofu, soaking up the other flavors.

4 red potatoes
2 shallots
½ bunch fresh basil
10 eggs
½ cup whole milk
2 tablespoons olive oil
½ cup sun-dried tomatoes
    (rehydrated with 1 cup
    water)
½ cup shredded mozzarella
    cheese
Fresh-cracked black pepper

Sun-Dried Tomato and Fresh Basil Frittata

*Sun-dried tomatoes are prepared at the end of July
or the start of August, when the sun is very hot. They are cut in half,
liberally salted, and left out in the sun for 4 or 5 days. You can dry
your own tomatoes in a 200°F oven for 8 hours.*

1. Preheat oven to 350°F. Peel the potatoes if desired. Peel and mince
   the shallots. Thinly slice the potatoes. Gently clean and slice the basil
   leaves. Beat the eggs in a bowl, and whisk in the milk.

2. Heat the oil to medium temperature in an ovenproof frying pan. Add
   the potatoes. Cover, and cook for 3 minutes. Turn the potatoes, cover,
   and cook for 3 more minutes. Add the shallots, stir, and cover. Continue
   cooking and turning the potatoes every 3 to 5 minutes until tender and
   lightly browned.

3. Pour in the egg mixture. Stir in the tomatoes, ¾ of the basil, the cheese,
   and black pepper.

4. Cover the pan, and place it in the oven. Bake for 15 minutes. Uncover,
   and bake for 5 minutes, until the egg is set. Serve sprinkled with the
   remaining basil and black pepper.

Mozzarella Cheese
*Mozzarella is a cheese that is commonly associated with Italian cooking.
It has a texture that is soft and elastic and its taste is sweet and milky.
The best way to buy it is fresh, in water, and it comes in various shapes
and sizes—braids, large and small balls, and so on.*

Asparagus–Egg White Frittata

This frittata is a very healthy option, especially for those who are trying to lower cholesterol intake.

Serves 10

2 tablespoons olive oil, divided
1 pound fresh asparagus
3 red onions
3 red potatoes
¼ pound prosciutto
18 egg whites
½ cup shredded provolone cheese
Fresh-cracked black pepper

1. Preheat oven to 350°F. Lightly grease a large baking pan with 1 tablespoon of the oil. Clean the asparagus and break off the tough ends. Peel and thickly slice the onions into rings.

2. Peel the potatoes if desired. Thinly slice the potatoes. Slice the prosciutto into thin ribbons. In a large bowl, whip the egg whites with an electric mixer until stiff peaks form.

3. Heat the remaining oil to medium temperature in a large frying pan. Add the potatoes, cover, and cook for 3 minutes. Turn the potatoes, cover, and cook for 3 more minutes. Add the onions, stir, and cover. Continue cooking and turning the potatoes every 3 to 5 minutes until tender and lightly browned.

4. Meanwhile, blanch the asparagus in boiling water for about 3 minutes, until just tender. Shock in ice water, and drain.

5. Place alternating layers of the cooked potatoes, asparagus, and cheese in the prepared baking pan. Pour the egg whites over the top to cover all the ingredients. Sprinkle with black pepper.

6. Bake for 15 to 20 minutes, uncovered, until the egg is thoroughly cooked. Serve with the shredded prosciutto over the top.

Preparing Asparagus
The best way to trim the ends of asparagus spears is to gently hold each end of the spear and bend until the spear breaks. Just don't throw away the ends. You can freeze the "woody" ends for later use in vegetable stock.

Serves 10

1 tablespoon olive oil
6 baking potatoes, baked and
    cooled
1 bunch scallions
4 plum tomatoes
¼ bunch fresh parsley
6 eggs
1 cup mascarpone cheese
Fresh-cracked black pepper

Baked Potato and Mascarpone Frittata

The mascarpone makes this a very rich frittata. You will likely only be able to eat a small amount at a time, so don't add too many side dishes.

1. Preheat oven to 350°F. Lightly grease a large baking pan with the oil. Peel the potatoes and slice lengthwise into 1-inch-thick rounds. Clean and slice the scallions. Clean and finely chop the tomatoes. Clean and gently chop the parsley. Beat the eggs in a bowl.

2. Arrange the potato slices in an even layer in the prepared baking pan. Sprinkle with the scallions, and dot with dollops of the mascarpone. Pour the eggs over the top.

3. Bake for 20 to 30 minutes, uncovered, until the egg is set. Top with the tomatoes, parsley, and black pepper.

Serves 10

1 tablespoon olive oil
1 pound penne pasta
2 cups fresh arugula
3 shallots
5 plum tomatoes
4 scallions
10 eggs
½ cup whole milk
½ pound goat cheese
Fresh-cracked black pepper

Pasta Frittata

The peppery taste of the arugula enhances the flavor of the goat cheese and eggs in this dish.

1. Preheat oven to 350°F. Grease large baking pan with the oil. Cook the pasta until al dente according to package directions, and drain. Gently clean the arugula. Peel and mince the shallots. Clean and slice the tomatoes lengthwise. Thinly slice the scallions. Beat the eggs in a bowl, and whisk in the milk.

2. Layer the pasta, arugula, shallots, tomatoes, and goat cheese in the prepared baking pan. Pour in the egg mixture, and sprinkle with pepper.

3. Cover, and bake for 20 minutes. Uncover, and bake until the egg is set, about 10 more minutes. Top with the scallions, and serve.

Cipolla Frittata
(Onion Frittata)

*You can use Spanish or yellow onions in this recipe
instead of Vidalia onions, if you prefer.*

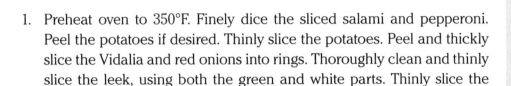

Serves 10

*¼ pound sliced Genoa salami
   or soppressata*
¼ pound sliced pepperoni
2 red potatoes
2 Vidalia onions
1 red onion
1 leek
½ bunch scallions
10 eggs
½ cup milk
2 tablespoons olive oil
¾ cup ricotta
Fresh-cracked black pepper

1. Preheat oven to 350°F. Finely dice the sliced salami and pepperoni. Peel the potatoes if desired. Thinly slice the potatoes. Peel and thickly slice the Vidalia and red onions into rings. Thoroughly clean and thinly slice the leek, using both the green and white parts. Thinly slice the scallions. Beat the eggs in a bowl, and whisk in the milk.

2. Heat the oil to medium temperature in a large ovenproof frying pan. Add the potatoes and all the onions. Cover, and cook for about 20 minutes, turning occasionally until the potatoes and onions are just tender. Add the leeks, cover, and cook for 3 minutes. Remove from heat.

3. Dot with dollop of the ricotta, and sprinkle the salami and pepperoni over the top. Pour in the egg mixture.

4. Place the pan in the oven and bake for 15 to 20 minutes, uncovered, until the egg is set. Top with the scallions and black pepper, and serve.

*1 large loaf crusty Italian
 bread
2 tablespoons olive oil,
 divided
2 yellow onions
½ pound pancetta
½ pound provolone
3 sprigs fresh basil
12 eggs
½ cup whole milk
Fresh-cracked black pepper*

Toasted Italian Bread Frittata

*This dish is great to prepare ahead of time and
serve as part of a brunch when entertaining.*

1. Preheat broiler. Slice the bread into 2-inch-thick slices, and toast in the oven until golden brown. Cut or tear the bread into large cubes. Change oven setting to bake, and preheat to 375°F. Lightly grease a large baking pan with 1 tablespoon of the oil.

2. Peel and thinly slice the onions. Finely dice the pancetta. Shred the provolone. Gently clean and slice the basil leaves. Beat the egg in a bowl, and whisk in the milk.

3. Heat the remaining oil in a large ovenproof frying pan. Sauté the onions for 3 minutes. Add the pancetta, and cook for 1 minute. Sprinkle in the cheese, ½ of the basil, and the bread. Immediately pour in the egg mixture, stir, and cover.

4. Cover the pan, and place in the oven. Bake for 20 minutes. Uncover, and bake for 5 to 10 minutes, until the egg is set. Sprinkle with the remaining basil and black pepper, and serve.

Chickpea and Escarole Frittata

You can get creative and substitute ingredients when making frittata.
Almost anything will taste good in a frittata.

Serves 10

2 red bell peppers
2 yellow onions
10 eggs
½ cup whole milk
2 tablespoons olive oil
3 cups cooked or canned
    chickpeas
4 cups steamed escarole
½ cup fresh-grated Parmesan
    cheese
Fresh-cracked black pepper

1. Preheat oven to 350°F. Clean and finely dice the red peppers. Peel and finely slice the onions. Beat the eggs in a bowl, and whisk in the milk.

2. Heat the oil to medium temperature in a large ovenproof frying pan. Add the onions and peppers, and sauté for 3 minutes. Add the chickpeas and escarole. Stir, and cook for 2 minutes. Add the egg mixture and the cheese, and stir to mix.

3. Cover the pan and place in the oven. Bake for 20 minutes. Uncover, and bake until the egg is set, about 5 to 10 minutes. Sprinkle with black pepper, and serve.

The Perfect Pan
Cast-iron frying pans are great to use when preparing a dish like frittata that calls for both stovetop and oven cooking. Just make sure that your cast-iron pan is properly cared for and seasoned.

Risotto Frittata

*This is a great recipe for using your leftover risotto from last night's dinner.
Of course, you can also make the risotto fresh for the recipe.*

1. Preheat oven to 350°F. Lightly grease a large baking pan with the oil. Clean the oregano and chop the leaves, reserving the tops for garnish. Beat the eggs, and whisk in the milk and chopped oregano.

2. Mix together the risotto and beans. Drop spoonfuls of the risotto-bean mixture into the prepared baking pan. Pour in the egg mixture.

3. Cover, and bake for 15 minutes. Uncover, and bake for 5 to 10 minutes, until the egg is set.

4. Sprinkle with black pepper, and garnish with the oregano tops. Serve hot.

Smashed Potato and Capicola Frittata

*To make smashed potatoes: Simmer 5 thoroughly cleaned, large potatoes in
water until al dente. Drain, and heat the potatoes in a hot pan or oven until
dry. "Smash" the potatoes with ¼ cup milk and ¼ cup butter.*

1. Preheat oven to 350°F. Lightly grease a large baking dish with the oil. Peel and finely mince the shallots. Clean and chop the parsley. Cut the sliced capicola into thin strips. Beat the eggs and egg whites in a bowl, and whisk in the milk.

2. In large bowl, mix together the potatoes, shallots, parsley, and egg mixture. Pour into the prepared baking dish. Sprinkle with red pepper flakes.

3. Cover, and bake for 20 minutes. Uncover, and bake for 5 to 10 minutes, until the egg is set.

Roasted Potato and Shallot Frittata

You can roast the potatoes and shallots ahead of time so there is less to do during the actual preparation of this dish.

Serves 10

4 tablespoons olive oil, divided
5 baking potatoes
5 shallots
5 large sprigs rosemary
10 eggs
½ cup whole milk
½ cup crumbled mascarpone cheese
Fresh-cracked black pepper

1. Preheat oven to 375°F. Lightly grease a large casserole dish with 1 tablespoon of the oil. Thoroughly clean the potatoes and cut into wedges. Peel and clean the shallots, and leave whole. Clean the rosemary and chop the leaves, reserving the top of 3 sprigs for garnish. Beat the eggs in a bowl, and whisk in the milk, cheese, and ½ of the rosemary leaves.

2. Combine the potatoes, shallots, remaining rosemary leaves, remaining oil, and black pepper in a roasting pan. Stir well to ensure that the potatoes and shallots are generously coated with the oil, rosemary, and pepper. Roast, uncovered, for 45 minutes.

3. Use a slotted spoon to transfer the potatoes and shallots to the greased casserole dish. Pour in the egg mixture.

4. Cover, and bake for 15 minutes. Uncover, and bake for 5 to 10 minutes, until the egg is set.

5. Sprinkle with the pepper, and garnish with the rosemary tops. Serve hot.

Serves 10

2 tablespoons olive oil
5 Idaho baking potatoes,
    baked and cooled
2 bunches scallions
2 red bell peppers
5 eggs
½ cup shredded mozzarella
    cheese
½ cup ricotta
Fresh-cracked black pepper

Frittata-Stuffed Baked Potatoes

*Bake and cool the potatoes ahead of time so they are easier
to handle when you're ready to prepare the dish.*

1. Preheat oven to 350°F. Lightly grease a baking pan with 1 tablespoon of the oil. Cut the potatoes in half lengthwise. Scoop out the insides of the potatoes, leaving about ½ inch of potato on the skin. Clean and finely chop the scallions and red peppers. Beat the eggs in a bowl.

2. In a large mixing bowl, thoroughly combine the potatoes, ½ of the scallions, the red peppers, eggs, ½ of the mozzarella, and the ricotta.

3. Stuff each potato skin with the potato mixture and place on the prepared pan. Sprinkle with the remaining mozzarella and the black pepper. Drizzle with the remaining oil.

4. Bake for 30 minutes, uncovered, until golden brown.

Cutting Cholesterol
There are a few things you can do to cut the cholesterol in most recipes. You can use more egg whites than yolks or use all egg whites and just add one yolk for color, if important. You can always use Egg Beaters or another egg substitute with less cholesterol, as well.

Beef and Tomato Frittata

This is a great summertime frittata.
Serve it for breakfast or lunch when you have company.

Serves 10

2 onions of choice
5 red potatoes
6 plum tomatoes
3 sprigs fresh marjoram or
    oregano
10 eggs
½ cup whole milk
1 cup shredded mozzarella
    cheese
1 tablespoon olive oil
1½ pounds lean ground beef
Fresh-cracked black pepper

1. Preheat oven to 350°F. Peel and dice the onions. Peel and thinly slice the potatoes. Clean and wedge the tomatoes. Clean and gently chop the marjoram leaves, reserving a few tops for garnish. Beat the egg in a bowl, and whisk in the milk, cheese, and half the chopped marjoram.

2. Heat the oil to medium temperature in a large ovenproof frying pan. Add the beef and potatoes, and sprinkle with black pepper. Cover, and cook for 30 minutes, stirring occasionally. Add the onions and the remaining marjoram, and cook for 5 minutes.

3. Thoroughly drain off all the grease. Add the tomatoes, pour in the egg mixture, and stir to mix.

4. Cover the pan and place in the oven. Bake for 15 minutes. Uncover, and bake for 5 to 10 minutes, until the egg is set.

5. Sprinkle with pepper, and garnish with the marjoram tops. Serve hot.

Serves 10

1 pound Italian sausage
4 large red potatoes
5 green bell peppers
2 large yellow onions
10 eggs
½ cup whole milk
¼ cup fresh-grated Asiago
    cheese
3 tablespoons olive oil
Fresh-cracked black pepper

Sausage and Pepper Frittata

This dish of sausage, peppers, onions, and eggs goes well with fresh crusty Italian bread. It can be served for brunch, lunch, or dinner.

1. Preheat oven to 375°F. Cut the sausage into 1-inch-thick slices. Peel the potatoes if desired. Cut the potatoes into ½-inch-thick slices. Clean and slice the bell peppers into thin strips. Peel and dice the onions. Beat the eggs in a bowl, and whisk in the milk and cheese.

2. Heat the oil to medium temperature in a large ovenproof frying pan. Add the sausage and potatoes. Cover, and cook for 5 minutes. Turn the sausage and potatoes, and cover. Continue cooking, turning the sausage and potatoes and stirring occasionally until the sausage is cooked and the potatoes are tender. Add the peppers and onions, and stir. Cover, and cook for 5 minutes.

3. Pour in the egg mixture, and stir to mix.

4. Place the pan in the oven. Bake for 15 to 20 minutes, until the egg is set. Sprinkle with black pepper and serve.

When to Grease a Pan
Some recipes ask you to grease a pan before baking the ingredients, while others don't. The reason is that dishes with a fair amount of fat in them, such as those with cheeses, will create their own layer of grease on the bottom. Those that are primarily made up of flour or have a lot of lean vegetables will have a tendency to stick to the baking dish if it isn't greased.

Stuffed Italian Pepper Frittata

Be sure to use Italian green peppers for this dish—they are lighter in color, smaller, and longer than green bell peppers. This dish has an impressive presentation, with the stuffed peppers set into the frittata.

Serves 10

2 tablespoons olive oil
2 large slices Italian bread, toasted
2 sprigs fresh sage or 1 tablespoon dried
2 large yellow onions
5 small fresh Italian peppers
1 pound ground pork
¼ cup fresh-grated Romano cheese
Fresh-cracked black pepper
10 eggs
1 cup milk

1. Preheat oven to 375°F. Lightly grease 2 large baking pans with the oil. Moisten the toasted bread with water and immediately squeeze out the water. Clean and chop the sage. Peel and finely dice the onions. Cut the green peppers in half lengthwise, and remove the seeds.

2. Mix together the pork, bread, sage, onions, cheese, and black pepper in a large mixing bowl. Stuff each pepper half with the pork mixture, and place stuffed side up in 1 of the prepared baking pans. Bake for 40 minutes, uncovered. Transfer the peppers to a rack to drain.

3. While the peppers cook, beat the eggs in a large bowl and whisk in the milk.

4. Arrange the peppers in the other prepared pan. Pour in the egg mixture.

5. Cover the pan, and bake for 15 minutes. Uncover, and bake for 5 to 10 minutes, until the egg is set. Sprinkle with black pepper, and serve.

2 pounds large shrimp
1 pound whole leeks
¼ pound bacon
3 large plum tomatoes
½ pound provolone cheese
5 eggs
5 egg whites
1 cup milk
1 tablespoon olive oil
Fresh-cracked black pepper

Shrimp Frittata

*This frittata is excellent for serving to company with
a green salad and crusty bread.*

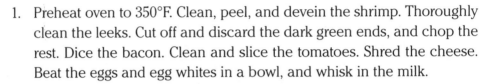

1. Preheat oven to 350°F. Clean, peel, and devein the shrimp. Thoroughly clean the leeks. Cut off and discard the dark green ends, and chop the rest. Dice the bacon. Clean and slice the tomatoes. Shred the cheese. Beat the eggs and egg whites in a bowl, and whisk in the milk.

2. Heat the oil to medium temperature in a large ovenproof frying pan. Sauté the leeks and bacon for 5 minutes, stirring occasionally. Drain off at least ½ of the fat.

3. Add the shrimp, tomatoes, cheese, and egg mixture. Stir to mix.

4. Cover the pan and place in the oven. Bake for 15 minutes. Uncover, and bake for 5 to 10 minutes, until the egg is set. Serve sprinkled with black pepper.

Shrimp Freshness

You want shrimp with a clean, oceanlike smell. Even a hint of ammonia is a bad sign. Frozen shrimp are fine, but buy them frozen and keep them frozen until you're ready to cook them. Never buy and then freeze fresh (or partially thawed) shrimp, and never thaw and refreeze shrimp.

Mushroom and Crab Frittata

Use only real crabmeat, not the pressed whitefish dyed red that is sold prepackaged. Real crabmeat is a bit more expensive but worth the cost.

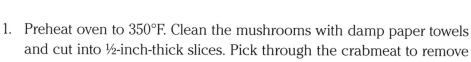

Serves 10

*1 pound button or field
    mushrooms
½ pound cooked crabmeat
4 large baking potatoes
2 leeks
½ bunch fresh parsley
12 eggs
½ cup whole milk
1 tablespoon olive oil
½ cup sour cream
Fresh-cracked black pepper*

1. Preheat oven to 350°F. Clean the mushrooms with damp paper towels and cut into ½-inch-thick slices. Pick through the crabmeat to remove any shells. Clean, peel, and grate the potatoes (keep in cold water to maintain the whiteness if not using immediately). Thoroughly clean the leeks, and chop the white and green parts. Clean and chop the parsley. Beat the eggs in a bowl, and whisk in the milk.

2. Heat the oil to medium temperature in a large ovenproof frying pan. Add the potatoes. Cover, and cook for 15 minutes, turning the potatoes occasionally. Add the mushrooms and leeks, and stir. Cover, and cook for 5 minutes. Remove from heat.

3. Add the crab and egg mixture. Dot with dollops of the sour cream, and sprinkle with black pepper.

4. Cover the pan and place in the oven. Bake for 15 minutes. Uncover, and bake for 5 to 10 minutes, until the egg is set. Serve hot.

Chapter 11

Meatballs and Sausages

Basic Beef Meatballs 200

Three-Meat Meatballs 201

Chicken Meatballs 202

Pork and Apple Meatballs 203

Salmon Balls 203

Shrimp Balls 204

Turkey and Fig Balls 205

Veal and Date Balls 206

Polpette con Pollo e Orzo (Chicken

Meatballs with Orzo) 207

Venison Meatballs 208

Fresh Cod Meatballs 209

Meatless Balls 210

Rosemary Chicken Meatballs . . 211

Agnello Polpette

(Lamb Meatballs) 212

Eggplant Meatballs 213

Basic Italian Pork Sausage . . . 214

Pollo Salsiccia con Origano (Chicken

Sausage with Oregano) . . . 214

Breakfast Pork Sausage 215

Seafood Sausage 215

Chicken and Sausage Casserole . . 216

Minted Lamb Sausage 217

Beef Sausage 217

Veal and Pepper Sausage 218

Salmon Sausage 218

Italian Beef and Sun-Dried

Tomato Sausage 219

Duck Sausage 219

Apple and Pork Sausage 220

Arugula, Mozzarella, and

Chicken Sausage 221

Rosemary Lamb Sausage 221

Smooth Chicken Liver Sausage 222

Whitefish Sausage 223

Vegetable and Bean Sausage . . 224

Turkey and Cranberry Sausage 224

Serves 10

5 thick slices day-old or
    toasted Italian bread
½ bulb garlic
¼ bunch fresh parsley
1½ pounds lean ground beef
1 egg, lightly beaten
¼ cup fresh-grated Parmesan
    or Romano cheese
Fresh-cracked black pepper

Basic Beef Meatballs

These classic meatballs are great served over pasta or as appetizers.
If served as appetizers, your guests might appreciate
smaller bite-size meatballs.

1. Soak the bread in water for 1 minute. Thoroughly squeeze out all the liquid. Peel and mince the garlic. Clean and chop the parsley.

2. In large mixing bowl, combine all the ingredients. Form the mixture into balls about 2 to 3 inches in size.

3. Bake or fry the meatballs: To bake, preheat oven to 375°F. Place the meatballs in a lightly greased baking pan, and cover. Bake for 30 minutes. Uncover, and brown for 5 to 10 minutes. To fry, heat about 1 tablespoon olive oil to medium temperature in a skillet. Fry for 30 minutes, uncovered and stirring occasionally, until cooked through.

4. Transfer the meatballs to paper towels to drain. Serve the meatballs plain, with sauce, or over pasta.

Using Bread
Day-old or two-day-old Italian bread is ideal to use for meatball and meat stuffing mixtures. If slightly stale bread is unavailable, you can simply toast some fresh bread, or use bread crumbs instead.

Three-Meat Meatballs

You can form your meatballs into any shape and size you like. However, if you make large meatballs, allow for more cooking time.

Serves 10

5 thick slices day-old or
  toasted Italian bread
2 sprigs fresh oregano
4 sprigs fresh parsley
2 shallots
½ bulb garlic
¾ pound ground veal
¾ pound lean ground pork
¾ pound lean ground beef
1 egg, lightly beaten
¼ cup fresh-grated Parmesan
  or Romano cheese
Fresh-cracked black pepper

1. Soak the bread in water for 1 minute. Thoroughly squeeze out all liquid. Clean and chop the oregano and parsley leaves. Peel and mince the shallots and garlic.

2. In a large mixing bowl, combine all the ingredients. Form into balls about 2 to 3 inches in size.

3. Bake or fry the meatballs: To bake, preheat oven to 375°F. Place the meatballs in a lightly greased baking pan, and cover. Bake for 30 minutes. Uncover, and brown for 5 to 10 minutes. To fry, heat about 1 tablespoon olive oil to medium temperature in a skillet. Fry for 30 minutes, uncovered and stirring occasionally, until cooked through.

4. Transfer the meatballs to paper towels to drain. Serve plain, with sauce, or over pasta.

5 thick slices day-old or
    toasted Italian bread
2 shallots
½ bulb garlic
1 cup mushrooms
1 lemon
¼ bunch fresh parsley
2 pounds ground chicken
2 egg whites
Fresh-cracked black pepper
1½ tablespoons olive oil
¼ cup dry white wine (not
    cooking wine)
2 tablespoons cold unsalted
    butter

Chicken Meatballs

*These meatballs are lower in fat and cholesterol than others.
Make some of these in addition to regular meatballs so
dieting family members can also enjoy the meal.*

1. Soak the bread in water for 1 minute. Thoroughly squeeze out all the liquid. Peel and mince the shallots and garlic. Clean and dice the mushrooms. Clean, zest, and juice the lemon. Clean and chop the parsley.

2. In a large mixing bowl, thoroughly combine the bread, shallots, garlic, mushrooms, lemon zest, ½ of the parsley, the chicken, egg whites, and black pepper. Form into 2-inch balls.

3. Heat the oil to medium temperature in a large sauté pan. Add the meatballs, and cover. Sauté for about 20 minutes until cooked through, turning occasionally to lightly brown on all sides.

4. Pour in the lemon juice and wine. Simmer, uncovered, until the liquid is reduced by half the volume. Reduce heat to low, and add the cold butter and parsley. Stir for 1 minute, and serve.

Substituting Onions

Onions can be used in many recipes in place of leeks, shallots, and even scallions, unless otherwise specified. You can also vary the type of onion you use in most recipes. Red onions have a strong, sweet flavor, while yellow and white onions are much milder varieties.

Pork and Apple Meatballs

The addition of apple to these meatballs gives them a slightly sweet flavor.
These are great to serve as part of an autumn meal.

1. Preheat oven to 375°F. Lightly grease a baking sheet with the oil. Soak the bread in water for 1 minute. Thoroughly squeeze out all the liquid. Peel and finely chop the onion. Peel and finely dice the apples. Clean and chop the oregano leaves.

2. In a large mixing bowl, thoroughly combine all the ingredients. Form the mixture into 2-inch balls.

3. Place the meatballs on the prepared baking sheet. Bake for about 30 minutes, until thoroughly cooked and golden brown.

4. Transfer the meatballs to paper towels to drain. Serve as desired.

Serves 10

1 tablespoon olive oil
5 thick slices day-old or
    toasted Italian bread
1 yellow onion
3 tart apples
2 sprigs fresh oregano
2 pounds lean ground pork
1 egg, lightly beaten
¾ cup chopped walnuts
Fresh-cracked black pepper

Salmon Balls

Prepare the polenta ahead of time to ensure that it's thoroughly
chilled when you prepare this recipe.

1. Preheat oven to 375°F. Lightly grease a baking pan with the oil. Finely flake the salmon. Clean and finely chop the red and Italian peppers. Peel and finely chop the onion. Clean and chop the parsley.

2. In a large mixing bowl, thoroughly combine all the ingredients. Form the mixture into 2-inch balls.

3. Place the balls in the prepared pan. Cover, and cook for about 7 minutes, until cooked through. Uncover, and cook for 5 more minutes to brown lightly.

4. Transfer the balls to paper towels to drain. Serve as desired.

Serves 10

1 tablespoon olive oil
2 pounds fresh salmon fillet
1 red bell pepper
1 Italian pepper
1 yellow onion
¼ bunch fresh parsley
½ recipe Basic Polenta (page
    162), chilled
1 egg, lightly beaten
Fresh-cracked black pepper

1 tablespoon olive oil
2 pounds fresh, chilled
    shrimp (or substitute any
    shellfish)
¼ bunch fresh parsley
½ recipe Basic Risotto (page
    140), chilled
1 egg, lightly beaten
½ teaspoon saffron threads
Fresh-cracked black pepper

Shrimp Balls

*Prepare the risotto ahead of time to be sure it's thoroughly chilled.
This will help when combining it with the shrimp.*

1. Preheat oven to 375°F. Lightly grease a baking pan with the oil. Clean, peel, and chop or grind the shrimp (keep the shrimp ice-cold). Clean and chop the parsley.

2. In a large mixing bowl, thoroughly combine all the ingredients. Form the mixture into 2-inch balls.

3. Place the balls in the prepared pan, and cover. Bake for about 8 minutes, until cooked through. Uncover, and bake for 3 more minutes to brown lightly. Serve as desired.

Food Safety

When preparing a dish that lists fish, seafood, or poultry as one of the ingredients, be sure to keep the fish, seafood, or chicken ice-cold during preparation to ensure food safety. If you will be doing a lot of handling or if the food will be on the counter for a long time, have a bowl with ice nearby to keep the ingredients while you are tending to other steps of the recipe.

Turkey and Fig Balls

For a fun variation on the classic Thanksgiving turkey, try serving these meatballs as part of the holiday feast.

Serves 10

5 thick slices day-old or toasted Italian bread
½ cup dried figs
1 yellow onion
2 sprigs fresh sage or 1 tablespoon dried sage
2 pounds ground turkey
1 egg, lightly beaten
½ cup chopped pecans
Fresh-cracked black pepper

1. Soak the bread in water for 1 minute. Thoroughly squeeze out all the liquid. Finely chop the figs. Peel and dice the onion. Clean and chop the sage leaves.

2. In a large mixing bowl, thoroughly combine all the ingredients. Form the mixture into balls about 2 to 3 inches in size.

3. Bake or fry the meatballs: To bake, preheat oven to 375°F. Place the meatballs in a lightly greased baking pan, and cover. Bake for 30 minutes. Uncover, and brown for 5 to 10 minutes. To fry, heat about 1 tablespoon olive oil to medium temperature in a skillet. Fry for 30 minutes, uncovered and stirring occasionally, until cooked through.

4. Transfer the meatballs to paper towels to drain. Serve plain, with sauce, or over pasta.

*5 thick slices day-old or
    toasted Italian bread
1 yellow onion
2 sprigs fresh oregano
2 sprigs fresh thyme
½ cup dried dates
¼ cup pine nuts
1 tablespoon olive oil
1½ pounds ground veal
½ recipe Basic Italian Pork
    Sausage (page 214),
    unformed and uncooked
1 egg, lightly beaten
Fresh-cracked black pepper*

Veal and Date Balls

*If you do not have dates on hand, raisins can be substituted.
However, it's a good idea to have figs in the house.
They complement many different kinds of meat.*

1. Soak the bread in water for 1 minute. Thoroughly squeeze out all the liquid. Peel and finely chop the onion. Clean and chop the oregano and thyme leaves. Finely dice the dates and pine nuts.

2. In a large mixing bowl, combine all the ingredients. Form the mixture into balls about 2 to 3 inches in size.

3. Bake or fry the meatballs: To bake, preheat oven to 375°F. Place the meatballs in a lightly greased baking pan, and cover. Bake for 30 minutes. Uncover, and brown for 5 to 10 minutes. To fry, heat about 1 tablespoon olive oil to medium temperature in a skillet. Fry for 30 minutes, uncovered and stirring occasionally, until cooked through.

4. Transfer the meatballs to paper towels to drain. Serve plain, with sauce, or over pasta.

Dates
Dates can be purchased either semidry/fresh, or dried. The semidry/ fresh type is softer and less sweet than the dried, and needs to be stored in the refrigerator unlike dried dates. Dates originated in North African and Middle Eastern cuisine, but because of the proximity of these areas to southern Italy, dates are used in some Italian cuisine as well.

Polpette con Pollo e Orzo
(Chicken Meatballs with Orzo)

The arugula and goat cheese in these meatballs makes them special, but in a pinch, you could use parsley and another soft cheese, such as fontina, instead.

Serves 10

½ small bunch fresh arugula
½ bulb garlic
½ pound goat cheese
1½ pounds ground chicken
1 cup cooked orzo pasta
1 egg, lightly beaten
Fresh-cracked black pepper

1. Clean and chop the arugula. Peel and mince the garlic. Crumble the goat cheese.

2. In a large mixing bowl, combine all the ingredients. Form the mixture into balls about 2 to 3 inches in size.

3. Bake or fry the meatballs: To bake, preheat oven to 375°F. Place the meatballs in a lightly greased baking pan, and cover. Bake for 30 minutes. Uncover, and brown for 5 to 10 minutes. To fry, heat about 1 tablespoon olive oil to medium temperature in a skillet. Fry for 30 minutes, uncovered and stirring occasionally, until cooked through.

4. Transfer the meatballs to paper towels to drain. Serve plain, with sauce, or over pasta.

5 thick slices day-old or
   toasted Italian bread
¼ bunch fresh parsley
½ bulb garlic
1½ pounds ground venison
   meat
½ recipe Basic Italian Pork
   Sausage (page 214),
   unformed and uncooked
1 egg, lightly beaten
¾ cup dried currants or
   raisins
½ cup chopped pine nuts
Fresh-cracked black pepper

Venison Meatballs

If you don't have venison available, you can substitute beef.

1. Soak the bread in water for 1 minute. Thoroughly squeeze out all the liquid. Clean and chop the parsley. Peel and mince the garlic.

2. In a large mixing bowl, combine all the ingredients. Form mixture into balls about 2 to 3 inches in size.

3. Bake or fry the meatballs: To bake, preheat oven to 375°F. Place the meatballs in a lightly greased baking pan, and cover. Bake for 30 minutes. Uncover, and brown for 5 to 10 minutes. To fry, heat about 1 tablespoon olive oil to medium temperature in a skillet. Fry for 30 minutes, uncovered and stirring occasionally, until cooked through.

4. Transfer the meatballs to paper towels to drain. Serve plain, with sauce, or over pasta.

Fresh Cod Meatballs

If you do not have mascarpone cheese, you can substitute cream cheese in a pinch.

Serves 10

1¾ pounds fresh cod fillet
5 thick slices day-old or
    toasted Italian bread
1 red bell pepper
2 Italian peppers
4 cloves garlic
1 egg, lightly beaten
¼ cup mascarpone cheese
Fresh-cracked black pepper
2 cups fresh-grated Romano
    cheese

1. Finely chop or grind the cod. Soak the bread in water for 1 minute. Thoroughly squeeze out all the liquid. Peel and finely dice the red and Italian peppers. Peel and mince the garlic.

2. In a large mixing bowl, combine all the ingredients *except* the Romano cheese. Form the mixture into balls about 2 to 3 inches in size. Roll the balls in the grated Romano.

3. Bake or fry the meatballs: To bake, preheat oven to 375°F. Place the meatballs in a lightly greased baking pan, and cover. Bake for 15 minutes. Uncover, and brown for 5 to 10 minutes. To fry, heat about 1 tablespoon olive oil to medium temperature in a skillet. Fry for 15 to 20 minutes, uncovered and stirring occasionally, until cooked through.

4. Transfer the meatballs to paper towels to drain. Serve plain, with sauce, or over pasta.

2 tablespoons olive oil
3 large carrots
3 yellow onions
3 stalks celery
½ bulb garlic
3 sprigs fresh oregano
2 cups cooked or canned
    cannellini beans
1 cup Basic Risotto (page 140)
2 eggs, lightly beaten
Fresh-cracked black pepper

Meatless Balls

Vegetarians and meat eaters alike will enjoy these.
Serve them over pasta, as you would meatballs, or as appetizers.

1. Peel and shred the carrots and onions. Clean and shred the celery. Peel and mince the garlic. Clean and chop the oregano. Mash the beans.

2. In a large mixing bowl, combine all the ingredients. Form the mixture into balls about 2 to 3 inches in size.

3. Bake or fry the veggie balls: To bake, preheat oven to 375°F. Place the balls in a generously greased baking pan, and cover. Bake for 15 minutes. Uncover, and brown for 5 to 10 minutes. To fry, heat about 1 tablespoon olive oil to medium temperature in a skillet. Fry for 15 to 20 minutes, uncovered and stirring occasionally, until cooked through.

4. Transfer the veggie balls to paper towels to drain. Serve plain, with sauce, or over pasta.

Soaking Beans

Soaking dried beans in water overnight makes them cook more quickly, but soaking is usually not necessary. Tiny beans like lentils never require soaking. Soaked beans tend to break apart more during cooking, which is fine for soup but not for bean salad. To soak beans, submerge them in at least 3 inches of water in a container large enough to allow the beans to expand, and refrigerate.

Rosemary Chicken Meatballs

Don't throw away leftover mashed potatoes!
This recipe gives you a great chance to use them.

Serves 10

2 shallots
½ bulb garlic
3 sprigs rosemary
2 pounds ground chicken
1 egg, lightly beaten
½ cup fresh-grated Parmesan
*   cheese*
1 cup mashed potatoes
Fresh-cracked black pepper

1. Peel and mince the shallots and garlic. Clean and chop the rosemary leaves.

2. In a large mixing bowl, combine all the ingredients. Form the mixture into balls about 2 to 3 inches in size.

3. Bake or fry the meatballs: To bake, preheat oven to 375°F. Place the meatballs in a lightly greased baking pan, and cover. Bake for 30 minutes. Uncover, and brown for 5 to 10 minutes. To fry, heat about 1 tablespoon olive oil to medium temperature in a skillet. Fry for 30 minutes, uncovered and stirring occasionally, until cooked through.

4. Transfer the meatballs to paper towels to drain. Serve plain, with sauce, or over pasta.

*5 thick slices day-old or
    toasted Italian bread*
3 shallots
½ bulb garlic
4 sprigs mint
1½ pounds ground lamb
*½ recipe Basic Italian Pork
    Sausage (page 214),
    unformed and uncooked*
1 egg, lightly beaten
Fresh-cracked black pepper

Agnello Polpette
(Lamb Meatballs)

*Serve this with Spelt Pasta (page 101), oil and balsamic vinegar,
and Roasted Garlic Paste (page 70).*

1. Soak the bread in water for 1 minute. Thoroughly squeeze out all the liquid. Peel and mince the shallots and garlic. Clean and chop the mint leaves.

2. In a large mixing bowl, combine all the ingredients. Form the mixture into balls about 2 to 3 inches in size.

3. Bake or fry the meatballs: To bake, preheat oven to 375°F. Place the meatballs in a lightly greased baking pan, and cover. Bake for 30 minutes. Uncover, and brown for 5 to 10 minutes. To fry, heat about 1 tablespoon olive oil to medium temperature in a skillet. Fry for 30 minutes, uncovered and stirring occasionally, until cooked through.

4. Transfer the meatballs to paper towels to drain. Serve plain, with sauce, or over pasta.

Eggplant Meatballs

You can roast the eggplant ahead of time to make for easy mixing.
Just be sure to cool the eggplant before you work with it.

Serves 10

1 tablespoon olive oil
1 large eggplant
2 shallots
3 cloves garlic
¼ bunch fresh parsley
½ cup shredded mozzarella
    cheese
¾ pound ground beef
½ recipe Basic Italian Pork
    Sausage (page 214),
    unformed and uncooked
3 thick slices day-old or
    toasted Italian bread
Fresh-cracked black pepper
1 egg

1. Preheat oven to 375°F. Lightly grease a baking sheet with the oil. Clean and slice the eggplant lengthwise. Place cut-side down on the prepared baking sheet. Roast for 40 minutes. Let cool completely and then mash.

2. Peel and mince the shallots and garlic. Clean and chop the parsley.

3. In a large mixing bowl, combine all the ingredients. Form the mixture into balls about 2 to 3 inches in size.

4. Bake or fry the meatballs: To bake, preheat oven to 375°F. Place the meatballs in a lightly greased baking pan, and cover. Bake for 30 minutes. Uncover, and brown for 5 to 10 minutes. To fry, heat about 1 tablespoon olive oil to medium temperature in a skillet. Fry for 30 minutes, uncovered and stirring occasionally, until cooked through.

5. Transfer the meatballs to paper towels to drain. Serve plain, with sauce, or over pasta.

Meatball Appetizers

Although you might not think of meatballs as a dish for entertaining, they make wonderful appetizers. Most meatball recipes can be adapted for use as appetizers by making the meatballs smaller, drizzling a pesto sauce over the top, inserting toothpicks, and placing them on a serving platter.

Serves 10

2½ pounds pork
½–¾ pound pork fat
1 bulb garlic
¼ cup fennel seeds
2 tablespoons dried basil
2 tablespoons dried oregano
Fresh-cracked black pepper
Kosher salt

Basic Italian Pork Sausage

This sausage is commonly known as Italian "sweet" sausage. Fennel seeds lend the characteristic taste to Italian sweet sausage.

1. Grind the meat and fat separately. Keep chilled. Peel and mince the garlic.

2. Mix together all the ingredients in a chilled bowl with chilled utensils. If using an electric mixer, be sure not to overblend the meat and fat.

3. Either stuff the mixture into casings or form into patties.

4. Use in desired preparation, or heat a small amount of oil or butter to medium temperature in a large sauté pan. Add the sausage, cover, and cook for about 30 minutes, turning at 5-minute intervals. Uncover and cook for about 10 to 15 minutes, until thoroughly browned.

Pollo Salsiccia con Origano
(Chicken Sausage with Oregano)

For a slight variation, form this mixture into small oval patties and quickly fry, drain on a paper towels, and serve with some fresh fruit as an appetizer.

Serves 10

2½ pounds chicken
¼–½ pound pork fat
½ bulb garlic
1 yellow onion
½ bunch fresh oregano
Fresh-cracked black pepper
Kosher salt

1. Grind the meat and fat separately. Keep chilled. Peel and mince the garlic and onion.

2. Mix together all the ingredients in a chilled bowl with chilled utensils. If using an electric mixer, be sure not to overblend the meat and fat.

3. Either stuff the mixture into casings or form into patties.

4. Use in desired preparation, or heat a small amount of oil or butter to medium temperature in a large sauté pan. Add the sausage, cover, and cook for about 30 minutes, turning at 5-minutes intervals. Uncover and cook for 10 to 15 minutes, until thoroughly browned.

Breakfast Pork Sausage

These fresh breakfast sausages are far better than any of the store-bought varieties. But just as conveniently, you can make a batch and freeze them for use on another day.

1. Grind the meat and fat separately. Keep chilled.

2. Mix together all the ingredients in a chilled bowl with chilled utensils. If using an electric mixer, be sure not to overblend the meat and fat.

3. Either stuff the mixture into casings or form into patties.

4. Use in desired preparation, or heat a small amount of oil or butter to medium temperature in a large sauté pan. Add the sausage, cover, and cook for about 30 minutes, turning at 5-minute intervals. Uncover and cook for 10 to 15 minutes, until thoroughly browned.

Serves 10

2½ pounds pork
¾ pound pork fat
2 heaping tablespoons dried sage
2 teaspoons onion powder
1½ teaspoons ground cinnamon
Fresh-cracked black pepper
Kosher salt

Seafood Sausage

This alternative to the classic pork sausage is great for seafood lovers. Serve over pasta, alone as appetizers, or drop in soup.

1. Remove the shells from the shellfish, and grind the meat. Keep chilled. Clean and finely chop the red pepper. Peel and mince the garlic and shallot. Clean and finely chop the parsley leaves.

2. Mix together all the ingredients in a chilled bowl using chilled utensils.

3. Either stuff the mixture into casings or form into patties.

4. Use in desired preparation, or heat a small amount of oil or butter to medium temperature in a large sauté pan. Add the sausage, cover, and cook for about 5 to 8 minutes, turning every 2 minutes or so. Uncover, and cook for 3 to 5 more minutes, until browned. Drain on paper towels.

Serves 10

2½ pounds shellfish of choice
1 red bell pepper
½ bulb garlic
1 shallot
½ bunch fresh parsley
3 eggs, lightly beaten
1 tablespoon all-purpose flour
Fresh-cracked black pepper
Kosher salt

1 (3-pound) whole chicken
¼ pound pork fat
1 cup shelled walnuts
½ bulb garlic
2 shallots
¼ bunch fresh parsley
1 egg, lightly beaten
1½ tablespoons fresh-grated
  Romano cheese
Fresh-cracked black pepper
Kosher salt

Chicken and Sausage Casserole

The French call this type of chicken preparation "galantine." It is time-consuming, but it makes for an impressive presentation and a great taste.

1. Thoroughly clean the chicken. Using a sharp knife, carefully remove the entire chicken skin, starting with back of chicken. (Try to keep the chicken skin in 1 large piece, as it will be the sausage casing in this preparation.) Keep the chicken and skin ice-cold throughout.

2. Carefully remove both breasts from the bone and keep whole. Debone the rest of the chicken and grind the meat. Grind the pork fat separately. Keep chilled.

3. Preheat oven to 375°F. Chop the walnuts. Peel and mince the garlic and shallots. Clean and chop the parsley.

4. In a chilled bowl, mix together the ground chicken, ground pork fat, walnuts, garlic, shallots, parsley, egg, cheese, black pepper, and salt using chilled utensils.

5. Lay out the chicken-skin flat, and place the whole chicken breasts on top. Spoon the sausage mixture over the breasts. Carefully fold the skin tightly around the breasts and sausage mixture, covering them completely.

6. Place the chicken "package" breast-side up (skin-seam-side down) in an ungreased loaf pan. Press to ensure no air bubbles are trapped inside. Bake for 1 to 1½ hours, until completely cooked. Drain off excess fat every 15 to 30 minutes.

7. Remove from oven and drain off excess fat. Let cool. Remove from loaf pan. Slice, and serve.

Minted Lamb Sausage

Lamb is considered a delicacy in most parts of Italy. It imparts a distinct flavor in this sausage recipe, but you may use beef or pork if you are not a fan of lamb.

1. Grind the lamb and pancetta separately. Keep chilled. Peel and mince the garlic. Clean and chop the mint leaves.

2. Mix together all the ingredients in a chilled bowl using chilled utensils. If using an electric mixer, be sure not to overblend the meat.

3. Either stuff the mixture into casings or form into patties.

4. Use in desired preparation, or heat a small amount of oil or butter to medium temperature in a large sauté pan. Add the sausage, cover, and cook for about 30 minutes, turning every 5 minutes or so. Uncover and cook for 10 to 15 minutes, until thoroughly browned. Drain on paper towels.

Serves 10

2¼ pounds lamb
¼–½ pound pancetta (or substitute bacon)
½ bulb garlic
½ bunch fresh mint
¼ cup pine nuts
½ cup raisins
1 egg, lightly beaten
Fresh-cracked black pepper
Kosher salt

Beef Sausage

You can substitute raisins for the currants and walnuts for the pistachios in this recipe. But use the original ingredients for an authentic flavor.

1. Grind the meat and fat separately. Keep chilled. Peel and mince the shallots and garlic.

2. Mix together all the ingredients in a chilled bowl with chilled utensils. If using an electric mixer, be sure not to overblend the meat and fat.

3. Either stuff the mixture into casings or form into patties.

4. Use in desired preparation, or heat a small amount of oil or butter to medium temperature in a large sauté pan. Add the sausage, cover, and cook for about 30 minutes, turning every 5 minutes or so. Uncover and cook for 10 to 15 minutes, until thoroughly browned. Drain on paper towels.

Serves 10

2¼ pounds lean beef
¼–½ pound pork fat
2 shallots
3 cloves garlic
1 egg, lightly beaten
2 tablespoons all-purpose flour
2½ heaping tablespoons ground cinnamon
½ teaspoon ground nutmeg
½ cup dried currants
½ cup chopped pistachios
Fresh-cracked black pepper
Kosher salt

Veal and Pepper Sausage

Serves 10

2 pounds veal
½–¾ pound pork fat
2 red bell peppers
2 green bell peppers
1 yellow onion
2 tablespoons dried
    marjoram or oregano
Fresh-cracked black pepper
Kosher salt

The classic combination of veal and peppers makes these sausages a big favorite. Serve these sausages for company—they're sure to be a crowd pleaser.

1. Grind the meat and fat separately. Keep chilled. Clean and finely dice the bell peppers. Peel and finely dice the onion.

2. Mix together all the ingredients in a chilled bowl with chilled utensils. If using an electric mixer, be sure not to overblend the meat and fat.

3. Either stuff the mixture into casings or form into patties.

4. Use in desired preparation, or heat a small amount of oil or butter to medium temperature in a large sauté pan. Add the sausage, cover, and cook for about 30 minutes, turning every 5 minutes or so. Uncover and cook for 10 to 15 minutes, until thoroughly browned. Drain on paper towels.

Salmon Sausage

Serves 10

2½ pounds salmon
½ bunch fresh parsley
½ cup Basic Risotto (page
    140), chilled
3 egg whites
¼ cup heavy cream
½ teaspoon ground mace (or
    substitute nutmeg)
Fresh-cracked black pepper
Kosher salt

You can use leftover risotto in this recipe, or make it fresh. Either way, the rice helps hold the fish together. Just make sure to chill the risotto completely before using.

1. Grind the salmon, keeping it cold throughout. Keep chilled. Clean and chop the parsley.

2. Mix together all the ingredients in a chilled bowl with chilled utensils. If using an electric mixer, be sure not to overblend.

3. Either stuff the mixture into casings or form into patties.

4. Use in desired preparation, or heat a small amount of oil or butter to medium temperature in a large sauté pan. Add the sausage, cover, and cook for about 15 minutes, turning every 3 minutes or so. Uncover and cook for 5 to 10 minutes, until thoroughly browned. Drain on paper towels.

Italian Beef and Sun-Dried Tomato Sausage

*For especially tender and flavorful beef, marinate in herbs and
wine 8 to 12 hours ahead of time.*

Serves 10

2½ pounds lean beef
½–¾ pound pork fat
½ bulb garlic
¼ pound Parmesan cheese
¼ pound Romano cheese
1 cup sun-dried tomatoes
*1 cup hearty red wine (not
   cooking wine)*
1 egg
1 tablespoon dried oregano
1 tablespoon dried basil
1 tablespoon dried parsley

1. Grind the beef and pork fat separately. Keep chilled. Peel and mince the garlic. Grate the cheeses. Rehydrate the tomatoes by soaking them in the wine for approximately 20 minutes, then squeeze out excess liquid.

2. Mix together all the ingredients in a chilled bowl with chilled utensils. If using an electric mixer, be sure not to overblend meat and fat.

3. Either stuff the mixture into casings or form into patties.

4. Use in desired preparation, or heat a small amount of oil or butter to medium temperature in a large sauté pan. Add the sausage, cover, and cook for about 30 minutes, turning every 5 minutes or so. Uncover and cook for 10 to 15 more minutes, until thoroughly browned. Drain on paper towels.

Duck Sausage

*This is a creative way to use duck, and these sausages make great appetizers
for a dinner party. Serve with a sauce of reduced orange juice.*

Serves 10

2½ pounds fresh duck meat
½ pound pork fat
½ bulb garlic
½ bunch scallions
*2 tablespoons fresh-grated
   orange zest*
½ teaspoon ground nutmeg
½ teaspoon ground cloves
Fresh-cracked black pepper
Kosher salt

1. Grind the meat and fat separately. Keep chilled. Peel and mince the garlic. Clean and chop the scallions.

2. Mix together all ingredients in a chilled bowl with chilled utensils. If using an electric mixer, be sure not to overblend the meat and fat.

3. Either stuff the mixture into casings or form into patties.

4. Use in desired preparation, or heat a small amount of oil or butter to medium temperature in a large sauté pan. Add the sausage, cover, and cook for about 30 minutes, turning every 5 minutes or so. Uncover and cook for 10 to 15 minutes, until thoroughly browned. Drain on paper towels.

2½ pounds pork
½–¾ pound pork fat
3 Granny Smith apples (or any tart apple)
¼ cup shelled almonds
2 tablespoons ground cinnamon
½ tablespoon ground nutmeg
½ tablespoon ground cloves
Fresh-cracked black pepper
Kosher salt

Apple and Pork Sausage

The apple gives this sausage a slightly sweet taste, and the almonds lend a slightly crunchy texture.

1. Grind the meat and fat separately. Keep chilled. Clean and finely dice the apples. Chop the almonds.

2. Mix together all the ingredients in a chilled bowl with chilled utensils. If using an electric mixer, be sure not to overblend meat and fat.

3. Either stuff the mixture into casings or form into patties.

4. Use in desired preparation, or heat a small amount of oil or butter to medium temperature in a large sauté pan. Add the sausage, cover, and cook for about 30 minutes, turning every 5 minutes or so. Uncover and cook for 10 to 15 minutes, until thoroughly browned. Drain on paper towels.

Handy Gadgets

Vegetable peelers come in handy for more than just peeling vegetables. You can use one to make garnishes, like Parmesan curls, or use it to scrape fruit when a recipe calls for the "zest" of lemon or orange. There is also a special tool called a "zester," which is used to extract zest, or very thin shreds of a fruit's hard skin.

Arugula, Mozzarella, and Chicken Sausage

The bacon is optional in this recipe, but if included it nicely counters the bitter taste of the arugula.

Serves 10

2 pounds chicken
¼ pancetta or bacon
2 small bunches fresh arugula
1 shallot
½ pound fresh mozzarella
1 egg, lightly beaten
Fresh-cracked black pepper
Kosher salt

1. Grind the chicken and pancetta separately. Keep chilled. Clean and roughly chop the arugula. Peel and mince the shallot. Shred the mozzarella.

2. Mix together all the ingredients in a chilled bowl with chilled utensils. If using an electric mixer, be sure not to overblend the meat and fat.

3. Either stuff the mixture into casings or form into patties.

4. Use in desired preparation, or heat a small amount of oil or butter to medium temperature in a large sauté pan. Add the sausage, cover, and cook for about 20 minutes, turning every 5 minutes or so. Uncover and cook for 10 to 15 minutes, until thoroughly browned. Drain on paper towel.

Rosemary Lamb Sausage

Try stuffing this sausage mixture into thinly sliced and lightly steamed squash, and bake with your favorite sauce.

Serves 10

2 pounds lamb
¼–½ pork fat
2 large baking potatoes
6 sprigs fresh rosemary
½ bulb garlic
Fresh-cracked black pepper
Kosher salt

1. Grind the lamb meat and pork fat separately. Keep chilled. Peel and shred the potatoes. Clean the rosemary and remove the "needles" from the stems (discard the stems). Peel and mince the garlic.

2. Mix together all the ingredients in a chilled bowl with chilled utensils. If using an electric mixer, be sure not to overblend meat and fat.

3. Either stuff the mixture into casings or form into patties.

4. Use in desired preparation, or a heat small amount of oil or butter to medium temperature in a large sauté pan. Add the sausage, cover, and cook for about 30 minutes, turning every 5 minutes or so. Uncover and cook for 10 to 15 minutes, until thoroughly browned. Drain on paper towels.

Smooth Chicken Liver Sausage

Don't let the word liver *turn you away. When mixed with the other ingredients, it takes on a whole new flavor.*

1. Peel and mince the garlic and shallots. Clean and chop the parsley. Peel and chop the hard-boiled eggs.

2. Heat the butter to medium temperature in a large sauté pan. Add the chicken liver, season with pepper and salt, and sauté for 15 minutes. Let cool. Blend chicken liver in a food processor until smooth.

3. Combine all the ingredients. Either stuff the mixture into casings or form into patties.

4. Use in desired preparation, or heat a small amount of oil or butter to medium temperature in a large sauté pan. Add the sausage, cover, and cook for about 10 minutes, turning every 3 minutes or so. Uncover and cook for 5 minutes or until thoroughly browned. Drain on paper towels.

Whitefish Sausage

These light sausages are ideal for a Christmas Eve appetizer or to accompany Spinach Pasta (page 105).

Serves 10

*2 pounds fresh whitefish
    fillets of choice*
½ bulb garlic
2 shallots
½ bunch fresh parsley
4 hard-boiled eggs
2 eggs, lightly beaten
½ cup chicken fat
2 tablespoons butter
Fresh-cracked black pepper
Kosher salt

1. Process the fish in a food processor until smooth. Keep chilled. Peel and mince the garlic and shallots. Clean and chop the parsley. Peel and chop the hard-boiled eggs.

2. Combine all the ingredients. Either stuff the mixture into casings or form into patties.

3. Use in desired preparation, or heat a small amount of oil or butter to medium temperature in a large sauté pan. Add the sausage, cover, and cook for about 10 minutes, turning every 3 minutes or so. Uncover and cook for about 5 minutes, until thoroughly browned. Drain on paper towels.

Got Milk?
Believe it or not, milk is commonly used when preparing fish. The combination of seasoned water and milk make a great poaching liquid. Just add white peppercorns, lemon juice, thin slices of onion, and fresh thyme before poaching fish.

Serves 10

1 yellow onion
2 cups cooked or canned
    chickpeas
2 cups cooked white rice
2 eggs, lightly beaten
2 cups steamed kale
2 tablespoons dried oregano
1 tablespoon dried basil
Fresh-cracked black pepper
Kosher salt

Vegetable and Bean Sausage

*You can substitute spinach for the kale and leftover risotto
for the rice called for in this recipe.*

1. Peel and dice the onion.

2. Mix together all the ingredients in a chilled bowl with chilled utensils. If using an electric mixer, be sure not to overblend.

3. Either stuff the mixture into casings or form into patties.

4. Use in desired preparation, or heat a small amount of oil or butter to medium temperature in a large sauté pan. Add the sausage, cover, and cook for about 30 minutes, turning every 5 minutes or so. Uncover and cook for 10 to 15 minutes, until thoroughly browned. Drain on paper towels.

Serves 10

2 pounds fresh turkey meat
½ pound pork fat
½ bunch fresh parsley
½ cup walnuts
½ cup dried cranberries
½ teaspoon ground nutmeg
½ teaspoon ground cloves
Fresh-cracked black pepper
Kosher salt

Turkey and Cranberry Sausage

*Though not an authentic Italian recipe, this turkey and cranberry sausage can
make a great addition to an Italian pasta dish.*

1. Grind the turkey meat and pork fat separately. Keep chilled. Clean and chop the parsley. Chop the walnuts.

2. Mix together all the ingredients in a chilled bowl with chilled utensils. If using an electric mixer, be sure not to overblend the meat and fat.

3. Either stuff the mixture into casings or form into patties.

4. Use in desired preparation, or heat a small amount of oil or butter to medium temperature in a large sauté pan. Add the sausage, cover, and cook for about 30 minutes, turning every 5 minutes. Uncover and cook for 10 to 15 minutes, until thoroughly browned. Drain on paper towels.

Chapter 12

Meat

Baked Pork Ribs 226

Sweet and Spicy Pork 226

Leg of Lamb 227

Fresh-Baked Ham and Potatoes 228

Marinated Venison Roast 229

Venison Kebabs 230

Spiced Oxtails 231

Italian Meat Loaf 231

Venison Bean Ragout 232

Osso Buco with Polenta Dumplings 233

Mama Theresa's Beef Braciola 234

Pork Terrine 235

Vitello al Forno (Baked Veal) 236

Lamb Loaf 237

Tender Beef Ravioli 238

Stuffed Pork Roast 238

Grilled Rack of Lamb 239

Easter Pizza Casserole 240

Chuck Steak Pot Roast 241

Baked Smoked Ham 242

Vitello alla Francese (French-Style Veal) 242

Vitello Brasato (Braised Veal) 243

Baked Pork Ribs

Enjoy these finger-licking ribs, Italian style.

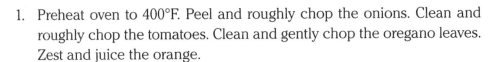

1. Preheat oven to 400°F. Peel and roughly chop the onions. Clean and roughly chop the tomatoes. Clean and gently chop the oregano leaves. Zest and juice the orange.

2. Heat the oil to medium-high temperature in a heavy-bottomed oven-proof pan. Brown the ribs and onions for 10 minutes. Add the tomatoes, and cook for 3 minutes. Add all the remaining ingredients.

3. Cover the pan, and place in the oven. Cook for 45 minutes. Uncover, and cook for 15 more minutes. Serve.

Sweet and Spicy Pork

*Serve this delicious pork with basic risotto or polenta and
a steamed vegetable of choice.*

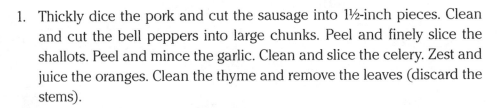

1. Thickly dice the pork and cut the sausage into 1½-inch pieces. Clean and cut the bell peppers into large chunks. Peel and finely slice the shallots. Peel and mince the garlic. Clean and slice the celery. Zest and juice the oranges. Clean the thyme and remove the leaves (discard the stems).

2. Heat the oil in a large skillet to medium-high temperature. Brown the pork and sausage on all sides. Add the bell peppers, shallots, garlic, celery, and ginger. Reduce heat to medium and sauté for 5 minutes.

3. Add the orange juice and zest, the thyme, and bay leaf. Season with salt and pepper, and simmer for 20 minutes, uncovered. Serve hot.

Leg of Lamb

*A large Dutch oven with a rack works best for cooking the lamb
in this dish. However, you can use any large baking dish with a rack.
Just wrap the lamb in foil to prevent the herbs from burning.*

Serves 10

1 bulb garlic
1 cup shelled walnuts
3 sprigs fresh rosemary
3 sprigs fresh mint
⅓ cup olive oil
1 (5-pound) leg of lamb
Kosher salt
Fresh-cracked black pepper
*1 cup pinot noir (or other red
    drinking wine of choice)*

1. Preheat oven to 350°F. Peel and mince half the garlic. Cut each of the remaining garlic cloves in half. Finely chop the walnuts. Clean and mince half the rosemary and mint. In a food processor, blend the minced garlic and minced herbs with the walnuts and half the oil.

2. Pierce the lamb with a sharp knife in several places. Insert 1 piece of the garlic, 1 rosemary leaf, and 1 mint leaf in each cut. Rub the herb-nut mixture on the outside of the lamb, and season with salt and pepper.

3. Grease a rack with the remaining oil and set in the bottom of a Dutch oven or a baking pan with a tight-fitting lid. Pour the wine into the bottom of the pan. Place the lamb on the rack.

4. Cover the pan tightly, and bake for 1½ hours. Remove the lid, and cook to desired doneness.

1 bulb garlic
8 sprigs fresh oregano
2 white onions
5 large Idaho potatoes
1 (5-pound) pork roast
    (bone-in)
Kosher salt
Fresh-cracked black pepper
1 tablespoon olive oil

Fresh-Baked Pork and Potatoes

This ham dish is great to serve to guests for a holiday meal.
Try it out this Christmas or New Year's Day.

1. Preheat oven to 375°F. Peel and cut the garlic cloves in half. Clean and remove the oregano leaves from the stems (discard the stems). Peel and cut the onions into large wedges. Scrub the potatoes and leave whole.

2. Pierce the pork with a sharp knife in several places and insert a piece of garlic and an oregano leaf in each cut. Season with salt and pepper. Place the pork roast on an oiled rack set in a Dutch oven or a baking pan with a tight-fitting lid. Cover, and roast for 1¼ to 1¾ hours.

3. Remove the pork with the rack. Pour the oil into the pan, and add the potatoes and onions. Return the pork to the pan, without the rack. Add any remaining herbs, and stir.

4. Roast, uncovered, for about 1 hour, until the potatoes are fork-tender and the pork is cooked through.

Potato Tips

To keep potatoes from budding, place an apple in the potato bag. For really smooth mashed potatoes, press cooked potatoes through a "ricer," which looks like an oversized garlic press, then fold in the milk, butter, and seasonings by hand. The ricer gets rid of lumps without overworking the potato into a glutinous gob. For a more home-style (lumpy) texture, use either a stiff whisk or potato masher to smash spuds.

Marinated Venison Roast

In order to properly marinate the venison in this recipe, you'll have to start preparation one day ahead of time.

Serves 10

3 Vidalia onions
2 shallots
1 bulb garlic
½ bunch fresh parsley
5 sprigs fresh thyme or ½ teaspoon dried
1 tablespoon ground cinnamon
2 bay leaves
Fresh-cracked black pepper
1 cup robust red table wine
2 cups Beef Stock (page 15)
1 (5-pound) venison roast
1 tablespoon olive oil

1. Peel and roughly chop the onions, shallots, and garlic. Clean and roughly chop the parsley and thyme leaves.

2. Combine all the ingredients *except* the venison and the oil in a large container with a lid or in a resealable plastic bag. Mix well. Add the venison to the mixture, turning the meat to coat completely with the marinade. Refrigerate for at least 8 hours or up to 1 day.

3. Preheat oven to 350°F. Heat a heavy-bottomed ovenproof pan with lid (such as a Dutch oven) on the stovetop over medium-high temperature and add the oil. Remove the meat from the marinade and sear until browned on all sides. Pour in the marinade and bring to a boil. Immediately cover, and place the pan in the oven.

4. Braise for 2½ hours. Remove the pan from the oven and place it on the stovetop. Transfer the venison to a pan with a rack, place in the oven, and bake for 30 minutes. While the meat roasts, reduce the marinade by half the volume over high heat on the stovetop. Once the meat is cooked, drizzle the reduced marinade over the top, and serve.

½ cup balsamic vinegar
1 tablespoon olive oil
1 teaspoon dried basil
1 teaspoon dried oregano
1 teaspoon dried parsley
Fresh-cracked black pepper
3 pounds venison loin
2 yellow onions
2 green bell peppers
    (optional)
1 large eggplant
½ pint grape tomatoes (or
    substitute cherry or
    wedged plum tomatoes)

Venison Kebabs

Allow some extra preparation time for this dish.
You need to soak wooden skewers in water to keep them from burning
when grilling. Marinate the venison for at least 3 hours prior to cooking.

1. To prepare the marinade, mix together the vinegar, oil, basil, oregano, parsley, and black pepper. Cut the venison into large chunks, and marinate for at least 3 hours.

2. Peel the onion and cut into large wedges. Clean and cut the bell peppers and eggplant into large pieces. Clean and dry the tomatoes.

3. Preheat the grill. Remove the meat from the marinade. Toss the vegetables lightly in the marinade, and discard the marinade. Thread the meat and vegetables onto skewers.

4. Grill the kebabs on each side until golden brown, about 2 minutes per side. Serve hot.

Grilling with Herbs
Next time you grill, instead of making a marinade with sprigs of fresh herbs (rosemary, sage, basil), put them directly on the hot coals when grilling. This will infuse the food you are grilling with the flavors of the herbs. Don't put the herbs on until the coals are white-hot and becoming ashy.

Spiced Oxtails

These oxtails must marinate in the refrigerator the night before.

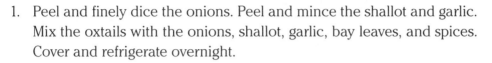

1. Peel and finely dice the onions. Peel and mince the shallot and garlic. Mix the oxtails with the onions, shallot, garlic, bay leaves, and spices. Cover and refrigerate overnight.

2. Preheat oven to 350°F. Heat the olive oil to medium-high temperature in a large Dutch oven (or heavy-bottomed ovenproof pot with a lid). Sear the oxtails on all sides. Add the wine, and reduce by half the volume. Pour in the stock, and bring to a boil.

3. Cover the pan and place in the oven. Braise for about 2½ hours, until cooked through. Serve hot.

Serves 10

2 yellow or white onions
1 shallot
½ bulb garlic
3½ pounds oxtails
2 bay leaves
½ teaspoon ground cloves
1½ teaspoons ground cinnamon
½ teaspoon ground nutmeg
Fresh-cracked black pepper
2 tablespoons olive oil
1 cup dry red wine (not cooking wine)
4 cups Beef Stock (page 15)

Italian Meat Loaf

This version of meat loaf, layered with spinach and mashed potatoes, is a bit more elegant and complex than standard meat loaf.

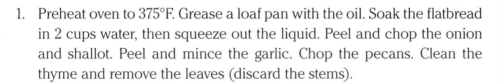

1. Preheat oven to 375°F. Grease a loaf pan with the oil. Soak the flatbread in 2 cups water, then squeeze out the liquid. Peel and chop the onion and shallot. Peel and mince the garlic. Chop the pecans. Clean the thyme and remove the leaves (discard the stems).

2. Mix together the flatbread, onions, shallot, garlic, pecans, thyme, beef, egg, currants, cinnamon, and pepper flakes.

3. Layer the smashed potatoes, spinach, and beef mixture in the prepared pan. Press firmly.

4. Bake for 45 minutes, uncovered. Drain off excess grease, and let cool slightly. Remove from loaf pan, slice, and serve.

Serves 10

1 teaspoon olive oil
3 pieces Basic Flatbread (page 80)
1 yellow onion
1 shallot
4 cloves garlic
¼ cup pecans
3 sprigs fresh thyme
1½ pounds ground beef
1 egg, lightly beaten
¼ cup dried currants
1 teaspoon ground cinnamon
¼ teaspoon red pepper flakes
1½ cups Roasted Garlic Smashed Potatoes (page 282)
2 cups steamed spinach

*1½ cups dried cannellini
beans
6 cups water
1½ pounds venison stew
meat
¼ pound pancetta
2 yellow onions
2 carrots
2 stalks celery
3 sprigs fresh thyme
2 tablespoons olive oil
1 cup dry red wine (not
cooking wine)
8 cups Beef Stock (page 15)
1 bay leaf
1½ tablespoons ground
cinnamon
½ teaspoon red pepper flakes*

Venison Bean Ragout

*Since you need to soak the beans in this recipe overnight,
you will have to start preparations a day in advance.*

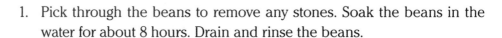

1. Pick through the beans to remove any stones. Soak the beans in the water for about 8 hours. Drain and rinse the beans.

2. Cut the venison into bite-size chunks. Thinly slice the pancetta. Peel and medium-dice the onions and carrots. Clean and medium-dice the celery. Clean the thyme and remove the leaves (discard the stems).

3. Heat the oil to medium temperature in a large stockpot. Add the pancetta and venison. Lightly brown for 5 minutes. Add the onions and carrots. Sauté for 5 minutes. Add the celery, and sauté for 5 more minutes. Pour in the wine, and reduce by half the volume.

4. Add the remaining ingredients. Simmer with the lid ajar for 1½ to 2 hours. Remove the bay leaf.

5. Serve alone or over pasta.

Osso Buco with Polenta Dumplings

*This version of osso buco is topped off with polenta dumplings
instead of the more-familiar gremolata.*

Serves 10

5 pounds veal shanks
1 bulb garlic
5 shallots
5 parsnips (or substitute
   carrots)
2 bulbs celeriac (or substitute
   5 stalks celery)
2 large leeks
3 pounds plum tomatoes
4 sprigs fresh thyme
½ bunch fresh parsley
2 tablespoons olive oil
½ cup red table wine
3 cups Beef Stock (page 15)
3 bay leaves
½ recipe Basic Polenta (page
   162), cooked
Kosher salt
Fresh-cracked black pepper

1. Preheat oven to 350°F. Rinse the veal shanks and pat dry with paper towels. Peel and thinly slice the garlic and shallots. Peel and roughly chop the parsnips and celeriac. Clean and roughly chop the leeks and tomatoes. Clean and roughly chop the thyme and parsley.

2. Heat the oil to medium-high temperature in a heavy-bottomed oven-proof pot with tight-fitting lid (such as a Dutch oven). Sear the shanks on all sides. Add the parsnips, celeriac, leeks, shallots, and garlic. Sauté for 5 minutes. Add the tomatoes, and stir.

3. Pour in the wine, and reduce by half the volume. Add the stock. Reduce heat to medium, and bring to simmer. Cover the pan and place in the oven. Braise for 4 hours, then add the herbs and simmer 30 more minutes.

4. Remove the pan from the oven and place on the stovetop over medium-high heat. Drop in heaping tablespoonfuls of the polenta. Cover, and cook for 15 to 20 minutes. Remove bay leaves.

5. Sprinkle to taste with salt and pepper. Ladle into bowls, and serve.

1 white onion
½ bulb garlic
½ bunch fresh parsley
2 hard-boiled eggs
½ pound capicola, thinly
*   sliced*
½ pound salami, thinly sliced
¼ pound pepperoni, thinly
*   sliced*
¼ pound fontina cheese
4 pounds beef braciola, thinly
*   sliced*
Fresh-cracked black pepper
2 tablespoons olive oil
1 cup Syrah (or other hearty
*   red wine of choice)*
4 cups Old World Gravy
*   (Long-Cooking Tomato*
*   Sauce) (page 64)*

Mama Theresa's Beef Braciola

Braciola makes a great leftover. Don't worry if you make too much for dinner—just reheat it for lunch the next day.

1. Peel and finely chop the onion. Peel and mince the garlic. Clean and chop the parsley. Peel and finely chop the hard-boiled eggs. Finely chop the capicola, salami, and pepperoni slices. Shred the cheese.

2. Lay out the beef and sprinkle with the onion, garlic, meats, egg, cheese, parsley, and pepper. Carefully roll up the meat and tie with butcher's twine.

3. Heat the oil to medium-high temperature in a skillet. Sear the tied meat on all sides. Reduce heat, and add the wine. Simmer, uncovered, for 90 minutes.

4. Reheat the tomato sauce. Serve the braciola with the tomato sauce over the top.

Pork Terrine

Serve with a baked apple. To prepare the apple: Core and slice off the top of the apple. Sprinkle with cinnamon. Place in a dish with a small amount of water and lemon juice, and cover with plastic wrap. Heat on high for about 5 minutes.

Serves 10

½ teaspoon olive oil
1½ pounds boneless pork
3 large Idaho baking
    potatoes
½ bunch fresh oregano
½ bulb garlic
1 eggplant
2 plum tomatoes
Fresh-cracked black pepper
¼ cup fresh-grated Romano
    cheese

1. Preheat oven to 375°F. Lightly grease a loaf pan with the oil. Cut the boneless pork into ½-inch-thick slices. Clean and slice the unpeeled potatoes as thinly as possible. Clean the oregano and remove the leaves (discard the stems). Peel and mince the garlic. Clean and slice the eggplant lengthwise. Clean and roughly chop the tomatoes.

2. Line the prepared pan with the pork, then add the potatoes, garlic, oregano, tomatoes, eggplant, black pepper, and Romano.

3. Cover with aluminum foil, and roast for 45 minutes. Remove from oven and uncover. Carefully drain off grease. Press down again and return to oven. Roast, uncovered, for 20 minutes.

4. Remove from oven, and let cool thoroughly. Slice, and serve at room temperature or reheat as desired.

Imported Is Best
When using canned tomatoes in a recipe that calls for fresh tomatoes, it is worth the extra expense and effort of seeking out and purchasing tomatoes imported from Italy. Look for cans of tomatoes that are labeled with "San Marzano." This means that they are grown in the San Marzano region of Italy and are known to be top-quality tomatoes.

Serves 10

4 tablespoons olive oil, divided
2 red bell peppers
2 yellow bell peppers
1 white onion
6 fresh sprigs marjoram
1½ pounds boneless veal, thinly sliced
1½ cups cooked brown rice
½ cup shredded fontina cheese
Fresh-cracked black pepper

Vitello al Forno (Baked Veal)

If you have some leftover rice or risotto in the house, feel free to use it in place of the brown rice called for in this recipe.

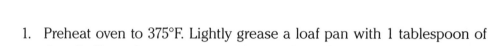

1. Preheat oven to 375°F. Lightly grease a loaf pan with 1 tablespoon of the oil. Clean the peppers, and leave whole. Peel and thickly slice the onion. Clean and gently chop the marjoram leaves.

2. Toss the peppers and onions in the remaining oil. Place on a large baking sheet. Roast for 10 to 20 minutes, until the onion is softened and the "skin" of the peppers blisters. Remove from oven and immediately seal the peppers in a plastic bag (this makes it easier to remove the skin). Place the onions on paper towels to drain. Gently remove the skins from the peppers. Cut the peppers in half, and remove the stems and seeds.

3. Layer the veal, peppers, rice, onions, marjoram, cheese, and black pepper in the prepared loaf pan.

4. Cover with aluminum foil, and roast for 45 minutes. Remove from oven and uncover. Carefully drain off grease. Return to the oven and roast, uncovered, for 20 minutes.

5. Remove from oven and let cool thoroughly. Slice, and serve at room temperature or reheat as desired.

Lamb Loaf

This is a delicious variation of the classic meat loaf. Even if you don't like regular meat loaf, give this a try. Its flavor may surprise and delight you.

Serves 10

2 tablespoons olive oil, divided
1¾ pounds lamb
½ bulb garlic
⅓ bunch fresh mint
½ cup walnuts
1 recipe Basic Pasta (page 100), unformed and uncooked
Fresh-cracked black pepper

1. Preheat oven to 350°F. Grease a loaf pan with 1 tablespoon of the oil. Cut the lamb into large cubes. Peel and mince the garlic. Clean and chop the mint leaves. Finely chop the walnuts.

2. Roll out the pasta dough on a floured surface into a sheet a few inches longer and wider than the top of the loaf pan.

3. Layer the lamb, garlic, mint, and walnuts in the loaf pan, and sprinkle with black pepper. Gently place the pasta dough over the top and tuck firmly around the ingredients.

4. Drizzle with the remaining olive oil. Cover with aluminum foil, and bake for about 45 minutes.

5. Let cool thoroughly. Slice, and serve at room temperature or reheat as desired.

Serves 10

1½ pounds filet mignon (or other tender cut of beef)
2 tablespoons ground cumin
Fresh-cracked black pepper
4 sprigs fresh parsley
6 cloves garlic
1 recipe Basic Pasta (page 100), unformed and uncooked
Extra-virgin olive oil

Tender Beef Ravioli

The beef used in this recipe must be very tender since it is sliced thinly and not ground. If the beef is too tough, you will have trouble slicing it.

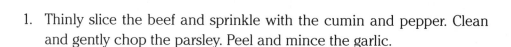

1. Thinly slice the beef and sprinkle with the cumin and pepper. Clean and gently chop the parsley. Peel and mince the garlic.

2. Roll out the dough on a floured surface into a sheet about ¼ inch thick. Cut into 3-inch squares. Place a spoonful of beef in the center of each square, and top with the garlic. Fold the squares in half, corner to corner to form a triangle, and seal tightly.

3. Bring a large pot of water to a slow boil. Add the pasta, and cook until al dente (the beef can be a bit rare). Drain.

4. Place on a warm serving plate, and drizzle with the oil. Sprinkle with the parsley and pepper, and serve.

Serves 10

3 boneless shoulder pork roasts
1 bulb fennel with tops
2 Granny Smith apples (or other tart variety)
1 white onion
1 pound raw sausage mixture of choice (see Chapter 11, page 199)
Fresh-cracked black pepper

Stuffed Pork Roast

The fennel and apples impart a wonderful fresh flavor to this pork roast. This dish makes a great autumn meal.

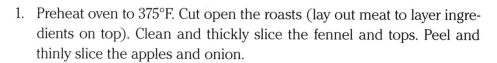

1. Preheat oven to 375°F. Cut open the roasts (lay out meat to layer ingredients on top). Clean and thickly slice the fennel and tops. Peel and thinly slice the apples and onion.

2. Lay out the roasts and layer with the sausage mixture, fennel, onion, and apples. Roll and tie securely with butcher's twine.

3. Place on a rack in a large roasting pan. Sprinkle with pepper. Cover, and roast for 2 hours then uncover and roast for ½ to 1 hour longer until the pork is thoroughly cooked. Untie, slice, and serve.

Grilled Rack of Lamb

Simple but delicious, this recipe depends on just the pure taste of the roast lamb with some basic seasoning. Serve with Roasted Garlic Smashed Potatoes (page 282).

Serves 10

5 pounds rack of lamb
½ bulb garlic
2 tablespoons olive oil
Fresh-cracked black pepper
Coarse salt

1. "French" the ends of the lamb rack by cutting away suet, fat, etc., from the bone ends just past the "center" chop area. Scrape the bones clean and cover the bare bone with foil. Preheat the grill.

2. Peel and mince the garlic. Mix together the garlic, oil, pepper, and salt.

3. Thoroughly rub the lamb with the garlic oil.

4. Grill the lamb on all sides to desired doneness (anywhere from 5 to 20 minutes), and serve.

Grilling Indoors

If you use your outdoor grill all summer, you are probably a little lost once the winter weather rolls in. However, there's a solution: grill pans provide that same grilled flavor and can be used indoors on your stovetop. Just remember to allow the grill pan to get hot before placing the food on it, just as you would with an outdoor grill.

Crust:
¼ cup butter
1½ cups all-purpose flour
3 tablespoons cold water
¼ cup olive oil

Casserole:
3 white onions
1 head fresh broccoli (or
    substitute any green
    vegetable)
½ pound cooked ham
½ recipe Basic Italian Pork
    Sausage (page 214)
6 eggs
2 cups heavy cream
¾ cup pot cheese
1 tablespoon olive oil

Easter Pizza Casserole

*Pot cheese, or farmer's cheese, is a mild white cheese made of curds from
soured skim milk. If pot cheese is unavailable, you can substitute goat cheese.*

1. Combine all the crust ingredients. Mix by hand or in a mixer with a dough hook at medium speed until a ball forms. Wrap dough in plastic wrap and let rest for 30 minutes in the refrigerator. Roll out the dough on a floured surface into a large rectangle. Place the dough in the bottom of a large baking pan.

2. Preheat oven to 375°F. Peel and thinly slice the onions. Roughly chop the broccoli into bite-sized pieces. Thickly dice the ham, and slice the sausage into ½-inch coins. Beat the eggs in a large bowl, then add the cream and cheese.

3. Heat the oil to medium temperature in a large sauté pan. Add the sausage and onion, and cook for 8 minutes. Add the broccoli, and cook for 3 more minutes. Remove from heat and drain on paper towels.

4. Place the ham and sausage mixture on top of the crust. Pour in the egg mixture. Bake for 1 hour, uncovered. Serve.

Chuck Steak Pot Roast

This hearty winter dish goes wonderfully with Browned Risotto Patties (page 143). The combination creates quite a feast!

Serves 10

4 yellow onions
1 pound carrots
1 bunch celery
4 tomatoes
1 bunch fresh parsley
3 sprigs fresh thyme
1 tablespoon olive oil
1 (4-pound) beef chuck roast
1 cup Cabernet Sauvignon
1 gallon Beef Stock (page 15)
1 bay leaf

1. Preheat oven 375°F. Peel and roughly chop the onions and carrots. Clean and roughly chop the celery and tomatoes. Clean and chop the parsley and thyme leaves.

2. Heat the oil to medium-high temperature in a heavy-bottomed oven-proof pot with a tight-fitting lid (such as a Dutch oven). Sear the meat on all sides. Add the onions, carrots, celery, and sauté for 5 minutes. Add the tomatoes.

3. Pour in the wine, and reduce by half the volume. Add the stock. Reduce heat to medium, and bring to a simmer. Cover the pan, and place in the oven. Braise for 4 hours.

4. Add the parsley, thyme, and bay leaf. Simmer for 30 more minutes with lid ajar. Serve.

"Sweating" Onions

Sweating onions means to cook them in a small amount of oil or butter over moderate heat, covered. This cooking method breaks down the rigid cell walls and allows the juices to escape without burning, which releases the full flavor of the onions. Many Italian recipes include this step.

Baked Smoked Ham

Serves 10

½ cup apple juice
½ cup honey
½ cup coarse-grained
  mustard
2 ripe pears
1 (5-pound) smoked ham

The fruity glaze contrasts nicely with the salty ham. For a different taste, substi-tute another fruit for the pears, such as apples or oranges.

1. Preheat oven to 350°F. Mix together the juice, honey, and mustard. Peel and thickly slice the pears and add to the juice mixture.

2. Spoon the glaze over the ham.

3. Cover, and bake for 1½ hours. Uncover, and bake for 30 more minutes.

Vitello alla Francese
(French-Style Veal)

Serves 10

½ bulb garlic
4 lemons
½ bunch fresh parsley
4 eggs
½ cup fresh-grated Parmesan
  cheese
Fresh-cracked black pepper
3½–4 pounds veal cutlets
½ cup all-purpose flour
¼ cup olive oil
½ cup cold unsalted butter

Francese refers to a style of cooking meat or poultry cutlets with a lemon-based sauce.

1. Peel and mince the garlic. Zest and juice the lemons. Clean and chop the parsley. Lightly beat the eggs.

2. Combine the egg, cheese, pepper, and ½ of the parsley. Dust the cutlets with the flour. Dip in the egg mixture, dip back in the flour, and shake off excess flour.

3. Heat the oil to medium temperature in a large sauté pan. Sauté the veal on one side, and turn. Add the lemon juice, zest, and cold butter. Sauté the veal until fully cooked.

4. Serve sprinkled with the remaining parsley.

Vitello Brasato (Braised Veal)

Never completely cover a braising dish. Instead, leave the lid ajar on the pot.
Serve this veal with polenta or a potato dish.

Serves 10

2½ pounds boneless veal
1½ pounds plum tomatoes
    (or 2½ cups canned)
2 yellow onions
3 carrots
3 stalks celery
½ bulb garlic
2 bay leaves
½ bunch fresh parsley
3 sprigs fresh thyme
3 sprigs fresh marjoram or
    oregano
2 tablespoons olive oil
2 cups dry red wine (not
    cooking wine)
2 cups Beef Stock (page 15)
Fresh-cracked black pepper

1. Preheat oven to 350°F. Cut the veal into large cubes. Clean and roughly chop the tomatoes. Peel and wedge the onions. Peel and slice the carrots. Clean and slice the celery. Peel and mince the garlic. Clean and gently chop the herbs.

2. Heat the oil to medium-high temperature in a large skillet. Add the veal, and brown for 8 minutes. Add the onions and carrots, and sauté for 3 minutes. Add the celery, tomatoes, and garlic, and sauté for 2 minutes.

3. Pour in the wine and reduce by half the volume. Add the stock, herbs, and pepper. Cover partially, and simmer on medium-low heat for 2 hours. Serve hot.

Braising Meat

Braising is a popular cooking method in Italian cuisine. For braising, you must use a deep pot with a heavy bottom, just big enough for the meat to fit in. If the pot is too big, the liquid will evaporate too quickly. The liquid should only cover the meat halfway, never completely. Always leave the cover ajar on the pot. Braising requires careful attention and a long cooking time.

Chapter 13

Poultry

Winter "Fruited" Chicken 246

Chicken Scaparelli 247

Pollo alla Cacciatora (Chicken Cacciatore) 248

Christmas Goose 249

Turkey Tetrazzini. 250

Pollo Rustico 251

Classic Chicken Parmesan 252

Ricotta Chicken Breasts 252

Stuffed Chicken 253

Turkey Piccata 254

Turkey with Mascarpone Sauce 255

Fruit-Braised Duck 256

Asiago Pollo con Prosciutto

   (Asiago Chicken with Prosciutto) 257

Layered Duck 258

Chicken Terrine 259

Polenta-Stuffed Turkey Breast 260

Seared Quail with Gorgonzola 261

Chicken Marsala 262

Chicken Fricassee 263

3 (1- to 2-pound) whole chickens
3 tart apples
3 pears
3 shallots
½ bulb garlic
3 sprigs fresh thyme
2 tablespoons olive oil
1 cup dry white wine (not cooking wine)
¼ cup walnuts
¼ cup dried fruit
2 bay leaves
1 cup apple cider
2 cups Chicken Stock (page 14)

Winter "Fruited" Chicken

This richly flavored chicken would be best complimented by a simple rice dish, such as Basic Risotto (page 140).

1. Preheat oven to 350°F. Clean and cut each chicken into 4 serving pieces: 2 breasts and 2 wings, or 2 thighs and 2 legs (reserve backbones for stock).

2. Clean and wedge the apples and pears. Peel and dice the shallots. Peel and mince the garlic. Clean the thyme and remove the leaves from the stems (discard the stems).

3. Heat the oil to medium-high temperature in an ovenproof pan on the stovetop. Brown the chicken pieces on all sides. Add the apples, pears, shallots, and garlic, and sauté for 1 minute. Add the remaining ingredients, and bring to a boil. Cover the pan, and immediately place in the oven.

4. Braise in the oven for 1 hour. Serve hot.

Chicken Scaparelli

Serve this dish with a crisp salad and a loaf of crusty Italian bread for a delicious, well-balanced meal.

Serves 10

*5 pounds bone-in chicken,
cut into serving pieces
(breasts, wings, thighs,
legs)*
3 Vidalia onions
½ bulb garlic
2 parsnips
1 carrot
2 stalks celery
¼ bunch fresh oregano
¼ bunch fresh marjoram
2 sprigs fresh thyme
½ bunch fresh parsley
¼ cup olive oil
Coarse salt
Fresh-cracked black pepper

1. Preheat oven to 375°F. Clean the chicken in ice-cold water. Pat dry with paper towels, and remove the skin if desired. Peel the onions, garlic, parsnips, and carrot. Clean the celery. Clean and dry the oregano, marjoram, and thyme. Remove the leaves and discard the stems. Roughly chop the parsley.

2. Finely chop the onions, garlic, parsnips, carrot, celery, and herbs, preferably in a food processor.

3. Pour the oil into a large roasting pan and add all the ingredients. Season with salt and pepper, stir, and cover.

4. Roast for 1 hour. Uncover, and roast for 20 more minutes. Serve immediately.

Cut the Fat
One way to reduce the fat in chicken recipes is to remove the skin from the chicken before cooking. This will lower the amount of fat in the chicken by more than half, leaving you with a much healthier but still delicious meal.

Serves 10

*5 pounds bone-in chicken,
cut into serving pieces
(breasts, thighs, wings,
legs)*
3 yellow onions
½ bulb garlic
2 stalks celery
12 plum tomatoes
1 pound fresh mushrooms
½ bunch fresh parsley
1 tablespoon olive oil
1 cup red table wine
2 cups Beef Stock (page 15)
1 tablespoon dried oregano
1 tablespoon dried basil
2 bay leaves
Fresh-cracked black pepper

Pollo alla Cacciatora
(Chicken Cacciatore)

*Cacciatora literally translates as "hunter's style." It connotes a dish made with
chopped tomatoes, mushrooms, herbs, and garlic sauce.*

1. Clean the chicken in ice-cold water and pat dry with paper towels. Peel and slice the onions. Peel and mince the garlic. Clean and slice the celery. Clean and wedge the tomatoes. Clean the mushrooms with a damp paper towel, and cut in half. Clean and roughly chop the parsley.

2. Heat the oil to medium-high temperature in a large heavy-bottomed pan. Brown the chicken pieces on all sides for about 5 minutes. Reduce heat to medium and add the onions, garlic, celery, tomatoes, and mushrooms. Stir, and sauté for 2 minutes.

3. Pour in the wine and reduce by half the volume. Add the remaining ingredients, and reduce heat to low. Simmer, uncovered, for 2 hours.

4. Serve with cooked pasta, polenta, risotto, or mashed potatoes.

Christmas Goose

When you make this festive Christmastime dish, it is a good idea to increase the quantity so you will have plenty of leftovers.

1. Preheat oven to 325°F. Thoroughly wash the goose with ice-cold salted water. Rinse thoroughly, and pat dry with paper towels. Remove the gizzards and gently loosen the skin from the breast.

2. Peel and cut the onions and parsnips into large wedges. Clean and cut the celery into large pieces. Peel the garlic and leave cloves whole. Peel the clementines and break into sections. Clean the parsley and thyme, and leave whole.

3. Gently place some of the clementine sections and ½ of the garlic cloves under the skin of the breast area on each side of the goose. Place the remaining clementine sections and garlic inside the cavity, along with the parsley and thyme.

4. Place the goose breast-side up on a rack in a large roasting pan. Arrange the onions, parsnips, and celery on either side of the bird. Pour in the pomegranate juice, wine, and stock. Sprinkle with the nutmeg and pepper. Cover tightly, and roast for 2½ hours. Baste every 30 minutes.

5. Uncover, and increase oven temperature to 400°F. Roast for 30 minutes or until nicely browned and cooked through (internal temperature should be 165°F). Serve.

Serves 10

1 (5- to 8-pound) goose
3 yellow onions
2 parsnips
2 stalks celery
1 bulb garlic
6 clementines (or substitute tangerines)
1 bunch fresh parsley
8 sprigs thyme
1 cup pomegranate juice
1 cup hearty red wine
1 cup Chicken Stock (page 14)
½ teaspoon fresh-ground nutmeg
Fresh-cracked black pepper

Serves 10

1 tablespoon olive oil

3 pounds boneless turkey
   meat, cooked

1 pound mushrooms

¾ cup melted unsalted butter,
   divided

½ cup all-purpose flour

1 cup Chicken Stock (page
   14), chilled

1 cup whole milk

½ cup fresh-grated Parmesan
   cheese

½ pound cooked pasta of
   choice (see Chapter 7,
   page 99)

¼ cup plain bread crumbs

Turkey Tetrazzini

Don't throw away leftover Thanksgiving turkey!
This recipe is a great way to use up those pesky leftovers.

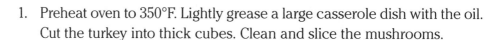

1. Preheat oven to 350°F. Lightly grease a large casserole dish with the oil. Cut the turkey into thick cubes. Clean and slice the mushrooms.

2. Heat ½ cup of the butter over medium temperature in a saucepan. Sauté the turkey until lightly golden. Add the mushrooms, and sauté for 2 minutes.

3. Add the flour to the pan, and mix with wooden spoon or whisk until the flour and butter in the pan form a roux (paste). Whisk in the stock, and cook until the mixture begins to thicken. Whisk in the milk, and cook until the mixture thickens into a sauce.

4. Remove from heat, and stir in the cheese and pasta. Transfer the mixture to the prepared casserole dish.

5. Mix together the remaining melted butter and the bread crumbs in a small bowl. Sprinkle over the top of the casserole. Bake for 20 minutes, uncovered. Serve hot.

Clarifying Butter

Fresh butter smokes and burns when added to a hot pan, so why do so many recipes suggest sautéing in butter? Because "clarified" butter is an ideal sauté medium. Fresh butter is an emulsion of butterfat, water, and milk proteins. Slowly heating whole butter divides these elements, enabling you to skim off the clarified butterfat, which is a clear, golden oil. This oil tolerates the high cooking temperatures needed to brown foods in a hot pan.

Pollo Rustico

This country-style roasted chicken goes well with any risotto, green vegetable, or salad.

Serves 10

1 (5-pound) whole chicken
2 red bell peppers
2 yellow bell peppers
2 white onions
2 sprigs fresh rosemary
1 sprig fresh sage
2 tablespoons olive oil
½ recipe Basic Italian Pork
    Sausage (page 214),
    unformed and uncooked
Fresh-cracked black pepper

1. Preheat oven to 350°F. Clean the chicken thoroughly in cold water and pat dry with paper towels. Remove any excess loose fat. Clean the bell peppers, and cut in half. Peel and cut the onions into large wedges. Clean the rosemary and sage and remove the needles and leaves (discard the stems). Gently tear the sage leaves in half.

2. Pour the oil into the bottom of a large roasting pan. Put the chicken in the pan. Scatter the sausage, peppers, onions, and herbs around the chicken. Sprinkle with pepper.

3. Cover the pan, and place in the oven. Cook for 30 minutes. Uncover, and stir. Increase heat to 425°F. Roast, uncovered, for 20 more minutes or until the chicken is golden brown and the juices run clear. Remove from oven, loosely cover with foil, and let rest for 10 minutes before carving.

Serves 10

3½ pounds skinless, boneless chicken
1 pound mozzarella or provolone cheese
3 eggs
¾ cup all-purpose flour
1 cup plain bread crumbs
2 tablespoons olive oil
2 cups Old World Gravy (Long-Cooking Tomato Sauce) (page 64)
2 teaspoons dried basil
2 teaspoons dried oregano
Fresh-cracked black pepper

Classic Chicken Parmesan

Yes, you can make this Italian restaurant favorite in your own kitchen! Leftovers make a nice "sub" sandwich on Italian bread.

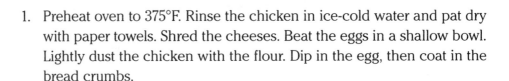

1. Preheat oven to 375°F. Rinse the chicken in ice-cold water and pat dry with paper towels. Shred the cheeses. Beat the eggs in a shallow bowl. Lightly dust the chicken with the flour. Dip in the egg, then coat in the bread crumbs.

2. Heat the oil to medium-high temperature in a large sauté pan. Quickly brown the breaded chicken on each side, and drain on paper towels.

3. Ladle ½ cup of the tomato sauce in the bottom of baking pan. Place the chicken in the pan in a single layer. Top with the cheese, and season with the basil, oregano, and pepper. Top with the remaining sauce.

4. Bake for 20 minutes. Serve with pasta.

Serves 10

1 tablespoon olive oil
10 large chicken breasts (bone-in, with wings attached if possible), cut in half
2 eggs
½ bunch fresh basil
2½ cups ricotta cheese
Fresh-cracked black pepper

Ricotta Chicken Breasts

Serve with Bread Salad (page 40) and Wilted Kale with Dried Currants and Walnuts (page 281).

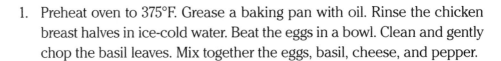

1. Preheat oven to 375°F. Grease a baking pan with oil. Rinse the chicken breast halves in ice-cold water. Beat the eggs in a bowl. Clean and gently chop the basil leaves. Mix together the eggs, basil, cheese, and pepper.

2. Form a "pocket" under the breast skin of each chicken breast by poking a small hole in the back area of the breast near the wing joint and gently lifting the skin with your finger. Stuff an even amount of the cheese mixture into each pocket with a pastry bag or spoon.

3. Place the chicken skin-side up in the prepared baking pan and roast for 1 hour, uncovered. Serve hot.

Stuffed Chicken

*Poultry needs to be cooked to a minimum internal temperature of 165°F.
Stuff only half the cavity so that the entire chicken
has an opportunity to cook fully.*

1. Preheat oven to 350°F. Grease a large baking pan with the oil. Rinse the chickens in ice-cold water, and pat dry with paper towels. Split into halves. Melt butter.

2. Cut the bread into large cubes. Peel and slice the onion. Peel and mince the garlic. Clean and chop the parsley and basil leaves. Clean the thyme and remove the leaves (discard the stems).

3. Mix together ½ cup of the melted butter, the bread, onion, garlic, parsley, basil, thyme, and black pepper.

4. Mound a couple of tablespoonfuls of the stuffing in half of the cavity of each chicken half, and place breast-side up in the prepared pan. Paint the skin with the butter mixture, and sprinkle with more black pepper.

5. Roast for 2½ hours, basting every 20 to 30 minutes, until the chickens' juices run clear and the chicken is cooked through. The chicken should reach an internal temperature of no less than 165°F (check the temperature at a joint with a meat thermometer).

Serves 10

1 tablespoon olive oil
2 (2- to 3-pound) whole
   chickens
¾ cup melted unsalted butter,
   divided
1 large loaf fresh Italian
   bread
1 white onion
½ bulb garlic
½ bunch fresh parsley
3 sprigs fresh basil
6 sprigs fresh thyme
Fresh-cracked black pepper

3–4 pounds boneless turkey meat
½ bunch fresh parsley
2 lemons
2 tablespoons olive oil
½ cup all-purpose flour
2 tablespoons capers, rinsed
1 cup Chicken Stock (page 14)
Fresh-cracked black pepper

Turkey Piccata

This "piccata" style of cooking meat very quickly in a pan with butter and lemon can also be used with chicken or veal.

1. Slice the turkey into serving-sized portions. Clean and gently chop the parsley. Zest and juice the lemons.

2. Heat the oil to medium temperature in a large sauté pan. Dust the turkey with the flour and shake off excess. Brown the turkey pieces on one side, then turn. Add the capers, lemon zest and juice, and the stock. Cook for 6 to 10 minutes longer, until browned and cooked through.

3. Sprinkle with the parsley and pepper, and serve.

Freezing Citrus Peels
Save the peels when you use lemons, limes, or oranges for juice or fruit and freeze them in a resealable bag. This way, when a recipe calls for citrus zest, you will have peels on hand, ready to grate or zest, right from the freezer. There's no need to thaw before using.

Turkey with Mascarpone Sauce

Because of the rich sauce this should be served with bland sides, such as Basic Risotto (page 140) or Basic Polenta (page 162) and a steamed vegetable.

Serves 10

1 tablespoon olive oil
4–5 pounds boneless turkey
Fresh-cracked black pepper
2 white onions
2 cups Mascarpone Cheese Sauce (page 69)

1. Preheat oven to 400°F. Grease a large roasting pan with the oil. Slice the turkey into thin "scaloppini-like" portions, and season with pepper. Peel and roughly chop the onions.

2. Place the onions in the prepared pan and top with the turkey. Cover, and roast for 20 minutes. Uncover and continue to roast 10-15 minutes longer.

3. While the turkey cooks, heat the cheese sauce.

4. Place the turkey and onions on a platter and drizzle with some sauce. Serve the remaining sauce on the side at the table.

1 (5-pound) duck
3 bay leaves
½ teaspoon dried thyme
½ teaspoon dried oregano
1 teaspoon dried parsley
Fresh-cracked black pepper
Kosher salt
½ cup dried fruit
½ cup almonds
1 teaspoon olive oil
1 cup hearty red drinking
  wine
2 cups grapefruit juice
2 cups Chicken Stock
  (page 14)
½ teaspoon ground nutmeg

Fruit-Braised Duck

*The dried fruit and nuts make an excellent complement to the duck meat.
Serve this with warm, crusty Italian bread.*

1. Rinse the duck in cold water and pat dry with paper towels. Cut each breast into 3 pieces, and remove the wings, legs, and thighs. Cut the back in half. Lay out all the pieces on a sheet pan, and sprinkle with the dried herbs, black pepper, and salt. Cover, and refrigerate overnight.

2. Rinse the duck of all the seasonings with cold water. Pierce the duck on all sides with a sharp knife. Roughly chop the dried fruit and almonds. Preheat oven to 275°F.

3. Heat the oil on high temperature in a large Dutch oven (or other heavy-bottomed ovenproof pot with a lid). Brown the duck pieces on all sides. Pour in the wine and reduce by half the volume.

4. Add the remaining ingredients. Cover the pan and place in the oven. Bake for 4 to 5 hours, until the duck is tender. Serve.

Asiago Pollo con Prosciutto
(Asiago Chicken with Prosciutto)

Be sure there is little or no salt in the stock you use for this dish. The prosciutto and Asiago cheese already provide plenty of salt.

Serves 10

3 pounds skinless, boneless chicken breasts
½ pound thinly sliced prosciutto
½ pound Asiago cheese
Fresh-cracked black pepper
2 tablespoons olive oil
½ cup Chicken Stock (page 14)
1 cup Oregano-Almond Pesto (page 73)

1. Rinse the chicken in cold water and pat dry with paper towels. Carefully slit the thickest part of each breast to form a pocket. Cut the sliced prosciutto into thin strips, and grate the cheese.

2. Carefully stuff each breast pocket with the prosciutto and cheese. Sprinkle the outside of the breasts with pepper.

3. Heat the oil to medium-high temperature in a large sauté pan. Brown the chicken on each side. Pour in the stock, and reduce heat to medium-low temperature. Cover, and cook for about 20 minutes, until the chicken is thoroughly cooked.

4. Serve with the pesto spooned over the top of the chicken (do not heat pesto).

2 tablespoons olive oil, divided
3 pounds boneless, skinless duck meat
Fresh-cracked black pepper
2 baked potatoes
2 large carrots
½ cup Rosemary Pesto (page 74)

Layered Duck

Grilling the duck and then baking it with the vegetables is a two-step process, but the final outcome of this dish is definitely worth the extra effort.

1. Preheat grill to medium-high temperature and preheat oven to 325°F. Lightly grease a loaf pan with 1 tablespoon of the oil. Lightly rub the outside of the duck with the remaining oil and season with pepper. Peel the potatoes and cut into thick slices. Peel and grate the carrots.

2. Brown the duck on both sides on the grill. Thinly slice the duck meat on the bias. Place the duck meat in the bottom of the prepared loaf pan. Layer the carrots, potatoes, and pesto on top (in that order).

3. Cover, and bake for 10 minutes. Serve hot.

Choosing Carrots
There are two main choices when it comes to carrots. You can either buy "horse" carrots, the large variety that must be peeled, or "baby" carrots, which usually come peeled, prewashed, and packaged in a bag. Horse carrots tend to be sweeter and juicier than baby carrots, which tend to be bland unless very fresh.

Chicken Terrine

This is a French-inspired recipe made in Northern Italy.
It is similar to the French dish, chicken galantine.

Serves 10

1 (3-pound) whole chicken
2 shallots
½ bulb garlic
4 large sprigs fresh basil
⅓ cup almonds (optional)
1 egg white
¼ cup fresh-grated Asiago
   cheese
¼ recipe sausage of choice
   (see Chapter 11, page
   199), unformed and
   uncooked
Fresh-cracked black pepper

1. Preheat oven to 375°F. Using a sharp knife, carefully remove the entire chicken skin, starting with the back of the chicken. (Try to keep the chicken skin in 1 large piece.) Line a loaf pan with the chicken skin, leaving excess skin hanging over one side.

2. Carefully remove both breasts from the bone and keep whole. Debone the rest of the chicken and chop the dark meat. Peel and mince the shallots and garlic. Clean and gently slice the basil. Chop the almonds.

3. Mix together the chopped dark meat, the shallots, garlic, basil, almonds, egg white, and cheese.

4. Place alternating layers of the chicken breasts and the sausage mixture in the loaf pan.

5. Carefully press the chopped chicken meat mixture on top. Sprinkle with black pepper. Fold the skin over the top and tuck skin into the pan around the sides.

6. Cover the pan with aluminum foil, and bake for 45 minutes. Remove from oven, and uncover. Carefully drain off grease. Press down the mixture again, and return to the oven. Bake, uncovered, for 20 minutes.

7. Remove from oven, and let cool thoroughly. Slice, and serve at room temperature or reheat as desired.

*1 (3- to 5-pound) turkey
    breast, with skin intact
¼ bunch fresh basil
¼ cup pine nuts
¼ recipe Basic Polenta (page
    162)
Fresh-cracked black pepper
¼ cup melted butter*

Polenta-Stuffed Turkey Breast

*The flavors of this dish are so intense that it is best served with
a simple steamed green vegetable or a salad.*

1. Preheat oven to 400°F. Rinse the turkey with cold water, and pat dry with paper towels. Gently loosen the skin from the breast by sliding your fingers in where the wing used to be. Loosen the edges, leaving the outer edge intact to form a pocket.

2. Clean the basil and remove the leaves (discard the stems). Chop the pine nuts. Mix together the pine nuts, polenta, and black pepper.

3. Stuff the polenta into the pocket between the meat and skin. Carefully place the basil leaves on top of the polenta.

4. Place the breast on a rack in a large roasting pan. Brush with the butter. Sprinkle with pepper and roast uncovered for 30 minutes.

5. Reduce temperature to 325°F, and roast for 2 more hours. Serve hot.

Seared Quail with Gorgonzola

Gorgonzola is a soft, creamy cheese with a strong taste. The cheese has areas of green, which come from the specially selected mold cultures added during the production process.

Serves 10

20 quail
10 plums
Kosher salt
Fresh-cracked black pepper
1 tablespoon olive oil
½ cup port wine
¾ cup Gorgonzola

1. Clean the quail in cold water and split in half at the back. Finely dice the plums. Carefully stuff the plums under the skins of the quail, and season with salt and pepper.

2. Heat the oil over medium-high heat in a large, deep frying pan. Sear the quail (in batches) skin-side down for 5 minutes. Turn the quail over, and reduce heat to medium-low.

3. Pour in the wine, top with the cheese, and cover. Slow-cook for 15 to 20 minutes. Serve hot.

Fresh Figs
Fresh figs make a delicious addition to almost any dish. They can be found at your local market in the produce section. They can be used in both sweet and savory dishes. Figs are often paired with Gorgonzola cheese, as the flavors complement each other nicely.

3½ pounds skinless, boneless
   chicken breasts
2 eggs
½ cup cold unsalted butter
2 cups fresh mushrooms
½ bulb garlic
½ cup all-purpose flour
¼ cup olive oil
1 cup Marsala wine

Chicken Marsala

*Authentic Marsala is finished with a small amount of the wine
and does not necessarily have mushrooms.*

1. Rinse the chicken and pat dry with paper towels. Place the breasts between layers of plastic wrap, and pound until thin. Beat the eggs in a bowl. Cut the butter into small pats. Clean and slice the mushrooms. Peel and mince the garlic.

2. Dust the chicken with the flour. Dip in the eggs, and return to the flour. Shake off excess flour.

3. Heat the oil to medium-high temperature in a large sauté pan. Add the chicken, and brown on one side. Turn over, and add the mushrooms and garlic.

4. Pour in the wine, and reduce to half the volume.

5. Add the pats of cold butter, and stir into the sauce. Serve the chicken with the sauce.

Chicken Fricassee

*This Italian version of stewed chicken is a favorite dish
in many Italian and Italian-American homes.*

～

3 pounds boneless chicken
2 white onions
1 bulb garlic
20 plum tomatoes
½ bunch fresh parsley
10 sprigs fresh thyme
3 tablespoons olive oil
1 cup Merlot
4 cups Chicken Stock (page
   14)
2 bay leaves
1 tablespoon fennel seeds
Fresh-cracked black pepper
¼ cup fresh-grated Parmesan
   cheese

1. Rinse the chicken in cold water and pat dry with paper towels. Peel and roughly chop the onions. Peel and mince the garlic. Clean and roughly chop the tomatoes. Clean the parsley and thyme, and leave whole.

2. Heat the oil to medium-high temperature in a large Dutch oven (or other heavy-bottomed pan with a lid). Brown the chicken on all sides. Add the onion and garlic, and lightly brown. Add the tomatoes, and stir for 2 minutes.

3. Pour in the wine, and reduce by half the volume. Add the stock, herbs, and spices. Reduce heat to low.

4. Cover, and simmer for 90 minutes. Serve sprinkled with the cheese.

Chapter 14

Fish and Seafood

Aragosta con Burro all'Aglio

    (Lobster with Garlic Butter) 266

Scallops Alfredo 267

Red Snapper with Peppers 268

Citrus-Braised Halibut 269

Cod Parmesan 270

Grilled Fish and Seafood Primavera 271

Orange-Poached Salmon with Prosciutto 272

Fish Casserole 273

Hearty Cioppino 274

Seafood Bake 275

Pasta con Alici (Pasta with Anchovy Sauce) 275

Baccalà in Saffron Marinara Broth 276

Shrimp Scampi 277

Cozze al Vino (Mussels in White Wine Broth) 277

20 long wooden skewers
10 small lobster tails
½ bulb garlic
½ bunch fresh parsley
½ pound unsalted butter
Kosher or sea salt
Fresh-cracked black pepper

Aragosta con Burro all'Aglio
(Lobster with Garlic Butter)

It's best to keep it simple when it comes to lobster. Some light seasoning and melted butter is enough to complement the natural flavor.

1. Soak the skewers for at least 20 minutes in water. Remove the lobster meat from the shells. Rinse the meat in ice-cold water, and pat dry. (Reserve the shells and freeze for use in another recipe, if desired.) Skewer each tail with 2 skewers (one at each end), then wrap the skewer ends in foil to prevent burning. Preheat grill (or broiler) to medium-high temperature.

2. While the grill heats, peel and mince the garlic. Clean and chop the parsley. Melt the butter in sauté pan over medium heat. Reduce heat to medium-low, and add the garlic. Sauté for 5 minutes.

3. Grill the lobster for about 3 minutes on each side.

4. Drizzle the lobster with the garlic butter, and sprinkle with the parsley, salt, and pepper. Serve.

Feast of the Seven Fishes
Christmas Eve is one of the most important religious holidays in Italy, and fish and seafood are the focus of the meal. Tradition demands that at least seven different fish dishes are prepared seven different ways and served at Christmas Eve dinner. Some think the tradition has its origin in the seven sacraments, but that is just speculation.

Scallops Alfredo

Make sure you use very fresh scallops for this dish.
Do not use bay scallops, as they will overcook.

Serves 10

2 tablespoons olive oil,
    divided
1 pound sea scallops
2 tablespoons unsalted butter
4 tablespoons all-purpose
    flour
½ cup dry white wine (not
    cooking wine)
1 cup Fish Stock (page 16)
1 cup heavy cream
½ cup shredded fontina
    cheese
Fresh-cracked black pepper

1. Preheat broiler on high. Lightly grease a large baking pan with 1 tablespoon of the oil. Rinse the scallops in cold water and pat dry with paper towels.

2. Melt the butter in a large saucepan over medium temperature, and add the remaining oil. Add the scallops, and sauté for 1 minute. Stir in the flour, and continue to stir for 1 minute.

3. Pour in the wine and stock, and simmer for 8 to 10 minutes. Whisk the mixture constantly until thickened.

4. While scallops simmer, reduce the heavy cream by half the volume in a small saucepan over medium-high heat.

5. Remove the scallops from heat, whisk in the cream, and stir in the cheese.

6. Ladle the scallops mixture into the prepared baking pan. Sprinkle with pepper, and brown quickly under the broiler.

5 small red snapper fillets
1 red bell pepper
1 yellow bell pepper
1 red onion
3 cloves garlic
3 sprigs fresh thyme
¼ cup barley flour (or substitute all-purpose flour)
2 tablespoons olive oil
Fresh-cracked black pepper
¼ cup wine vinegar

Red Snapper with Peppers

Serve this dish with Basic Risotto (page 140) and fresh crusty Italian bread.

1. Gently clean the fish in ice-cold water and pat dry with paper towels. Clean and finely slice the bell peppers. Peel and finely slice the onion and garlic. Clean the thyme, remove the leaves, and discard the stems (reserve 1 sprig for garnish).

2. Lightly flour the fillets. Heat the oil to medium temperature in a large sauté pan. Sauté the fish for 2 minutes, and turn. Add the peppers, onions, garlic, thyme leaves, black pepper, and vinegar.

3. Cover, and cook for 5 to 10 minutes, until the fish is flaky and the peppers are lightly cooked. Serve on a platter garnished with the thyme sprig.

How to Tell if Fish Is Fresh

For one thing, fresh fish has virtually no smell. With whole fish, the body should be rigid and the flesh firm. The skin should not be dry and the scales should be shiny and tightly connected to the body. With fillets, the flesh should be white or rosy, with iridescent reflections.

Citrus-Braised Halibut

*Since the citrus flavor is very strong in this dish, the best choice
for a side is Basic Risotto (page 140).*

Serves 10

1¾ pounds halibut fillet
1 large yellow onion
3 cloves garlic
4 large oranges
½ bunch fresh parsley
3 sprigs fresh thyme
2 tablespoons olive oil
¼ cup all-purpose flour
½ cup Fish Stock (page 16)
½ cup dry white wine (not
    cooking wine)
1 bay leaf
1 teaspoon capers, rinsed
Fresh-cracked black pepper

1. Preheat oven to 350°F. Rinse the halibut with ice-cold water, and pat dry with paper towels. Cut into large chunks. Peel and cut the onion into large wedges. Peel the garlic and cut each clove in half. Zest and juice the oranges. Clean the parsley and thyme, remove the leaves, and keep leaves whole.

2. Heat the oil to high temperature in a Dutch oven or other heavy-bottomed ovenproof pan with a lid. Dust the fish with the flour. Sear until brown on both sides.

3. Add all the remaining ingredients *except* the capers and pepper. Bring to a quick boil, cover, and place the pan in the oven. Braise for 20 minutes or until the fish flakes.

4. Place the fish on a serving platter and drizzle with the pan juices. Sprinkle with the capers and pepper. Serve with cooked parsley and thyme from the pan for garnish.

3 tablespoons olive oil, divided

10 (6-ounce) thick pieces fresh cod fillet

2 pounds plum tomatoes

½ bunch fresh basil

¼ cup Roasted Garlic Paste (page 70)

Fresh-cracked black pepper

2 egg whites

½ cup durum wheat (semolina) flour

¼ cup all-purpose flour

2 teaspoons baking powder

½ pound provolone cheese, thinly sliced

Cod Parmesan

Serve this dish with a simple side of pasta, risotto, or a steamed vegetable and some fresh Italian bread.

1. Preheat oven to 400°F. Lightly grease a baking pan with 1 tablespoon of the oil. Rinse the fish in ice-cold water and thoroughly dry with paper towels. Clean and finely dice the tomatoes. Clean and slice the basil.

2. Combine the tomatoes, basil, garlic paste, and pepper. Whisk the egg whites in a small bowl. In separate bowl, sift together the flours and baking powder. Dip the fish in the flour, then in the egg whites, then back in the flour.

3. Heat the remaining oil to medium temperature in a large sauté pan. Lightly brown the fish on both sides. Place the fish in the prepared baking pan. Top with the cheese. Bake for about 10 minutes, or until the cheese browns and the fish flakes.

4. To serve, place the fish on serving plates and top each with 2 heaping tablespoonfuls of the tomato mix.

Grilled Fish and Seafood Primavera

A good fish market will clean shrimp and other fresh seafood for you if you order in advance. This will save you some work in the kitchen.

Serves 10

½ pound large fresh shrimp
1 pound fresh tuna
½ pound fresh sea scallops
1 eggplant
2 red bell peppers
2 stalks celery
2 white onions
½ bulb garlic
3 sprigs fresh basil
¼ cup olive oil
½ cup Fish Stock (page 16)
½ cup dry white wine (not
    cooking wine)
¼ pound cold unsalted butter
1 pound cooked pasta of
    choice (see Chapter 7,
    page 99)
½ cup fresh-grated Romano
    cheese
Fresh-cracked black pepper

1. Preheat grill to medium-high temperature. Peel and devein the shrimp. Thoroughly clean the tuna, scallops, and shrimp with ice-cold water. Pat dry with paper towels, and keep chilled.

2. Clean the eggplant, bell peppers, and celery. Slice the eggplant lengthwise into 1½-inch-thick slices. Cut the bell peppers in half and remove the seeds. Peel and thickly slice the onions about ½ inch thick. Peel and mince the garlic. Clean and gently slice the basil.

3. Mix together the garlic and oil. Dip the shrimp, tuna, scallops, eggplant, bell peppers, celery, and onions in the oil. Shake off excess oil.

4. Grill the oiled seafood and vegetables for about 5 to 8 minutes, turning every 1 to 2 minutes, until the vegetables are al dente and the shellfish is cooked. Continue to grill the tuna to desired doneness.

5. Cut the eggplant, peppers, and celery into strips. Cut the onion rings in half. Thinly slice the tuna.

6. Heat the stock and wine in a saucepan, and bring to a boil. Boil for 2 minutes. Remove from heat, and stir in the butter.

7. Mix together all the ingredients. Sprinkle with fresh-cracked black pepper, and serve.

Fish and Seafood

Fish and seafood are staple foods in Italy. Italians seem to prefer fish to any other food. Remember that Italy is basically a peninsula and is surrounded by water on three sides. The most common cooking methods in Italy are roasting and grilling. Fish "stews" such as Zuppa di Pesce are also popular, and stuffed fish dishes are common as well.

2 pounds salmon fillet
½ bulb garlic
4 oranges
1 teaspoon olive oil
¼ pound prosciutto, very
    thinly sliced
½ cup raisins
Fresh-cracked black pepper

Orange-Poached Salmon with Prosciutto

*You can "moist bake" or poach fillets in the oven instead of the usual method
of poaching on the stovetop in a pot of simmering liquid.*

1. Preheat oven to 375°F. Rinse the salmon in cold water and pat dry with paper towels. Cut the salmon into 10 equal serving portions. Keep chilled. Peel and mince the garlic. Zest and juice 2 of the oranges. Cut the remaining 2 oranges into slices ½ inch thick. Lightly grease a large baking dish with oil.

2. Lay out the prosciutto on a clean surface. Place a salmon fillet on top of each slice. Sprinkle with the garlic and orange zest, place 2 orange slices on top of each, and sprinkle with the raisins. Wrap the prosciutto around the salmon, enclosing the stuffing. Place the prosciutto bundles in prepared baking dish. Pour in the orange juice. Sprinkle with pepper.

3. Cover, and poach in the oven for 20 to 30 minutes, until the fish flakes. Serve.

Fish Casserole

This is a simple dish that can be served at room temperature or chilled.

1. Preheat oven to 400°F. Grease a loaf pan with the oil. Peel and finely chop the onion. Finely chop the bread. Beat the eggs.

2. Line the prepared loaf pan with the salmon, allowing excess to hang over one side. Place layers of the cod, onion, Pepperoncino Gremolata, then the bread in the pan. Repeat layers, and pour the egg over the top. Wrap the excess salmon over the top, and press down to compress all the ingredients.

3. Pour the cheese sauce over the top. Cover with foil, and bake for 30 minutes. Uncover, and bake for 10 more minutes.

4. Remove from oven and let rest for 30 minutes. Serve.

Pesce Fritto (Fried Fish)

Olive oil is the best medium for frying fish. With the exception of anchovy, fish for frying should not weigh more than 3 ounces. Fish should be dipped in milk, water, or egg, and then coated in flour before frying. After frying, drain off excess fat by placing on paper towels.

Serves 10

1 tablespoon olive oil
1 large white onion
½ loaf crusty Italian bread
2 eggs
1½ pounds salmon fillet
1½ pounds cod fillet
2 cups Italian Pepperoncino
    Gremolata (page 76)
2 cups Mozzarella and Ricotta
    Cheese Sauce (page 68)

12 dozen littleneck clams
½ pound fresh sea scallops
½ pound fresh large shrimp
½ pound fresh halibut fillet
½ pound fresh cod fillet
10 Roma tomatoes
2 white onions
½ pound parsnips
½ bunch celery
½ bunch fresh parsley
1 cup Old World Gravy (Long-
*   Cooking Tomato Sauce)*
*   (page 64)*
2 cups Fish Stock (page 16)
1½ teaspoons saffron thread
Fresh-cracked black pepper

Hearty Cioppino

The saffron makes this a wonderfully fragrant seafood stew.
Serve with fresh Italian bread and a crisp salad.

1. Clean the clams and scallops in ice-cold water. Peel, devein, and clean the shrimp. Cut the halibut and cod into large chunks. Clean and cut each tomato into quarters. Peel and cut the onions and parsnips into large wedges. Clean and cut the celery into large chunks. Clean and finely chop the parsley.

2. Place the tomatoes, tomato sauce, stock, saffron, onions, parsnips, celery, parsley, and black pepper in a large stockpot. Simmer, with lid ajar, for 1½ hours.

3. Fifteen minutes before cooking time is complete, add all the seafood.

4. Serve with focaccia of choice, if desired (see Chapter 6, page 79).

Shrimp Quality
Size doesn't generally affect taste and texture when it comes to shrimp—freshness and origin do. The best, sweetest shrimp are from Ecuador and South America. Most shrimp are frozen within hours of being caught; otherwise, they lose their firm texture and sweet flavor. Stores thaw just what they think they will sell that day.

Seafood Bake

Only use fresh seafood whenever possible.
Frozen seafood rarely retains all of its original texture and flavor.

Serves 10

2 tablespoons olive oil, divided
½ pound crabmeat
½ pound sea scallops
2 red bell peppers
½ bunch chives
½ recipe Basic Risotto (page 140)
Fresh-cracked black pepper

1. Preheat oven to 375°F. Lightly grease a loaf pan with 1 tablespoon of the oil. Pick through the crabmeat to remove any shells. Thinly slice the scallops. Clean and finely mince the bell peppers. Finely slice the chives.

2. Spread a thin layer of risotto in the prepared loaf pan; then alternate layers of crab, bell pepper, scallops, chives, black pepper, and risotto. Repeat the process 2 more times, ending with a top layer of risotto.

3. Drizzle the top with the remaining oil, and cover with foil. Bake for 25 minutes. Uncover and cook for 10 more minutes, until the top is browned. Serve sprinkled with black pepper.

Pasta con Alici
(Pasta with Anchovy Sauce)

Anchovy are bluish-green in color, except for the silver stomach, and they do not have scales. They can be marinated, fried, or baked.

Serves 10

3 large cloves garlic
½ bunch fresh parsley
1 lemon
1½ tablespoons olive oil
2 tablespoons cold unsalted butter
¼ cup anchovy fillets
½ cup dry white wine (not cooking wine)
1 cup Fish Stock (page 16)
1 recipe Basic Pasta (page 100), cut into linguini and cooked al dente
Fresh-cracked black pepper

1. Peel and mince the garlic. Clean and chop the parsley. Zest and juice the lemon.

2. Heat the oil to medium temperature in a medium-sized saucepan. Add the butter and garlic, and sauté 2 minutes. Add the anchovy, and toss in the oil for 1 minute. Add the lemon juice and wine, and let reduce for 1 minute. Add the stock. Cook for 5 minutes.

3. Add the pasta and toss thoroughly. Sprinkle with the parsley, lemon zest, and pepper. Serve in heated bowls.

1½ pounds baccalà (salted cod)
2 shallots
½ bulb garlic
1 pound plum tomatoes
½ bunch fresh parsley
1 tablespoon olive oil
1 teaspoon saffron threads
½ cup dry white wine (not cooking wine)
1 cup Fish Stock (page 16)
2 tablespoons fresh-grated Parmesan cheese
Fresh-cracked black pepper

Baccalà in Saffron Marinara Broth

This unique dish is very fragrant, due to the saffron.
Serve with plenty of Italian bread for dipping.

1. Lightly pound the baccalà to soften. Soak the baccalà in ice-cold water in a large plastic container for at least 2 days (4 days is better) in the refrigerator. Pour off the water every 8 to 12 hours, rinse the fish, and add fresh ice-cold water. Pat fish dry.

2. Peel and mince the shallots and garlic. Clean and chop the tomatoes. Clean and gently chop the parsley.

3. Heat the oil to medium temperature in a large saucepan. Add the fish, shallots, garlic, and tomatoes. Sauté for 5 minutes. Add the saffron and wine; let the wine reduce by half the volume. Pour in the stock, and cook for approximately 20 minutes, uncovered.

4. Serve in shallow bowls sprinkled with the cheese, parsley, and pepper.

Baccalà

Baccalà, or salt cod, is a common dish in Italy. Fresh whole cod is boned and its sides salt cured and preserved in wood barrels. Before cooking, soften the cod by pounding on it with a wooden mallet or pestle. Soak the softened fish in cold water for a minimum of 2 days (4 to 5 days is better) to remove the salt. Change the water 3 times a day, and gently rinse the fish each time under clean water.

Shrimp Scampi

Shrimp scampi must be served right from the stove for the best texture. If it has to sit, the shrimp becomes slightly soggy as it soaks up the sauce.

Serves 10

1 pound medium-sized shrimp (20– 30 count)
½ bulb garlic
1 large lemon
½ bunch fresh parsley
2 tablespoons olive oil
Fresh-cracked black pepper
½ cup dry white wine (not cooking wine)
½ cup Fish Stock (page 16)
¼ cup cold unsalted butter

1. Peel and devein the shrimp (leave the tails intact). Rinse in cold water and pat dry with paper towels. Peel and mince the garlic. Zest and juice the lemon. Clean and chop the parsley.

2. Heat the oil to medium temperature in a large sauté pan. Season the shrimp with pepper and add to the hot oil. Sauté for 1 minute, stirring constantly. Add the garlic, then lemon juice and wine, stirring constantly. Sauté for 1 minute, then add the stock. Cook for 3 minutes.

3. Add the cold butter, stir, and remove from heat. Sprinkle with the lemon zest and parsley, and serve.

Cozze al Vino
(Mussels in White Wine Broth)

Serve this with bruschetta (sliced Italian bread rubbed with garlic and olive oil and toasted). Bruschetta is great for sopping up the broth in this dish.

Serves 10

3 dozen fresh mussels
2 shallots
½ bulb garlic
3 sprigs fresh thyme
3 sprigs fresh basil
3 sprigs fresh parsley
2 tablespoons olive oil
1 bay leaf
2 tablespoons unsalted butter
1 cup dry white wine (not cooking wine)
1 cup Fish Stock (page 16)
Fresh-cracked black pepper

1. Thoroughly clean the mussels. Peel and mince the shallots and garlic. Clean the thyme and basil and gently chop the leaves. Clean and chop the parsley.

2. Heat the oil to medium temperature in a large saucepan. Add the mussels, shallots, garlic, half the herbs, the bay leaf, butter, wine, and stock.

3. Cover, and simmer for 8 to 10 minutes, until the mussels open. (Discard any mussels that do not open.)

4. Remove from heat. Serve sprinkled with the remaining herbs and black pepper.

Chapter 15

Vegetables

Cavolfiore Fritto (Fried Cauliflower) 280

Wilted Kale with Dried Currants and Walnuts 281

Broccoli with Romano Bread Crumbs 281

Roasted Garlic Smashed Potatoes 282

Roasted Butternut Squash Stew 283

Celeriac Alfredo 283

Verdure al Forno (Baked Vegetable Casserole) 284

Broccoli Raab Parmesan 285

Finochio Ripieni con Salsicce

  (Sausage-Stuffed Fennel) 286

Patate Fritti (Fried Potatoes) 286

Roasted Red Peppers 287

Grilled Vegetables 288

Rolled Squash 289

Carciofi Ripieni (Stuffed Artichokes) 290

Pecan Broccoli 291

Green Bean Bundles 292

Sautéed Beets with Shallots 293

Asparagi alla Milanese (Milan-Style Asparagus) . . . 294

Parsley Peas 294

Baked Sweet Potatoes with Pear 295

Zucchini Patties 295

Escarole Stew 296

Carrot and Citrus Casserole 297

Serves 10

1 head fresh cauliflower,
    blanched and shocked
4 eggs
¼ cup fresh-grated Asiago
    cheese
¼ cup whole milk
½ cup all-purpose flour
½ cup fresh bread crumbs
½ bunch fresh parsley
¼ cup olive oil
Fresh-cracked black pepper

Cavolfiore Fritto
(Fried Cauliflower)

You can also use the batter in this recipe for frying a number of other vegetables, such as blanched broccoli, mushrooms, peppers, and asparagus.

1. Cut the cauliflower into bite-sized florets. Beat the eggs in a medium-sized bowl, and mix in the cheese and milk. Combine the flour and bread crumbs. Clean and chop the parsley.

2. Heat the oil to medium temperature in a large fry pan with a lid. Dip the florets in the egg mixture, then dust with the bread crumb mixture. Place in the hot oil and set the lid ajar. Sauté on all sides until lightly brown and fork-tender, about 10 minutes.

3. Drain on a rack lined with paper towels. Sprinkle with parsley and pepper. Serve hot.

Blanch and Shock
To blanch and shock vegetables, quickly cook in boiling water to al dente. Then immediately remove from the water and shock in ice water until completely cold. Drain the vegetables, season, and serve, or prepare as the recipe directs.

Wilted Kale
with Dried Currants and Walnuts

The slightly bitter taste of the kale is offset by the sweetness of the currants.
The nuts create a nice crunchy texture.

1. Rinse the kale in cold water and pat dry.

2. Place the kale, vinegar, currants, and walnuts in a large stockpot. Cover, and bring to low simmer. Cook for 5 to 10 minutes or until the greens are just wilted.

3. Immediately remove from heat and drizzle with the honey and oil. Sprinkle with salt and pepper, and serve.

Serves 10

3 bunches fresh kale (or substitute any other fresh green)
2 cups balsamic vinegar
1 cup dried currants
1 cup chopped walnuts
¼ cup honey
¼ cup extra-virgin olive oil
Kosher salt
Fresh-cracked black pepper

Broccoli with Romano Bread Crumbs

Blanching and shocking the broccoli helps maintain its green color.
If a vegetable isn't shocked with cold water when it comes out of the boiling pot, it will continue to "cook" even after it's been drained.

1. Preheat oven to 375°F. Grease a large casserole dish with 1 tablespoon of the oil. Clean the broccoli and cut lengthwise. Quickly blanch the broccoli in boiling water until just al dente, then drain. Shock in ice water, and drain thoroughly.

2. Place the broccoli in the prepared casserole dish. Mix together the remaining oil, the butter, bread crumbs, and cheese in a bowl. Sprinkle the bread crumb mixture on top of the broccoli.

3. Bake for 15 minutes or until the bread crumbs are lightly browned and the broccoli is warm. Serve sprinkled with pepper.

Serves 10

¼ cup olive oil, divided
2 heads fresh broccoli
¼ cup melted unsalted butter
⅓ cup bread crumbs
⅓ cup fresh-grated Romano cheese
Fresh-cracked black pepper

2 pounds potatoes
¼ cup Roasted Garlic Paste
   (page 70)
¼ cup unsalted butter
¼ cup heavy cream
Kosher salt
Fresh-cracked black pepper

Roasted Garlic Smashed Potatoes

*Cooking potatoes whole instead of cutting them
up decreases absorption of water. Quick-drying in a hot oven
after boiling them helps remove water, too.*

1. Clean and peel the potatoes. Fill a large ovenproof pot with water and bring to a boil. Add the potatoes, and boil for 5 minutes. Lower heat to a simmer and continue to cook for 40 minutes or until tender. Drain, return the whole potatoes to the pot, and return to the stovetop for a few minutes to dry out (or place in a hot oven for 5 to 10 minutes).

2. Mash the potatoes, then fold in the remaining ingredients until well mixed. Serve.

Mashing Potatoes

Mashing potatoes in a standing mixer seems like an easy way to break up most lumps and evenly incorporate butter, seasonings, and milk. However, it's all too easy to overmash them, which quickly turns starches into gluey gluten. The key is to "smash" (or whip) them by hand or with a mixer just enough to break up the lumps, then fold in the butter, milk, and seasonings by hand.

Roasted Butternut Squash Stew

Butternut squash is the closest equivalent to the native Italian zucca,
a round, bumpy-skinned squash with flesh resembling that
of a pumpkin in texture and color.

1. Preheat oven to 375°F. Peel and roughly chop the squash, onions, and carrots. Clean and chop the celery. Clean the thyme and parsley, and remove the leaves (discard the stems).

2. Toss the vegetables and fresh herbs in the oil. Place in a roasting pan and roast for 45 minutes, uncovered.

3. Remove from the oven and place all the ingredients in a large stockpot. Simmer for 1½ hours, uncovered. Let cool. Purée until smooth.

4. Serve with steamed greens, if desired.

Serves 10

2 butternut squash
2 yellow onions
3 carrots
2 stalks celery
2 sprigs fresh thyme
¼ bunch fresh parsley
¼ cup olive oil
2 tablespoons ground cumin
½ teaspoon ground mace or
    nutmeg
1 bay leaf
Fresh-cracked black pepper
6 cups Chicken Stock (page
    14)

Celeriac Alfredo

Sometimes called Verona celery, celeriac (celery root)
can be eaten raw; cut into sticks and sautéed with oil, vinegar,
pepper and salt; or fried, plain or with breading.

1. Preheat oven to 375°F. Grease a large baking dish with the oil. Peel and thinly slice the celeriac. Peel and mince the garlic.

2. Bring a large pot of water to a boil, and cook the celeriac until fork-tender (al dente).

3. Layer the celeriac, garlic, and Alfredo sauce in the prepared pan. Sprinkle with the pesto and pepper.

4. Cover, and bake for 15 minutes. Uncover, and bake for 15 more minutes. Serve hot.

Serves 10

1 tablespoon olive oil
2 bulbs fresh celeriac
½ bulb garlic
2 cups Easy Alfredo Sauce
    (page 69)
½ cup Sage Pesto (page 74)
Fresh-cracked black pepper

Serves 10

1 large eggplant
3 red bell peppers
2 yellow onions
1 pound fresh spinach
3 cloves garlic
1½ cups ricotta cheese
¼ cup fresh-grated Parmesan
   cheese
½ cup shredded mozzarella
   cheese
1 egg
Fresh-cracked black pepper
¼ cup olive oil

Verdure al Forno
(Baked Vegetable Casserole)

This is a truly customizable dish.
You can substitute nearly any vegetable for those listed.

1. Preheat a grill or broiler to medium-high temperature. Cut the eggplant lengthwise into ½-inch-thick slices. Cut the bell peppers in half. Peel and cut the onions into ½-inch-thick slices. Clean the spinach. Peel and mince the garlic.

2. Combine the ricotta, ½ of the Parmesan cheese, ½ of the mozzarella, the egg, garlic, and pepper. Preheat oven to 350°F. Grease a loaf pan with 1 tablespoon of the oil.

3. Toss the vegetables in the remaining oil. Grill the vegetables for 2 minutes on each side, until just tender (al dente).

4. In the prepared pan, alternate layers of the vegetables and thin layers of the cheese mixture, starting with a layer of eggplant on the bottom. Grind fresh-cracked pepper over each layer and repeat until all the ingredients are used. Top with the remaining mozzarella and Parmesan, and finish with another grinding of black pepper.

5. Cover, and bake for 20 to 25 minutes, until thoroughly heated and the cheese is melted. Serve hot.

Eggplant
When selecting eggplant (melanzana) in the market, look for firm ones with a smooth texture. Whenever a recipe calls for eggplant slices to be breaded or coated in flour and then fried, you can choose to bake them on a baking sheet instead for less mess and much less fat.

Broccoli Raab Parmesan

This bitter variety of broccoli is very popular in Southern Italy. It is often boiled prior to other preparation to cut the bitter taste. It is commonly sautéed in oil and garlic and seasoned with lemon juice, salt, and pepper.

1. Preheat oven to 375°F. Clean the broccoli raab. Trim and discard the very ends of the stems. Peel and thickly slice the onions. Shred provolone. Pour 1 tablespoon of the oil into the bottom of a large ovenproof pan.

2. Place the broccoli and onion in the prepared pan and season with pepper. Stir thoroughly. Roast for 12 minutes, uncovered, and remove from oven.

3. Pour half of the sauce in the bottom of a separate baking dish. Arrange the broccoli and onion in the bottom of pan. Sprinkle with the provolone. Drizzle with the remaining sauce, then drizzle with the remaining oil.

4. Sprinkle with pepper. Bake for 10 minutes, uncovered, and serve.

Serves 10

2 heads fresh broccoli raab
2 Vidalia onions
½ pound provolone
2 tablespoons olive oil, divided
Fresh-cracked black pepper
1½ cups Old World Gravy (Long-Cooking Tomato Sauce) (page 64)

Finochio Ripieni con Salsicce
(Sausage-Stuffed Fennel)

*Fennel and pork sausage are a natural combination,
but this recipe reverses the usual method of stuffing sausage with
fennel seeds. Here, the fennel holds the sausage stuffing.*

1. Clean and trim the fennel bulbs (cut off the stalks; use only the bottom bulb). Boil until al dente. Remove, drain, and let cool.

2. Preheat oven to 375°F. Grease a large baking dish with the oil. Carefully slice the bulbs in half; keep the base (root piece) intact on each half. This should aid in keeping the "leaves" together.

3. Carefully stuff each leaf layer with the sausage mixture.

4. Place each stuffed half in the prepared baking dish cut-side down. Cover, and bake for 45 minutes. Uncover and bake 15 minutes longer.

5. Drain off excess fat. Serve hot.

Patate Fritti
(Fried Potatoes)

*Enjoy these potato pancakes hot and crispy, immediately after cooking.
Sprinkle with Parmesan cheese, if desired.*

1. Peel and shred the potatoes. Peel and mince the garlic.

2. Mix together the potatoes and garlic. Form the mixture into oval pancakes, about 4 by 2 inches in size.

3. Heat the oil to medium-high in a large sauté pan. Fry the pancake until golden brown and crisp on each side. Fry in batches if necessary to avoid overcrowding the pan.

4. Season with salt and pepper, and serve.

Roasted Red Peppers

Homemade roasted red peppers taste so much better than store-bought canned or jarred varieties—and they're extremely simple to make!

4 peppers

4 whole red peppers
¼ cup olive oil

1. Preheat oven to 400°F (or preheat grill on high). Toss the whole peppers (stem and all) in the olive oil. Roast on a baking sheet pan until the skin starts to blister.

2. Immediately place the peppers in a bowl of ice water, or place in a plastic bag and seal immediately (this makes it easy to peel them).

3. After 5 minutes, peel off and discard the skins. Use, or store in the refrigerator for later use.

Pleasing Peppers

Making your own roasted red peppers is a great idea. They're a common ingredient in many different types of cooking, and they store well in the refrigerator. If you set aside some time to make a batch—even on a day when you won't be using them—they'll be ready for you when you need them.

3 large baking potatoes
4 red bell peppers
2 large onions (any type)
¼ cup olive oil
*2 cups Old World Gravy
(Long-Cooking Tomato
Sauce) (page 64)*
2 cups steamed spinach
*½ cup Roasted Garlic Paste
(page 70)*
1 cup ricotta cheese
Fresh-cracked black pepper

Grilled Vegetables

*This one-pot vegetable "lasagna" dish is the Italian version of a French dish.
It makes a great side to any roast chicken or meat dish.*

1. Preheat oven to 350°F. Preheat grill to medium-high temperature. Clean and slice the potatoes lengthwise into ½-inch-thick slices. Clean, cut, and seed the bell peppers. Peel and cut the onions into ½-inch-thick rings.

2. Lightly "grease" the potatoes, peppers, and onions by brushing with the olive oil. Grill until fork-tender.

3. While the veggies grill, preheat the sauce in a small saucepan.

4. Layer all the ingredients in a casserole dish, starting with a few ladlefuls of the sauce on the bottom and alternating layers of vegetables, ricotta, and sauce. Sprinkle with black pepper.

5. Bake for 20 minutes or just until heated through and bubbling. Serve.

Rolled Squash

Only cook the squash until it is just tender enough to roll—if overcooked, it will fall apart when handled. Leaving peels on the eggplant, zucchini, and yellow squash will help them hold their shape.

Serves 10

1 large eggplant
2 large zucchini
1 large yellow squash
1 medium butternut squash
Coarse salt
1½ cups cheese sauce of choice (see Chapter 5, page 63)
1 cup Traditional Pesto (page 71)

1. Preheat oven to 375°F. Clean and slice the eggplant, zucchini, and yellow squash lengthwise. Peel and slice the butternut squash, scoop out the insides, and rinse the seeds. Toss the seeds in the salt and toast lightly on greased baking sheet for about 10 minutes.

2. Partially steam the butternut squash on the stovetop or in the microwave until just fork-tender. Drain off liquid.

3. Coat the inside of a loaf pan with half of the cheese sauce. Then layer the eggplant, zucchini, yellow squash, and butternut squash in the pan. Top with more cheese sauce (leave a little for the end), and ½ cup of the pesto.

4. Carefully fold over the sliced squash to form a roll and top with the remaining pesto and cheese sauce. Cover, and bake for 20 minutes.

5. Uncover, and cook for 10 minutes. Serve sprinkled with toasted seeds.

1 loaf fresh Italian bread
½ bulb garlic
1 cup fresh mushrooms
1 lemon
¼ bunch fresh parsley
1 tablespoon olive oil
5 whole artichokes
1 tablespoon all-purpose
*   flour*
¼ cup fresh-grated Asiago
*   cheese*
½ cup melted unsalted butter
½ cup Chicken Stock (page
*   14)*
½ cup dry white wine (not
*   cooking wine)*
Fresh-cracked black pepper

Carciofi Ripieni
(Stuffed Artichokes)

When buying artichokes, look for a rich green color and tight heads.
The outside leaves should not be dry.

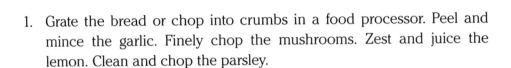

1. Grate the bread or chop into crumbs in a food processor. Peel and mince the garlic. Finely chop the mushrooms. Zest and juice the lemon. Clean and chop the parsley.

2. Preheat oven to 350°F. Lightly grease a baking pan with the oil. Clean the artichokes and cut each in half lengthwise, leaving the stem attached on each side. Snip off the tips of each leaf to remove the prickly end and scoop out the "choke" (the white/purple threadlike center). Dip the artichokes in water mixed with the lemon juice, then dust with the flour.

3. Mix together the bread, garlic, mushrooms, lemon zest, parsley, cheese, and butter. Stuff each artichoke leaf with a small amount of the bread mixture, and fill the center portion where the choke was removed. Arrange the artichokes upright in the prepared baking pan, spaced apart.

4. Pour in the stock and wine. Cover the pan with foil, and bake for 30 minutes. Uncover the pan, and bake for 15 minutes to lightly brown the tops. Serve sprinkled with fresh-cracked black pepper.

Artichokes
Artichokes are the flowers of a large plant and are available November through May. There are two varieties—those without thorns ("unarmed") known as "Roman," and the prickly type, which have little thorns at the triangular tip of each leaf. The soft heart or center of the artichoke can be eaten raw or cooked and sprinkled with olive oil, salt, and pepper.

Pecan Broccoli

For this dish, it is important that the broccoli is cooked al dente, or just firm to the bite. Soggy or limp broccoli will be overwhelmed by the crunchiness of the pecans.

Serves 10

3 tablespoons olive oil, divided
4 heads broccoli
1 cup shelled pecans
¼ cup honey
Fresh-cracked black pepper
¼ cup balsamic vinegar

1. Preheat oven to 375°F. Lightly grease a large oblong baking pan with 1 tablespoon of the oil. Clean and split the broccoli, and cut into long spears.

2. Roughly chop the pecans and toss in a small bowl with the remaining oil, the broccoli, honey, and lots of black pepper.

3. Spread the broccoli mixture in an even layer in the prepared baking pan. Roast for 15 to 20 minutes, uncovered, until the broccoli is cooked al dente.

4. Place the cooked broccoli spears on a serving platter. Drizzle with the balsamic vinegar, and serve.

3 tablespoons olive oil, divided
1½ pounds fresh green beans
Kosher salt
Fresh-cracked black pepper
¼ recipe Basic Flatbread (page 80), unformed and uncooked
1 cup Cannellini Bean Purée (page 70)

Green Bean Bundles

The preparation of these green beans raises a simple vegetable side to a great dish for entertaining. It makes the portions easy to serve and creates an attractive presentation.

1. Preheat oven to 375°F. Lightly grease a sheet pan with 1 tablespoon of the oil. Clean the green beans and snap off the stem ends. Blanch the green beans and shock in ice water. Drain.

2. Toss the green beans in the remaining olive oil and season with salt and pepper.

3. Roll out the dough into a sheet ½ inch thick. Cut into strips about 1 inch wide and 6 inches long. Gather the green beans into bundles of 6 to 8 beans, wrap them in the dough strips, tie, and press to seal.

4. Place the bundles on the prepared baking sheet, and bake for 15 minutes. While the green bean bundles roast, heat the Cannellini Bean Purée.

5. To serve, spoon the purée onto a serving platter, and top with the green bean bundles.

Sautéed Beets with Shallots

The bright color in this dish gives it a great presentation. It makes a good accompaniment to any roasted meat dish.

Serves 10

1½ pounds fresh beets
4 pounds fresh shallots
¼ cup seedless red grapes
2 tablespoons olive oil
Kosher salt
Fresh-cracked black pepper
½ cup light-bodied red table wine

1. Peel and thinly slice the beets. Peel and finely chop the shallots. Cut the grapes in half.

2. Heat the oil to medium temperature in a large sauté pan. Add the beets and shallots, and season with salt and pepper. Cover, and cook for 20 minutes, stirring frequently.

3. Pour in the wine and cook for 10 minutes, stirring continuously.

4. Add the grapes, and reduce heat to low. Cover, and cook for 5 minutes. Serve hot.

Shallots

Shallots are onionlike vegetables that can be substituted in many recipes for onions and scallions. Shallots generally have two sections, or "lobes," which should be separated before peeling. Shallots can be cooked various ways, just like onions.

Serves 10

2 cups water
2 pounds asparagus
1 egg
3 tablespoons unsalted butter
¼ cup fresh-grated Parmesan
    cheese

Asparagi alla Milanese
(Milan-Style Asparagus)

*This dish is a dressed-up version of basic steamed asparagus.
The butter, egg, and cheese add extra color and flavor.*

1. Bring the water to a boil in a large saucepan. Break off the "woody" ends of the asparagus (holding each spear at each end and bending until the asparagus spear breaks).

2. Place the asparagus in the water, cover, and steam until al dente. While the asparagus is steaming, fry the egg.

3. Remove the asparagus from the water, drain, and place on a serving platter. Place pats of the butter on top and evenly distribute the butter over the asparagus as it melts. Place the fried egg over the asparagus tips. Serve sprinkled with the cheese.

Parsley Peas

Serves 10

1½ pounds fresh peas
¼ bunch fresh parsley
4 cups Vegetable Stock (page
    16)
Fresh-cracked black pepper
Kosher salt

*To create your own variations of this recipe, try it with other herbs
in place of the parsley, such as mint or basil.*

1. Shuck the peas. Clean and chop the parsley.

2. Bring the stock to a slow simmer on the stovetop. Add the peas, and cook until al dente.

3. Remove from heat, and add the parsley, pepper, and salt. Serve hot.

Aw, Shucks!
Wondering what shuck means? As a noun, a shuck is a husk, pod, or shell. To shuck, as a verb, is to remove the husk, pod, or shell. So, when you shuck peas, you simply remove the peas from the pods. Easy, right?

Baked Sweet Potatoes with Pear

This tasty side dish goes very well with smoked meats or other salty main dishes.

1. Preheat oven to 375°F. Lightly grease a large oblong pan with the oil. Peel and thinly slice the sweet potatoes and pears.

2. Spread a layer of sweet potatoes and then a layer of the pears in the prepared pan. Sprinkle the fennel seeds over the top. Dot with pats of the butter, and sprinkle with the pepper. Pour the pear nectar over the top.

3. Cover, and bake 1 hour. Serve hot.

Serves 10

1 tablespoon olive oil
2 pounds sweet potatoes
4 pears (any type)
1 teaspoon fennel seeds
3 tablespoons unsalted butter
Fresh-cracked black pepper
1 cup pear nectar

Zucchini Patties

This can be served as an appetizer or a side dish. It also makes a great entrée, if you are having vegetarians over for dinner.

1. Clean and shred the zucchini. Peel and mince the shallots and garlic. Beat the eggs.

2. Mix together the zucchini, shallots, garlic, eggs, cheese, milk, flour, and pepper. Form the mixture into small oval patties.

3. Heat the oil to medium-high temperature in a large skillet. Fry the patties on each side.

4. Drain the patties on paper towels, and serve.

Serves 10

1½ pounds fresh zucchini
2 shallots
3 cloves garlic
4 eggs
½ cup fresh-grated Parmesan cheese
½ cup whole milk
½ cup all-purpose flour
Fresh-cracked black pepper
½ cup olive oil

Serves 10

4 heads escarole
3 large Idaho potatoes
3 white onions
2 carrots
2 stalks celery
½ bulb garlic
¼ cup walnuts
6 sprigs fresh thyme
*1 cup cooked or canned
     chickpeas*
*8 cups Vegetable Stock (page
     16)*
2 bay leaves
Fresh-cracked black pepper
*1 teaspoon extra-virgin olive
     oil*

Escarole Stew

*Escarole is a leafy green that is frequently used in Italian cooking.
Serve this stew with crusty Italian bread for dipping.*

1. Clean the escarole and separate the leaves. Peel and thickly wedge the potatoes, onions, and carrots. Clean and roughly chop the celery. Peel the garlic and leave the cloves whole. Chop the walnuts. Clean the thyme and remove the leaves (discard the stems).

2. Place all the ingredients *except* the escarole and olive oil in a large stockpot and simmer at medium heat for 1 hour, uncovered.

3. Add the escarole, and simmer for 5 minutes.

4. Adjust seasoning to taste. Drizzle with the olive oil, and serve.

The Right Pot
When a recipe instructs you to use a "heavy-bottomed" pot, that's your clue that a thin pot may result in a burned flavor. Thick bottoms conduct heat more evenly and retain heat better, causing fewer "hot spots" where the flame or electric element contacts the pan. Hot spots burn certain foods, no matter how carefully you stir.

Carrot and Citrus Casserole

This slightly sweet casserole is colorful and nutritious. Serve as an appetizer or accompaniment to a roasted meat entrée.

Serves 10

2 tablespoons unsalted butter
3 large oranges
2 pounds fresh baby carrots
½ cup dried currants (or
    substitute raisins)
¼ cup brown sugar
½ cup long-cooking oats

1. Preheat oven to 375°F. Lightly grease a casserole dish with ½ tablespoon of the butter. Zest and juice the oranges.

2. Layer the carrots, currants, orange juice, zest, the remaining butter, the brown sugar, and oats in the prepared casserole dish.

3. Cover, and bake for 1 hour. Uncover, and bake for 15 minutes. Serve hot.

Chapter 16

Desserts

Scaweelies 300

Tordillas 301

Geenaweelies 302

Classic Biscotti 303

Italian Bread Pudding 304

Sweet Potato Pudding 305

Pear-Filled Calzones 306

Cinnamon Rolls 307

Grapefruit and Pomegranate Bars 308

Momma Theresa's Zucchini Cake 309

Oatmeal Muffins 309

Mustastoy 310

Fig Tart 310

Port Cookies 311

Almond Loaf 312

Keith's "No Dairy" Apple Cake 313

Anisette Cookies 314

Scaweelies

Serves 10

1 cup butter or shortening
1 tablespoon granulated
    sugar
6 eggs, lightly beaten
1½ ounces anisette liqueur
3 cups all-purpose flour
4 cups vegetable or corn oil
4 cups honey

*This is a family rendition of a classic Italian cookie. Store Scaweelies
in a container lined with aluminum foil or plastic wrap and keep covered.*

1. Cream together the butter, sugar, eggs, and anisette.

2. Mix the flour with the butter mixture by hand or in a mixer with a dough hook for 3 to 5 minutes at medium speed, until wet and dry ingredients are fully incorporated. Cover the dough with plastic wrap or a clean towel and allow to rest for 1 hour in the refrigerator.

3. Knead the dough slightly; then roll out on floured board to ½-inch thickness. Form into braids, twists, or other shape.

4. Heat the oil to medium-high temperature in a large, deep, heavy-bottomed pan. Fry the dough until lightly golden. Transfer to paper towels to drain.

5. Heat the honey to medium temperature in a heavy-bottomed saucepan. Dip each Scaweelie in the honey, and allow excess honey to drip off. Place on wax paper. Serve slightly warm, but be sure honey has cooled enough not to burn the mouth.

Tordillas

Though called something different in every family, these are classic Italian Christmas pastries. Of course, they're a delicious treat all year round.

Serves 10

3 cups all-purpose flour
2 tablespoons baking powder
1 pinch iodized salt
¼ cup granulated sugar
1 cup shortening
6 eggs, lightly beaten
½ cup port wine
4 cups vegetable or corn oil
4 cups honey

1. Sift together the flour, baking powder, and salt in a large mixing bowl. In a separate bowl, cream together the sugar and shortening, then add the eggs and wine. Make a well in the center of the flour mixture, and pour in the egg mixture. Mix by hand or in a mixer with a dough hook at medium speed until the dough forms into a ball. Cover the dough with plastic wrap or a clean towel and allow to rest for at least 1 hour (no longer than 3 hours) in the refrigerator.

2. Pull off pieces of the dough in portions equal to about 2 tablespoons. Roll into little ovals using your hands. Continue until all the dough is used up.

3. Heat the oil to medium-high temperature in a deep, heavy-bottomed skillet. Fry each ball until light golden brown. Drain on paper towels.

4. Heat the honey to medium temperature in a saucepan. Dip each ball in the honey, carefully shaking off excess, and place on wax paper. Serve slightly warm, but be sure honey has cooled enough not to burn the mouth.

Italian Sweets
Italian cuisine is not really known for its sweet dishes. Most sweet dishes are tied to holy days, feasts, weddings, and other celebrations. Pastries, gelato (ice cream), and biscotti are the most common types of Italian desserts.

Serves 10

½ cup chopped walnuts
½ cup semisweet chocolate
    chips
½ cup raisins
½ cup sweet jam (any flavor)
1 recipe Scaweelies dough
    (page 300), unformed
    and uncooked
4 cups honey

Geenaweelies

*Geenaweelies (a family name for these cookies) are made with the
Scaweelies dough and stuffed with various fillings. This variation includes
chocolate and walnuts, but you can add whatever you like.*

1. Mix together the nuts, chocolate chips, raisins, and jam.

2. Roll out the dough on a floured surface into a sheet ½ inch thick. Cut into 3-inch squares.

3. Place small spoonfuls of the chocolate chip mixture in the center of each dough square. Wet the edges of the squares lightly with water. Fold the dough over from corner to corner to form a triangle. Seal by pressing the edges together with fork tines. (You can also make circles of dough and seal them on top of each other with the filling in the middle.)

4. Heat the oil to medium-high temperature in a large, deep, heavy-bottomed pan. Fry the pastries until lightly golden. Drain on paper towels.

5. Heat the honey to medium temperature in a heavy-bottomed sauce-pan. Dip the Geenaweelies in the honey and allow excess honey to drip off. Place on wax paper, and let cool slightly so that honey does not burn the mouth. Serve.

Classic Biscotti

It is the twice-baked aspect that gives biscotti that characteristic crunch. There are numerous variations of this recipe, but these are the classic almond and anisette flavor.

Serves 10

1½ cups unsalted butter
¾ cup granulated sugar
¾ cup light brown sugar
2 eggs, lightly beaten
¼ cup anisette liqueur
3½ cups all-purpose flour
½ teaspoon baking powder
½ teaspoon baking soda
½ cup sliced almonds

1. Preheat oven to 375°F. Lightly grease baking pan with ½ teaspoon of butter. Cream together the butter and sugars. Add the eggs and anisette. Sift together the flour, baking powder, and baking soda into a separate, large bowl.

2. Mix together the butter and flour mixtures until well mixed and a dough forms. Fold in the almonds.

3. Divide the dough into 2 equal parts and form each into an oval-shaped mound about 2 inches high. Place the dough mounds on a baking sheet.

4. Bake for 20 minutes. Slice the mounds lengthwise into 2-inch-thick pieces. Return to the oven and bake for 5 minutes.

5. Remove from the oven and let cool slightly. Store in an air-tight container.

About Biscotti

Biscotti are baked twice for extra crunch—first as a log and then in slices. You can put any dried fruit or nut in biscotti. Pistachios and hazelnuts work especially well. Use dried cherries or apricots instead of raisins for a nice variation. Biscotti keep well, so they make a great holiday gift for friends and family.

Serves 10

¼ cup unsalted butter
1 large loaf day-old or
    toasted Italian bread
6 eggs
2 cups whole milk
2 cups heavy cream
¼ cup anisette liqueur
    (optional)
¼ cup honey
¼ cup granulated sugar

Italian Bread Pudding

Many cultures have their own version of bread pudding—everyone seeks a use for day-old bread. This is the Italian version of this popular dessert.

1. Preheat oven to 375°F. Lightly grease an oblong 13" × 9" baking pan with 1 teaspoon of the butter. Melt the remaining butter. Tear the bread into large chunks, and combine with melted butter in a bowl.

2. Beat the eggs in a large bowl, and whisk in the milk, cream, liqueur, honey, and sugar.

3. Place the bread mixture in the prepared pan. Pour the egg mixture over the top, and stir.

4. Bake for 30 minutes, uncovered. Stir, and return to the oven. Bake for about 15 to 20 minutes longer until set. Serve warm with whipped cream, if desired.

Sweet Potato Pudding

The technique of heating eggs through without actually cooking them is called "tempering." This technique is applied in step 2 of this recipe.

Serves 10

¼ cup unsalted butter
5 large sweet potatoes
8 eggs
½ cup all-purpose flour
½ cup honey
4 cups whole milk
4 cups half-and-half
½ cup raisins (optional)

1. Preheat oven to 375°F. Lightly grease a large casserole dish with 1 teaspoon of the butter. Melt the remaining butter.

2. Clean and pierce the sweet potatoes with a fork. Place in the prepared baking pan. Bake for about 1 hour or until fork-tender, uncovered. Allow to cool. Peel the potatoes and cut into large chunks.

3. Beat the eggs in a bowl, and stir in the flour and ¼ cup of the honey. Mix together the milk, half-and-half, the melted butter, and the remaining honey in a stainless steel bowl.

4. Bring 4 cups of water to a boil in a large pot. Place the bowl with the milk mixture on top of the pot and heat. Carefully ladle small amounts of the heated milk mixture into the egg mixture, whisking constantly until the egg mixture is warm. (This will slowly heat but not cook the eggs.)

5. When the egg mixture is warm, quickly whisk it into the remaining milk mixture (still on the pot), and cook until the mixture thickens.

6. Remove the bowl from the heated pot, and mix in the potatoes and raisins. Transfer the potato mixture to the prepared casserole dish and bake for 20 minutes. Serve with drizzled honey.

Serves 10

1 (¼-ounce) packet dry active
    yeast
¼ cup warm water (no hotter
    than 115°F)
1 pound all-purpose flour
Pinch iodized salt
2 cups warm milk
5 ripe pears
1 lemon
¼ cup unsalted butter
¼ cup honey
½ teaspoon ground cloves
Cooking spray
½ cup confectioners' sugar

Pear-Filled Calzones

*This dessert calzone is a refreshing variation of the standard
ricotta cheese calzone you're used to.*

1. Stir the yeast into the warm water. Let stand for 3 to 5 minutes, until foamy. Mix with a few spoonfuls of the flour. Sift together the remaining flour and salt onto a board.

2. Make a "well" in the center of the flour, and pour in the yeast mixture. Gently mix by hand or in a mixer with a dough hook until a soft ball forms. Knead for 5 minutes. Divide the dough into 10 small balls, and place on a floured board. Cover with plastic wrap, and let rest for 1 hour.

3. While the dough rests, peel, core, and slice the pears. Zest and juice the lemon. Cut the butter into 10 portions.

4. Mix together the milk, pears, lemon juice, and honey. Sprinkle with the cloves.

5. Preheat oven to 375°F. Roll out the dough balls approximately 1 inch thick on a floured surface. Fill each with the pear mixture, and top with a pat of the butter. Fold over the dough and seal firmly. Let rest on the floured board, covered, for about 1 hour.

6. Lightly grease a baking sheet with the cooking spray. Gently place the calzones on the pan, and bake for 30 to 40 minutes. Remove from oven, place on a plate, and sprinkle with the confectioners' sugar.

Cinnamon Rolls

Homemade cinnamon rolls are vastly superior to those you can buy in the store. Make these for breakfast, as a snack, or as part of a brunch buffet.

1. Prepare the dough: Stir the yeast into the water. Let stand for 3 to 5 minutes, until frothy. Sift together the flour, sugar, and salt. Mix together the eggs and cooled milk. Combine the yeast water, flour mixture, and egg mixture, and mix until a ball forms. Allow the dough to rest for 1 hour in a greased bowl in a warm place.

2. While the dough rests, combine all the filling ingredients in a bowl. Mix together all the frosting ingredients in a separate bowl. Store the frosting in the refrigerator. Preheat oven to 375°F.

3. Punch down the dough once it has doubled in size. Roll out on a floured surface into a ½-inch-thick rectangle. Paint the dough with the filling mixture and roll it up into a log. Cut the log into 3-inch sections. Place on a greased sheet pan.

4. Bake for 45 minutes until brown. Let cool slightly, and frost. Serve.

Vanillas of the World

The best-quality vanilla beans and extracts come from Tahiti and Madagascar. Cheaper (and often watery) extracts come from Mexico. Major U.S. brands are not as finessed as most exotic imports, but these provide reliable vanilla flavor. For best results, pay more for higher-quality vanilla.

Dough:
1 (¼-ounce) packet dry active yeast
½ cup warm water
3 cups all-purpose flour
¼ cup brown sugar
Pinch iodized salt
3 eggs
1 cup scalded milk (cooled thoroughly)

Filling:
1 cup melted unsalted butter
3 tablespoons ground cinnamon
½ cup granulated sugar

Frosting:
1 cup confectioners' sugar
1 teaspoon vanilla extract
1½ cups whole milk

Serves 10

2½ cups all-purpose flour
1¼ cups unsalted butter
¾ cup confectioners' sugar
1 ripe pomegranate
5 eggs
½ cup fresh grapefruit juice
2½ cups granulated sugar
1¼ teaspoons baking powder

Grapefruit and Pomegranate Bars

*Always wear an old shirt or apron when working with pomegranates,
as the bright red juice can stain.*

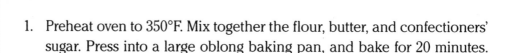

1. Preheat oven to 350°F. Mix together the flour, butter, and confectioners' sugar. Press into a large oblong baking pan, and bake for 20 minutes. Remove from oven and let cool slightly.

2. While the crust bakes, cut open the pomegranate and remove the seeds. Discard the skin and other material.

3. Beat the eggs in a bowl, and mix in the grapefruit juice, sugar, and baking powder. Fold in the pomegranate seeds. Pour the mixture over the crust. Bake for 20 to 25 minutes, until the top is set. Allow to cool before cutting into bars.

Chinese Apple
The pomegranate is a large, round, maroon fruit, sometimes called a Chinese apple. When opened, it is full of edible seeds that are tart and slightly crunchy. Pomegranate is somewhat expensive, but it's worth the cost for special occasions and recipes.

Momma Theresa's Zucchini Cake

If you have a lot of zuccini left over at the end of the summer, use it to make this delicious cake. Serve warm with whipped cream.

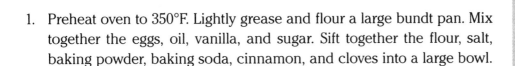

Serves 10

3 eggs
1 cup vegetable oil
3 teaspoons vanilla extract
1½ cups granulated sugar
3 cups all-purpose flour
1 teaspoon salt
1 teaspoon baking powder
1 teaspoon baking soda
1 teaspoon ground cinnamon
2 teaspoons ground cloves
2 medium zucchini
1 cup chopped walnuts

1. Preheat oven to 350°F. Lightly grease and flour a large bundt pan. Mix together the eggs, oil, vanilla, and sugar. Sift together the flour, salt, baking powder, baking soda, cinnamon, and cloves into a large bowl. Clean and finely shred the zucchini.

2. Mix together the wet and dry ingredients, then fold in the zucchini and walnuts.

3. Pour the batter into the pan and bake for 1 hour. Serve warm.

Oatmeal Muffins

Store these hearty muffins in an airtight container and enjoy them toasted with butter for the next few days.

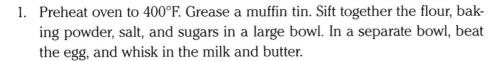

Serves 10

1 cup all-purpose flour
1¼ tablespoons baking powder
¼ teaspoon salt
¼ cup granulated sugar
¼ cup light brown sugar
1 egg
¾ cup whole milk
¼ cup melted unsalted butter
1 cup uncooked oatmeal
½ cup chopped dried fruit
½ cup chopped nuts of choice

1. Preheat oven to 400°F. Grease a muffin tin. Sift together the flour, baking powder, salt, and sugars in a large bowl. In a separate bowl, beat the egg, and whisk in the milk and butter.

2. Combine the wet and dry ingredients, then fold in the oatmeal, fruit, and nuts. Pour the batter into the greased muffin tin, filling each about halfway. Bake for about 20 minutes. Serve.

Serves 10

2 cups honey
3 eggs
¼ cup granulated sugar
2 teaspoons baking powder
½ cup whole milk
¼ cup unsalted butter
4 cups all-purpose flour
1 cup chopped walnuts

Mustastoy

This sweet bread, called something different in every family, makes a great breakfast or snack. You can substitute other nuts for walnuts, if you prefer.

1. Preheat oven to 275°F (low-heat oven). Lightly grease a baking sheet. Mix together all the ingredients. Cover the dough with plastic wrap or a clean towel and allow to rest for ½ hour.

2. Form the dough into small oval loaves, and place on the greased baking sheet.

3. Bake for 1 hour. Let cool before serving.

Serves 10

2 cups all-purpose flour
1¼ cups cold unsalted butter
¾ cup granulated sugar
10 whole fresh figs

Fig Tart

*You can use either the white or dark figs for this recipe—
just be sure they're fresh figs.*

1. Preheat oven to 375°F. Mix together the flour, butter, and sugar. Roll out the dough and place in a large ungreased tart pan.

2. Clean and cut the figs in half. Place the figs, cut-side down, on the tart crust.

3. Bake for 20 minutes.

Port Cookies

Most Italian recipes include wine,
but this one is actually named after it!

1. Preheat oven to 375°F. Cream together the butter and granulated sugar. Beat the egg in a separate bowl, and mix into the butter mixture along with the honey and wine. Sift together the flours, salt, and baking soda. Combine the wet and dry ingredients.

2. Roll the dough into tablespoon-sized balls. Place on an ungreased baking sheet, and bake for 8 to 10 minutes.

3. While cookies bake, mix ¼ cup light brown sugar with nutmeg and cloves.

4. Remove cookies from oven and roll in spiced brown sugar. Cool and serve.

For Any Occasion
These cookies are favorites to serve at holiday gatherings and family celebrations. Don't worry about an overwhelming alcohol taste—the alcohol burns off during the baking process. So, the kids are certainly welcome to enjoy these tasty treats!

Serves 10

½ cup unsalted butter, naturally softened
1 tablespoon granulated sugar
1 egg
¼ cup honey
¼ cup port wine
1 cup whole-wheat flour
1 cup all-purpose flour
¼ teaspoon iodized salt
¼ teaspoon baking soda
¼ cup light brown sugar
¼ teaspoon ground nutmeg
¼ teaspoon ground cloves

Serves 10

2¼ cups all-purpose flour
1 tablespoon baking powder
½ cup unsalted butter
1 cup granulated sugar
3 eggs
¾ cup whole milk
1 tablespoon almond extract
½ cup chopped or slivered
   almonds

Almond Loaf

Almonds are common ingredients in sweet Italian dishes.
Enjoy this bread for breakfast or as a snack with tea.

1. Preheat oven to 350°F. Lightly grease and flour a loaf pan. Sift together the flour and baking powder. Cream together the butter and sugar. Beat the egg, then add the milk and almond extract.

2. Combine the flour, butter mixture, and egg mixture. Fold in the nuts. Pour into the greased loaf pan.

3. Bake for 40 to 45 minutes. Serve warm.

Just a Spoonful of Sugar

When grinding almonds for a sweet recipe, put a spoonful of sugar in with the almonds to be ground. This prevents the almonds from getting too oily and forming a paste while being processed. Just be sure not to add too much sugar, especially if there is other sugar in the recipe.

Keith's "No Dairy" Apple Cake

*To vary the flavor of this cake, you can substitute pears
or other fresh fall or winter fruits.*

⁓

1. Preheat oven to 350°F. Grease and lightly flour a bundt pan. Peel and slice the apples. Mix with 5 tablespoons of the granulated sugar and all of the cinnamon.

2. Sift together the flour, the remaining 2 cups granulated sugar, and the baking powder. Beat the eggs in a mixing bowl, and whisk in the oil, orange juice, and vanilla.

3. Mix together the wet and dry ingredients until smooth. Fold in the apples and pine nuts. Pour the batter into the prepared pan.

4. Bake for 60 minutes or until cooked through.

5. Sprinkle with the confectioners' sugar, and serve.

Serves 10

6 large apples
2 cups, plus 5 tablespoons
   granulated sugar
2 teaspoons ground
   cinnamon
2 cups all-purpose flour
1 tablespoon baking powder
4 eggs
1 cup vegetable oil
¼ cup orange juice
2½ teaspoons vanilla extract
½ cup pine nuts
¼ cup confectioners' sugar

Serves 10

2 cups all-purpose flour
1 tablespoon baking powder
2 eggs
6 tablespoons unsalted butter
⅓ cup whole milk
½ cup granulated sugar
1 teaspoon anisette liqueur

Anisette Cookies

For frosting: whip together ½ cup unsalted butter, 1 cup whole milk, 2 cups confectioners' sugar, and ½ teaspoon vanilla extract.

1. Preheat oven to 350°F. Sift together the flour and baking powder. Beat the egg, then add the butter, milk, sugar, and anisette.

2. Mix together the dry and wet ingredients to form a dough.

3. Form by rolling into cigar-sized rolls. Using your finger, spiral the dough into a "beehive" shape. Place on an ungreased baking sheet.

4. Bake for 10–12 minutes. Let cool slightly. Frost if desired, and serve.

Appendix: Recipe Menus

New Year's Day

Artichoke Leaves (page 58)
Fig and Gorgonzola Salad (page 44)
Braised Duck Risotto (page 154)
Green Bean Bundles (page 292)
Verdure al Forno (Baked Vegetable Casserole) (page 284)
Spelt Pasta with Spicy Old World Gravy (Fra Diavlo) (pages 101 and 65)
Italian Bread Pudding (page 304)

Easter Sunday

Garlic Soup (page 27)
Fresh Crab with Arugula Salad (page 43)
Wilted Kale Salad with Roasted Shallots (page 38)
Leg of Lamb (page 227)
Easter Pizza Casserole (page 240)
Sausage-Filled Shallots (page 59)
Roasted Potato and Garlic Gnocchi (page 120)
Gorgonzola Browned Pears (page 59)
Easter Egg Bread (page 91)

Thanksgiving

Polenta-Stuffed Turkey Breast (page 260)
Roasted Garlic Smashed Potatoes (page 282)
Baked Sweet Potatoes with Pear (page 295)
Carciofi Ripieni (Stuffed Artichokes) (page 290)
Herbed Flatbread (page 85)
Broccoli Raab Parmesan (page 285)
Italian Bread Pudding (page 304)

Recipe Menus (continued)

Christmas Eve

Christmas Eve Salad (page 45)
Clam-Stuffed Portobellos (page 50)
Frittura di Paranza (Pan-Fried Smelts) (page 60)
Baccalà in Saffron Marinara Broth (page 276)
Shrimp Scampi (page 277)
Red Snapper and Pepper Risotto (page 156)
Seafood Polenta (page 177)
Mushroom and Crab Frittata (page 197)
Fresh Vegetable Dip with Crusty Italian Bread (page 51)
Cavolfiore Fritto (Fried Cauliflower) (page 280)
Classic Biscotti (page 303)
Keith's "No Dairy" Apple Cake (page 313)

Christmas Brunch

Breakfast Egg Polenta (page 171)
Tender Beef Ravioli (page 238)
Breakfast Pork Sausage (page 215)
Cinnamon Rolls (page 307)
Melon and Prosciutto (page 52)
Four-Cheese Frittata (page 182)
Garlic and Olive Bruschetta (page 54)
Broccoli with Romano Bread Crumbs (page 281)
Occo Buco with Polenta Dumplings (page 233)
Hearty Cold Antipasto Salad (page 46)
Christmas Goose (page 249)
Scaweelies (page 300)
Tordillas (page 301)
Geenaweelies (page 302)

Index

Acini di Pepe, 109
  Pork Soup with Acini di Pepe, 30
Agnello Polpette (Lamb Meatballs), 213
Almond Loaf, 312
Anisette Cookies, 314
Antipasti, *see* Appetizers
Appetizers, 49–62
  about, 34, 52; meatballs as, 213
  Antipasto Salad, 34
  Artichoke Leaves, 58
  Baked Mixed Cheese Hors d'oeuvres, 53
  Cheese-Filled Prunes, 62
  Clam-Stuffed Portobellos, 50
  Creamy Crab Appetizers, 52
  Fresh Vegetable Dip with Crusty Italian
    Bread, 51
  Frittura di Paranza (Pan-Fried Smelts), 60
  Garlic and Olive Bruschetta, 54
  Gorgonzola Browned Pears, 59
  Grilled Pork Cubes, 62
  Hearty Cold Antipasto Salad, 46
  Lobster Capicola, 61
  Marinated Beef Skewers, 55
  Melanzane Marinate (Pickled Eggplants),
    51
  Melon and Prosciutto, 52
  Orange Shrimp, 56
  Oregano Pork Ribs, 56
  Pomodori Ripieni (Stuffed Roma
    Tomatoes), 57
  Sausage-Filled Shallots, 59
  Seafood Sausage Bread, 58
  Spicy Chicken Wings, 55
Apples
  Apple and Pork Sausage, 220
  Baby Greens with Apple and
    Mascarpone, 43
  Keith's "No Dairy" Apple Cake, 313
  Pork and Apple Meatballs, 203
  Stuffed Pork Roast, 238
  Winter "Fruited" Chicken, 246
Aragosta con Burro all'Aglio (Lobster with
  Garlic Better), 266
Artichokes
  about, 290
  Artichoke Leaves, 58
  Carciofi Ripieni (Stuffed Artichokes), 290
  Carciofi Ripieni con Risotto (Artichokes
    Stuffed with Risotto), 144
Arugula
  Arugula, Mozzarella, and Chicken
    Sausage, 221
  Baked Spaghetti Tart, 132

Eggplant Arugula Salad, 47
Fresh Crab with Arugula Salad, 43
Fresh Vegetable Dip with Crusty Italian
  Bread, 51
Polpette con Pollo e Orzo (Chicken
  Meatballs with Orzo), 207
Asiago Pollo con Prosciutto (Asiago Chicken
  with Prosciutto), 257
Asparagus
  about, 185
  Asparagi alla Milanese (Milan-Style
    Asparagus), 294
  Asparagus–Egg White Frittata, 185
Aunt Gloria's Italian Green Bean Salad, 37

Baby Greens with Apple and Mascarpone,
  43
Baccalà in Saffron Marinara Sauce, 276
Baccalà with Pasta and Fresh Peas, 126
Baked Mixed Cheese Hors d'oeuvres, 53
Baked Pork Ribs, 226
Baked Potato and Mascarpone Frittata, 186
Baked Smoked Ham, 242
Baked Spaghetti Tart, 132
Baked Sweet Potatoes with Pear, 295
Balsamic vinegar, 60
Barley Flatbread, 89
Basic Beef Meatballs, 200
Basic Cheese Pizza, 95
Basic Flatbread, 80
Basic Frittata, 180
Basic Italian Pork Sausage, 214
Basic Pasta, 100
Basic Polenta, 162
Basic Risotto, 140
Basil
  about, 57
  Fresh Basil Pasta, 106
  Sun-Dried Tomato and Fresh Basil
    Frittata, 184
Beans
  about: cooking for soups, 25; soaking
    of, 210
  Aunt Gloria's Italian Green Bean Salad, 37
  Bean and Sausage Soup, 26
  Bowtie Pasta with Braised Beans and
    Greens, 134
  Cannellini Bean Purée, 70
  Cannellini Bean Salad, 36
  Citrus Green-Bean Salad, 48
  Fagioli Pasta (Bean Pasta), 107
  Green Bean Bundles, 292
  Meatless Meatballs, 210

Pasta e Fagioli (Pasta and Bean Soup), 25
Vegetable and Bean Sausage, 224
Venison Bean Ragout, 232
Beef
  Basic Beef Meatballs, 200
  Beef and Polenta Casserole, 175
  Beef and Tomato Frittata, 193
  Beef Sausage, 217
  Beef Stock, 15
  Chuck Steak Pot Roast, 241
  Eggplant Meatballs, 213
  Italian Beef and Sun-Dried Tomato
    Sausage, 219
  Italian Meat Loaf, 231
  Mama Theresa's Beef Braciola, 234
  Marinated Beef Skewers, 55
  Meat Ravioli, 137
  Pasta con Ragu Bolognese, 133
  Seared Filet Mignon Risotto, 147
  Seasoned Beef Risotto, 151
  Tender Beef Ravioli, 238
  Three-Meat Meatballs, 201
Beets
  Chilled Beet Soup, 29
  Sautéed Beets with Shallots, 293
Bell peppers, *see* Peppers, bell
Biscotti, Classic, 303
Bowtie Pasta with Braised Beans and
  Greens, 134
Braised dishes
  about, 243
  Braised Veal and Pepper Risotto, 149
  Braised Veal with Polenta Dumplings, 174
Bread Pudding, Italian, 304
Breads, *see* Flatbreads/Pizza/Focaccia
Bread Salad, 40
Bread Sticks, 96
Breakfast Pork Sausage, 215
Broccoli
  Broccoli with Romano Bread Crumbs, 281
  Easter Pizza Casserole, 240
  Pecan Broccoli, 291
Broccoli raab
  Broccoli Raab Parmesan, 285
  Gorgonzola Polenta Cakes with Braised
    Broccoli Raab, 168
  Grilled Broccoli Raab and Alfred Risotto,
    142
Browned Risotto Patties, 143
Brown Sauce, 75
Bruschetta
  about, 3
  Garlic and Olive Bruschetta, 54

Butter
    clarifying of, 250
    sweet and salted, 155

Cabbage, Savoy Salad, 41
Caesar Salad, 33
Capicola
    about, 61
    Lobster Capicola, 61
    Mama Theresa's Beef Braciola, 234
    Smashed Potato and Capicola Frittata, 190
Carciofi Ripieni (Stuffed Artichokes), 290
Carciofi Ripieni con Risotto (Artichokes Stuffed with Risotto), 144
Carrots, and Citrus Casserole, 297
Cauliflower, Fried, 280
Celeriac
    Celeriac Alfredo, 283
    Celeriac Misto, 42
Cheeses, see also Gorgonzola; Mascarpone
    about: aged varieties, 67; curls of, 30; mozzarella, 184
    Asiago Pollo con Prosciutto (Asiago Chicken with Prosciutto), 257
    Baked Mixed Cheese Hors d'oeuvres, 53
    Cheese-Filled Prunes, 62
    Cheese Tortellini, 136
    Cheese Tortellini Salad, 45
    Fontina and Parmesan Polenta with Sun-Dried Tomatoes, 170
    Fresh Mozzarella and Tomato Salad, 35
    Mozzarella and Ricotta Cheese Sauce, 68
Chicken, see Poultry
Chickpeas
    Chickpea and Escarole Frittata, 189
    Chickpea Flatbread, 82
Chilled Beet Soup, 29
Chilled Marinated Whitefish, 48
Christmas dishes
    Christmas Eve dinner, 266
    Christmas Eve Salad, 45
    Christmas Goose, 249
Chuck Steak Pot Roast, 241
Chutney
    Fruit Chutney, 77
    Minty Fruit Chutney, 76
Cinnamon-Nutmeg Polenta with Dried Fruit and Nuts, 173
Cinnamon Rolls, 307
Cioppino, 24
    Hearty Cioppino, 274
Cipolla Frittata (Onion Frittata), 187
Citrus dishes, see also Oranges
    about: zest of, 254
    Citrus-Braised Halibut, 269
    Citrus Green-Bean Salad, 48
    Grapefruit and Pomegranate Bars, 308
Clam-Stuffed Portobellos, 50

Classic Biscotti, 303
Classic Chicken Parmesan, 252
Classic Fettuccine Alfredo, 129
Cookies, see Desserts
Corn, Polenta with Roasted, 164
Cornmeal, see also Polenta
    Cornmeal Flatbread, 88
    Cornmeal Pasta, 110
Cozze al Vino (Mussels in White Wine Broth), 277
Creamy Clam Risotto, 154
Creamy Crab Appetizers, 52
Creamy Polenta, 163
Crusty Egg Bread, 92

Dandelion Egg Drop, 26
Dates, 206
Deep-Fried Pasta, 135
Desserts, 299–314
    Almond Loaf, 312
    Anisette Cookies, 314
    Cinnamon Rolls, 307
    Classic Biscotti, 303
    Fig Tart, 310
    Grapefruit and Pomegranate Bars, 308
    Greenaweelies, 302
    Italian Bread Pudding, 304
    Keith's "No Dairy" Apple Cake, 313
    Momma Theresa's Zucchini Cake, 309
    Mustastoy, 310
    Oatmeal Muffins, 309
    Pear-Filled Calzones, 306
    Port Cookies, 311
    Scaweelies, 300
    Sweet Potato Pudding, 305
    Tordillas, 301
Duck, see Poultry

Easter dishes
    Easter Egg Bread, 91
    Easter Pizza Casserole, 240
Easy Alfredo Sauce, 69
Eggless Pasta, 103
Eggplant
    about: blanching and shocking, 284
    Eggplant Arugula Salad, 47
    Eggplant Pasta, 112
    Grilled Vegetable Frittata, 183
    Melanzane Marinate (Pickled Eggplants), 51
    Pork Terrine, 235
    Roasted Eggplant Purée, 72
    Rolled Squash, 289
    Venison Kebabs, 230
    Verdure al Forno (Baked Vegetable Casserole), 284

Eggs, see also Frittata
    about: cholesterol and, 192; pasteurization, 33; separating of, 101; testing for freshness, 104
    Crusty Egg Bread, 92
    Easter Egg Bread, 91
    Egg White Pasta, 104
    Polenta with Poached Eggs, 172
    Savory Breakfast Egg Polenta, 171
Equipment
    frittata pans, 189
    greasing of pans, 194
    knives, 81
    parchment paper, 121
    pots, 296
    risotto pans, 140
    slow cooker, 175
    vegetable peelers, 220
    wooden spoons, 27
    zester, 220
Escarole
    Chickpea and Escarole Frittata, 189
    Escarole Stew, 296

Fagioli Pasta (Bean Pasta), 107
Fennel
    about, 42
    Finochio Ripieni con Salsicce (Sausage-Stuffed Fennel), 286
Fettuccine Alfredo con Capesante, 130
Figs
    about: black and white, 44; fresh, 261
    Fig and Gorgonzola Salad, 44
    Fig Tart, 310
    Turkey and Fig Balls, 205
Finochio Ripieni con Salsicce (Sausage-Stuffed Fennel), 286
Fish, see also Seafood
    about: baccalà, 276; cooking in milk, 223; fresh, 268; fried, 273; as staple, 271
    Baccalà in Saffron Marinara Sauce, 276
    Baccalà with Pasta and Fresh Peas, 126
    Chilled Marinated Whitefish, 48
    Citrus-Braised Halibut, 269
    Cod Parmesan, 270
    Fish Casserole, 273
    Fish Stock, 16
    Fresh Cod Meatballs, 209
    Frittura di Paranza (Pan-Fried Smelts), 60
    Grilled Fish and Seafood Primavera, 271
    Grilled Tuna Salad, 40
    Hearty Cioppino, 274
    Hearty Fish Soup with Pesto, 23
    Lemon Scampi Cod Risotto, 158
    Orange-Poached Salmon with Prosciutto, 272
    Pasta con Alici (Pasta with Anchovy Sauce), 275

Pasta Stuffed with Fresh Cod in Saffron Broth, 128
Red Snapper and Pepper Risotto, 156
Red Snapper with Peppers, 268
Salmon Balls, 203
Salmon Pasta, 116
Salmon Sausage, 218
Stewed Fish with Polenta, 169
Whitefish Sausage, 223
Zuppa di Pesce (Fish Soup), 19
Flatbreads/Pizza/Focaccia, 79–97
about: focaccia dough, 93; yeast for, 90
Barley Flatbread, 89
Basic Cheese Pizza, 95
Basic Flatbread, 80
Bread Sticks, 96
Chickpea Flatbread, 82
Cornmeal Flatbread, 88
Crusty Egg Bread, 92
Easter Egg Bread, 91
Easter Pizza Casserole, 240
Fried Dough, 90
Frisedda, 96
Garlic and Herb Focaccia, 93
Garlic Knots, 97
Herbed Flatbread, 85
Onion Flatbread, 83
Roasted Garlic Flatbread, 84
Saffron Flatbread, 87
Sicilian Pizza, 95
Spelt Flatbread, 86
Whole-Wheat Flatbread, 81
Whole-Wheat Focaccia, 94
Focaccia, see Flatbreads/Pizza/Focaccia
Fontina
Baked Mixed Cheese Hors d'oeuvres, 53
Fontina and Parmesan Polenta with Sun-Dried Tomatoes, 170
Four-Cheese Frittata, 182
Fra Diavolo (Spicy Old World Gravy), 65
Fresh-Baked Ham and Potatoes, 228
Fresh Basil Pasta, 106
Fresh Cod Meatballs, 209
Fresh Crab with Arugula Salad, 43
Fresh Mozzarella and Tomato Salad, 35
Fresh Tomato Salad, 32
Fresh Vegetable Dip with Crusty Italian Bread, 51
Fried Dough, 90
Fried Green Tomatoes and Mascarpone Polenta, 166
Frisedda, 96
Frittata, 179–197
about, 180
Asparagus–Egg White Frittata, 185
Baked Potato and Mascarpone Frittata, 186
Basic Frittata, 180
Beef and Tomato Frittata, 193

Bell Pepper Frittata, 181
Chickpea and Escarole Frittata, 189
Cipolla Frittata (Onion Frittata), 187
Four-Cheese Frittata, 182
Frittata-Stuffed Baked Potatoes, 192
Grilled Vegetable Frittata, 183
Mushroom and Crab Frittata, 197
Pasta Frittata, 186
Risotto Frittata, 190
Roasted Potato and Shallot Frittata, 191
Sausage and Pepper Frittata, 194
Shrimp Frittata, 196
Smashed Potato and Capicola Frittata, 190
Stuffed Italian Pepper Frittata, 195
Sun-Dried Tomato and Fresh Basil Frittata, 184
Toasted Italian Bread Frittata, 188
Frittura di Paranza (Pan-Fried Smelts), 60
Fruit-Braised Duck, 256
Fruit Chutney, 77

Garlic
about, 97
Garlic and Herb Focaccia, 93
Garlic and Olive Bruschetta, 54
Garlic Knots, 97
Garlic-Saffron Polenta Triangles, 167
Garlic Soup, 27
Roasted Garlic Flatbread, 84
Roasted Garlic Pasta, 108
Roasted Garlic Paste, 70
Roasted Garlic Smashed Potatoes, 282
Roasted Potato and Garlic Gnocchi, 120
Gnocchi, 119
Roasted Potato and Garlic Gnocchi, 120
Goose, see Poultry
Gorgonzola
Baked Mixed Cheese Hors d'oeuvres, 53
Fig and Gorgonzola Salad, 44
Gorgonzola Browned Pears, 59
Gorgonzola Polenta Cakes with Braised Broccoli Raab, 168
Seared Quail with Gorgonzola, 261
Stuffed Shells, 131
Grapefruit and Pomegranate Bars, 308
Gravy, see Sauces
Greenaweelies, 302
Green Bean Bundles, 292
Greens, see also Arugula; Kale; Spinach
about: buying and storing, 35; kinds of, 46
Baby Greens with Apple and Mascarpone, 43
Bowtie Pasta with Braised Beans and Greens, 134
Chickpea and Escarole Frittata, 189
Escarole Stew, 296
Grilled dishes
about: grilling indoors, 239

Grilled Broccoli Raab and Alfredo Risotto, 142
Grilled Fish and Seafood Primavera, 271
Grilled Pork Cubes, 62
Grilled Portobello Mozzarella Polenta, 165
Grilled Rack of Lamb, 239
Grilled Tuna Salad, 40
Grilled Vegetable Frittata, 183
Grilled Vegetables, 288

Ham, Baked Smoked, 242
Hearty Cioppino, 274
Hearty Cold Antipasto Salad, 46
Hearty Fish Soup with Pesto, 23
Herbs, see also Basil
about: dried, 66; fresh, 54, 71; frozen, 5; grilling with, 230; grinding, 173
Herbed Flatbread, 85
Tomato and Parmesan Risotto, 145
Homemade pasta, see Pasta, homemade
Hors d'oeuvres, see Appetizers

Italian Beef and Sun-Dried Tomato Sausage, 219
Italian Bread Pudding, 304
Italian cuisine, 1–11
basic ingredients of, 7
cooking techniques of, 8–11
regional nature of, 2–6
Italian Meat Loaf, 231
Italian Pepperoncini Gremolata, 76

Kale
Wilted Kale Salad with Roasted Shallots, 38
Wilted Kale with Dried Currants and Walnuts, 281
Keith's "No Dairy" Apple Cake, 313

Lamb
Agnello Polpette (Lamb Meatballs), 212
Grilled Rack of Lamb, 239
Lamb Loaf, 237
Lamb Risotto, 150
Leg of Lamb, 227
Minted Lamb Sausage, 217
Minty Polenta Encrusted Lamb Chops, 176
Rosemary Lamb Sausage, 221
Lasagna, see Pasta, homemade
Layered Duck, 258
Leeks
about: cleaning of, 151
Shrimp Frittata, 196
Leg of Lamb, 227
Lemon Scampi Cod Risotto, 158
Lentil Soup, 22

Mama Theresa's Beef Braciola, 234
Marinated Beef Skewers, 55
Marinated Venison Roast, 229
Mascarpone
    about, 53
    Baby Greens with Apple and
        Mascarpone, 43
    Baked Mixed Cheese Hors d'oeuvres,
        53
    Fried Green Tomatoes and Mascarpone
        Polenta, 166
    Mascarpone Cheese Sauce, 69
    Stuffed Shells, 131
    Turkey with Mascarpone Sauce, 255
Meatballs, 199–213
    Agnello Polpette (Lamb Meatballs), 213
    Basic Beef Meatballs, 200
    Chicken Meatballs, 202
    Eggplant Meatballs, 213
    Fresh Cod Meatballs, 209
    Meatless Meatballs, 210
    Minestrone with Meatballs, 20
    Polpette con Pollo e Orzo (Chicken
        Meatballs with Orzo), 207
    Pork and Apple Meatballs, 203
    Risotto-Encased Meatballs, 146
    Rosemary Chicken Meatballs, 211
    Salmon Balls, 203
    Shrimp Balls, 204
    Three-Meat Meatballs, 201
    Turkey and Fig Balls, 205
    Veal and Date Balls, 206
    Venison Meatballs, 208
Meatless Meatballs, 210
Meats, see specific meats
Melanzane Marinate (Pickled Eggplants),
    51
Melon and Prosciutto, 52
Minestrone with Meatballs, 20
Minted Lamb Sausage, 217
Minty Fruit Chutney, 76
Minty Polenta Encrusted Lamb Chops, 176
Momma Theresa's Zucchini Cake, 309
Mozzarella
    Fresh Mozzarella and Tomato Salad, 35
    Mozzarella and Ricotta Cheese Sauce, 68
Mushrooms
    about: cleaning of, 50
    Chicken Marsala, 262
    Clam-Stuffed Portobellos, 50
    Grilled Portobello Mozzarella Polenta,
        165
    Mushroom and Crab Frittata, 197
    Pollo alla Cacciatora (Chicken
        Cacciatore), 248
Mustastoy, 310

New World Fresh Sauce, 66
Nuts, 173

Oatmeal Muffins, 309
Old World Gravy (Long-Cooking Tomato
    Sauce), 64
Olive oil, 2, 36
Onions
    about: red, 37; substitutes for, 202;
        sweating of, 241
    Cipolla Frittata (Onion Frittata), 187
    Grilled Vegetables, 288
    Onion Flatbread, 83
Oranges
    Carrot and Citrus Casserole, 297
    Citrus Polenta, 172
    Orange-Poached Salmon with Prosciutto,
        272
    Orange Shrimp, 56
Oregano-Almond Pesto, 73
Oregano Pork Ribs, 56
Osso Buco with Polenta Dumplings, 233
Oxtails, Spiced, 231

Pancetta
    Lentil Soup, 22
    Minted Lamb Sausage, 217
    Minty Polenta Encrusted Lamb Chops,
        176
    Venison Bean Ragout, 232
Parsley Peas, 294
Parsnips
    Braised Veal and Pepper Risotto, 149
    Chicken Scaparelli, 247
    Christmas Goose, 249
Pasta, dried
    about: amount of sauce for, 106, 110;
        cooking tips, 110; quality of, 113;
        testing for doneness, 108
    Cheese Tortellini Salad, 45
    Chicken Orzo, 18
    Minestrone with Meatballs, 20
    Pasta e Fagioli (Pasta and Bean Soup), 25
    Pasta Frittata, 186
    Pasta with Rich Broth, 29
    Polpette con Pollo e Orzo (Chicken
        Meatballs with Orzo), 207
    Tomato Soup with Fried Pasta Garnish, 21
    Vegetable Broth with Roasted Rigatoni,
        28
Pasta, homemade, 99–137
    about: cooking ravioli, 124
    Acini di Pepe, 109
    Baccalà with Pasta and Fresh Peas, 126
    Baked Spaghetti Tart, 132
    Basic Pasta, 100
    Bowtie Pasta with Braised Beans and
        Greens, 134
    Cheese Tortellini, 136
    Chicken Pasta, 115
    Classic Fettuccine Alfredo, 129
    Cornmeal Pasta, 110

Deep-Fried Pasta, 135
Eggless Pasta, 103
Eggplant Pasta, 112
Egg White Pasta, 104
Fagioli Pasta (Bean Pasta), 107
Fettuccine Alfredo con Capesante, 130
Fresh Basil Pasta, 106
Gnocchi, 119
Lobster Ravioli, 124
Meat Ravioli, 137
Pasta con Alici (Pasta with Anchovy
    Sauce), 275
Pasta con Ragu Bolognese, 133
Pasta Dumplings, 132
Pasta Stuffed with Fresh Cod in Saffron
    Broth, 128
Pasta-Wrapped Shrimp with Pesto, 125
Pork-Filled Pasta Shells, 127
Roasted Garlic Pasta, 108
Roasted Potato and Garlic Gnocchi, 120
Saffron and Shallot Pasta, 113
Salmon Pasta, 116
Scallop Pasta, 117
Spelt Pasta, 101
Spinach Pasta, 105
Strawberry Pasta, 114
Stuffed Rigatoni, 121
Stuffed Shells, 131
Tender Beef Ravioli, 238
Tomato Pasta, 111
Traditional Lasagna, 122
Vegetarian Lasagna, 123
Walnut Pasta, 118
Whole-Wheat Pasta, 102
Patate Fritti (Fried Potatoes), 286
Pears
    Baked Sweet Potatoes with Pear, 295
    Gorgonzola Browned Pears, 59
    Pear-Filled Calzones, 306
    Winter "Fruited" Chicken, 246
Peas
    Baccalà with Pasta and Fresh Peas, 126
    Parsley Peas, 294
Pecan Broccoli, 291
Pepper, fresh-cracked, 72
Peppers, bell
    about, 160
    Bell Pepper Frittata, 181
    Braised Veal and Pepper Risotto, 149
    Chickpea and Escarole Frittata, 189
    Grilled Vegetable Frittata, 183
    Grilled Vegetables, 288
    Pollo Rustico, 251
    Red Snapper and Pepper Risotto, 156
    Risotto Seafood Pepper Cakes, 160
    Roasted Red Peppers, 287
    Sausage and Pepper Frittata, 194
    Sweet and Spicy Pork, 226
    Veal and Pepper Sausage, 218

Verdure al Forno (Baked Vegetable Casserole), 284
Vitello alla Francese (French-Style Veal), 236
Pesto, *see* Sauces
Pizza, *see* Flatbreads/Pizza/Focaccia
Polenta, 161–177
about, 167
Basic Polenta, 162
Beef and Polenta Casserole, 175
Braised Veal with Polenta Dumplings, 174
Cinnamon-Nutmeg Polenta with Dried Fruit and Nuts, 173
Citrus Polenta, 172
Creamy Polenta, 163
Fontina and Parmesan Polenta with Sun-Dried Tomatoes, 170
Fried Green Tomatoes and Mascarpone Polenta, 166
Garlic-Saffron Polenta Triangles, 167
Gorgonzola Polenta Cakes with Braised Broccoli Raab, 168
Grilled Portobello Mozzarella Polenta, 165
Minty Polenta Encrusted Lamb Chops, 176
Osso Buco with Polenta Dumplings, 233
Polenta-Stuffed Turkey Breast, 260
Polenta with Poached Eggs, 172
Polenta with Roasted Corn, 164
Polenta with Stock, 163
Savory Breakfast Egg Polenta, 171
Seafood Polenta, 177
Stewed Fish with Polenta, 169
Sweet Breakfast Egg Polenta, 171
Pollo alla Cacciatora (Chicken Cacciatore), 248
Pollo Rustico, 251
Pollo Salsiccia con Origano (Chicken Sausage with Oregano), 214
Polpette con Pollo e Orzo (Chicken Meatballs with Orzo), 207
Pomegranate, and Grapefruit Bars, 308
Pomodori Ripieni (Stuffed Roma Tomatoes), 57
Pork
Apple and Pork Sausage, 220
Baked Pork Ribs, 226
Basic Italian Pork Sausage, 214
Breakfast Pork Sausage, 215
Eggplant Meatballs, 213
Finochio Ripieni con Salsicce (Sausage-Stuffed Fennel), 286
Fra Diavolo (Spicy Old World Gravy), 65
Fresh-Baked Pork and Potatoes, 228
Grilled Pork Cubes, 62
Meat Ravioli, 137
Old World Gravy (Long-Cooking Tomato Sauce), 64

Oregano Pork Ribs, 56
Pasta con Ragu Bolognese, 133
Pork and Apple Meatballs, 203
Pork-Filled Pasta Shells, 127
Pork Soup with Acini di Pepe, 30
Pork Terrine, 235
Risotto-Encased Meatballs, 146
Stuffed Italian Pepper Frittata, 195
Stuffed Pork Roast, 238
Sweet and Spicy Pork, 226
Three-Meat Meatballs, 201
Port Cookies, 311
Potatoes, *see also* Sweet potatoes
about: mashing, 282; tips on, 228
Baked Potato and Mascarpone Frittata, 186
Escarole Stew, 296
Fresh-Baked Pork and Potatoes, 228
Frittata-Stuffed Baked Potatoes, 192
Gnocchi, 119
Grilled Vegetables, 288
Patate Fritti (Fried Potatoes), 286
Pork Terrine, 235
Roasted Garlic Smashed Potatoes, 282
Roasted Potato and Garlic Gnocchi, 120
Roasted Potato and Shallot Frittata, 191
Smashed Potato and Capicola Frittata, 190
Poultry, 245–263
about: reducing fat, 247
Arugula, Mozzarella, and Chicken Sausage, 221
Asiago Pollo con Prosciutto (Asiago Chicken with Prosciutto), 257
Braised Duck Risotto, 154
Chicken and Oregano Risotto, 153
Chicken and Sausage Casserole, 216
Chicken Fricasse, 263
Chicken Marsala, 262
Chicken Meatballs, 202
Chicken Orzo, 18
Chicken Pasta, 115
Chicken Saltimbocca Risotto, 152
Chicken Scaparelli, 247
Chicken Stock, 14
Chicken Terrine, 259
Christmas Goose, 249
Classic Chicken Parmesan, 252
Duck Sausage, 219
Fruit-Braised Duck, 256
Layered Duck, 258
Pasta with Rich Broth, 29
Polenta-Stuffed Turkey Breast, 260
Pollo alla Cacciatora (Chicken Cacciatore), 248
Pollo Rustico, 251
Pollo Salsiccia con Origano (Chicken Sausage with Oregano), 214

Polpette con Pollo e Orzo (Chicken Meatballs with Orzo), 207
Ricotta Chicken Breasts, 252
Rosemary Chicken Meatballs, 211
Seared Quail with Gorgonzola, 261
Smooth Chicken Liver Sausage, 222
Spicy Chicken Wings, 55
Stracciatella, 17
Stuffed Chicken, 253
Stuffed Rigatoni, 121
Turkey and Cranberry Sausage, 224
Turkey and Fig Balls, 205
Turkey and Walnut Risotto, 155
Turkey Piccata, 254
Turkey Tetrazzini, 250
Turkey with Mascarpone Sauce, 255
Winter "Fruited" Chicken, 246
Prosciutto
Asiago Pollo con Prosciutto (Asiago Chicken with Prosciutto), 257
Asparagus–Egg White Frittata, 185
Crusty Egg Bread, 92
Melon and Prosciutto, 52
Prunes, Cheese-Filled, 62

Quail, *see* Poultry

Ravioli, *see* Pasta, homemade
Rice, *see* Risotto
Ricotta Chicken Breasts, 252
Risotto, 139–160
about: cooking of, 145; pans for, 140; patties, 157; rice varieties, 148
Basic Risotto, 140
Braised Duck Risotto, 154
Braised Veal and Pepper Risotto, 149
Browned Risotto Patties, 143
Carciofi Ripieni con Risotto (Artichokes Stuffed with Risotto), 144
Chicken and Oregano Risotto, 153
Chicken Saltimbocca Risotto, 152
Creamy Clam Risotto, 154
Grilled Broccoli Raab and Alfredo Risotto, 142
Lamb Risotto, 150
Lemon Scampi Cod Risotto, 158
Lobster Risotto, 159
Red Snapper and Pepper Risotto, 156
Risotto-Encased Meatballs, 146
Risotto Frittata, 190
Risotto Seafood Pepper Cakes, 160
Roasted Carrot Risotto, 141
Seafood Risotto, 157
Seared Filet Mignon Risotto, 147
Seasoned Beef Risotto, 151
Spicy Risotto, 146
Stewed Veal Risotto, 148
Tomato and Parmesan Risotto, 145
Turkey and Walnut Risotto, 155

Roasted dishes
  Roasted Butternut Squash Stew, 283
  Roasted Carrot Risotto, 141
  Roasted Eggplant Purée, 72
  Roasted Garlic Flatbread, 84
  Roasted Garlic Pasta, 108
  Roasted Garlic Paste, 70
  Roasted Garlic Smashed Potatoes, 282
  Roasted Potato and Garlic Gnocchi, 120
  Roasted Potato and Shallot Frittata, 191
  Roasted Red Peppers, 287
Rolled Squash, 289
Rosemary Chicken Meatballs, 211
Rosemary Lamb Sausage, 221
Rosemary Pesto, 74

Saffron
  about, 24
  Baccalà in Saffron Marinara Sauce, 276
  Garlic-Saffron Polenta Triangles, 167
  Pasta Stuffed with Fresh Cod in Saffron
    Broth, 128
  Saffron and Shallot Pasta, 113
  Saffron Flatbread, 87
  Stewed Fish with Polenta, 169
Sage Pesto, 74
Salads, 31–48
  about: oil on, 36
  Antipasto Salad, 34
  Aunt Gloria's Italian Green Bean Salad, 37
  Baby Greens with Apple and
    Mascarpone, 43
  Bread Salad, 40
  Caesar Salad, 33
  Cannellini Bean Salad, 36
  Celeriac Misto, 42
  Cheese Tortellini Salad, 45
  Chilled Marinated Whitefish, 48
  Christmas Eve Salad, 45
  Citrus Green-Bean Salad, 48
  Eggplant Arugula Salad, 47
  Fig and Gorgonzola Salad, 44
  Fresh Crab with Arugula Salad, 43
  Fresh Mozzarella and Tomato Salad, 35
  Fresh Tomato Salad, 32
  Grilled Tuna Salad, 40
  Hearty Cold Antipasto Salad, 46
  Lobster Salad, 39
  Savoy Cabbage Salad, 41
  Wilted Kale Salad with Roasted Shallots,
    38
Salmon, see Fish
Salsa Besciamella (Béchamel Sauce), 67
Salt, 68, 86
Sauces, 63–77
  about: thickening of, 75
  Brown Sauce, 75
  Cannellini Bean Purée, 70
  Easy Alfredo Sauce, 69

Fra Diavolo (Spicy Old World Gravy), 65
Fruit Chutney, 77
Hearty Fish Soup with Pesto, 23
Italian Pepperoncini Gremolata, 76
Mascarpone Cheese Sauce, 69
Minty Fruit Chutney, 76
Mozzarella and Ricotta Cheese Sauce, 68
New World Fresh Sauce, 66
Old World Gravy (Long-Cooking Tomato
  Sauce), 64
Oregano-Almond Pesto, 73
Pasta-Wrapped Shrimp with Pesto, 125
Roasted Eggplant Purée, 72
Roasted Garlic Paste, 70
Rosemary Pesto, 74
Sage Pesto, 74
Salsa Besciamella (Béchamel Sauce), 67
Traditional Pesto, 71
Walnut Pesto, 73
Sausage, 214–224
  about: basics of making, 10–11
  Apple and Pork Sausage, 220
  Arugula, Mozzarella, and Chicken
    Sausage, 221
  Basic Italian Pork Sausage, 214
  Bean and Sausage Soup, 26
  Beef Sausage, 217
  Breakfast Pork Sausage, 215
  Chicken and Sausage Casserole, 216
  Duck Sausage, 219
  Finochio Ripieni con Salsicce (Sausage-
    Stuffed Fennel), 286
  Fra Diavolo (Spicy Old World Gravy), 65
  Italian Beef and Sun-Dried Tomato
    Sausage, 219
  Minted Lamb Sausage, 217
  Old World Gravy (Long-Cooking Tomato
    Sauce), 64
  Pollo Salsiccia con Origano (Chicken
    Sausage with Oregano), 214
  Rosemary Lamb Sausage, 221
  Salmon Sausage, 218
  Sausage and Pepper Frittata, 194
  Sausage-Filled Shallots, 59
  Seafood Sausage, 215
  Smooth Chicken Liver Sausage, 222
  Stuffed Pork Roast, 238
  Turkey and Cranberry Sausage, 224
  Veal and Pepper Sausage, 218
  Vegetable and Bean Sausage, 224
  Whitefish Sausage, 223
Sautéed Beets with Shallots, 293
Savory Breakfast Egg Polenta, 171
Savoy Cabbage Salad, 41
Scaweelies, 300
Seafood
  about: shrimp, 196, 274
  Aragosta con Burro all'Aglio (Lobster
    with Garlic Better), 266

Christmas Eve Salad, 45
Cioppino, 24
Clam-Stuffed Portobellos, 50
Cozze al Vino (Mussels in White Wine
  Broth), 277
Creamy Clam Risotto, 154
Creamy Crab Appetizers, 52
Fettuccine Alfredo con Capesante, 130
Fresh Crab with Arugula Salad, 43
Grilled Fish and Seafood Primavera, 271
Hearty Cioppino, 274
Lobster Capicola, 61
Lobster Ravioli, 124
Lobster Risotto, 159
Lobster Salad, 39
Mushroom and Crab Frittata, 197
Orange Shrimp, 56
Pasta-Wrapped Shrimp with Pesto, 125
Scallop Pasta, 117
Scallops Alfredo, 267
Seafood Bake, 275
Seafood Polenta, 177
Seafood Risotto, 157
Seafood Sausage, 215
Seafood Sausage Bread, 58
Shrimp Balls, 204
Shrimp Frittata, 196
Shrimp Scampi, 277
Zuppa di Pesce (Fish Soup), 19
Seared Filet Mignon Risotto, 147
Seared Quail with Gorgonzola, 261
Seasoned Beef Risotto, 151
Semolina, 100
Shallots
  about, 293
  Roasted Potato and Shallot Frittata, 191
  Saffron and Shallot Pasta, 113
  Sausage-Filled Shallots, 59
  Sautéed Beets with Shallots, 293
  Wilted Kale Salad with Roasted Shallots,
    38
Shrimp, see Seafood
Sicilian Pizza, 95
Smashed Potato and Capicola Frittata, 190
Smooth Chicken Liver Sausage, 222
Soups, 13–30
  about: discarding solids, 17; removing fat
    from, 14, 20
  Bean and Sausage Soup, 26
  Beef Stock, 15
  Chicken Orzo, 18
  Chicken Stock, 14
  Chilled Beet Soup, 29
  Cioppino, 24
  Dandelion Egg Drop, 26
  Fish Stock, 16
  Garlic Soup, 27
  Hearty Fish Soup with Pesto, 23
  Lentil Soup, 22

Minestrone with Meatballs, 20
Pasta e Fagioli (Pasta and Bean Soup), 25
Pasta with Rich Broth, 29
Pork Soup with Acini di Pepe, 30
Stracciatella, 17
Tomato Soup with Fried Pasta Garnish, 21
Vegetable Broth with Roasted Rigatoni, 28
Vegetable Stock, 16
Zuppa di Pesce (Fish Soup), 19
Spelt Flatbread, 86
Spelt Pasta, 101
Spiced Oxtails, 231
Spicy Chicken Wings, 55
Spicy Risotto, 146
Spinach
    Italian Meat Loaf, 231
    Spinach Pasta, 105
    Verdure al Forno (Baked Vegetable Casserole), 284
Squash, see also Zucchini
    Roasted Butternut Squash Stew, 283
    Rolled Squash, 289
Stewed Fish with Polenta, 169
Stewed Veal Risotto, 148
Stock, see Soups
Stracciatella, 17
Strawberry Pasta, 114
Stuffed Chicken, 253
Stuffed Italian Pepper Frittata, 195
Stuffed Pork Roast, 238
Stuffed Rigatoni, 121
Stuffed Shells, 131
Sun-dried tomatoes
    Italian Beef and Sun-Dried Tomato Sausage, 219
    Sun-Dried Tomato and Fresh Basil Frittata, 184
Sweet and Spicy Pork, 226
Sweet Breakfast Egg Polenta, 171
Sweet potatoes
    Baked Sweet Potatoes with Pear, 295
    Sweet Potato Pudding, 305

Tender Beef Ravioli, 238
Three-Meat Meatballs, 201
Toasted Italian Bread Frittata, 188
Tomatoes
    about: canned, 235; choosing, 32
    Beef and Tomato Frittata, 193
    Braised Veal with Polenta Dumplings, 174
    Chicken Fricasse, 263
    Fontina and Parmesan Polenta with Sun-Dried Tomatoes, 170
    Fra Diavolo (Spicy Old World Gravy), 65
    Fresh Mozzarella and Tomato Salad, 35
    Fresh Tomato Salad, 32
    Fried Green Tomatoes and Mascarpone Polenta, 166
    New World Fresh Sauce, 66

Old World Gravy (Long-Cooking Tomato Sauce), 64
Osso Buco with Polenta Dumplings, 233
Pomodori Ripieni (Stuffed Roma Tomatoes), 57
Stewed Fish with Polenta, 169
Tomato and Parmesan Risotto, 145
Tomato Pasta, 111
Tomato Soup with Fried Pasta Garnish, 21
Vitello Brasato (Braised Veal), 243
Tordillas, 301
Traditional Lasagna, 122
Traditional Pesto, 71
Turkey, see Poultry

Vanilla, 307
Veal
    Braised Veal and Pepper Risotto, 149
    Braised Veal with Polenta Dumplings, 174
    Minestrone with Meatballs, 20
    Osso Buco with Polenta Dumplings, 233
    Pasta con Ragu Bolognese, 133
    Stewed Veal Risotto, 148
    Three-Meat Meatballs, 201
    Veal and Date Balls, 206
    Veal and Pepper Sausage, 218
    Vitello alla Francese (French-Style Veal), 236, 242
    Vitello Brasato (Braised Veal), 243
    Verdure al Forno (Baked Vegetable Casserole), 284
Vegetables, 279–297. See also Eggplant; Greens; Zucchini
    about: blanching and shocking, 280; carrot varieties, 258; cooking prior to making soup, 22
    Asparagi alla Milanese (Milan-Style Asparagus), 294
    Asparagus–Egg White Frittata, 185
    Baccalà with Pasta and Fresh Peas, 126
    Baked Sweet Potatoes with Pear, 295
    Broccoli Raab Parmesan, 285
    Broccoli with Romano Bread Crumbs, 281
    Carciofi Ripieni (Stuffed Artichokes), 290
    Carrot and Citrus Casserole, 297
    Cavolfiore Fritto (Fried Cauliflower), 280
    Celeriac Alfredo, 283
    Celeriac Misto, 42
    Chilled Beet Soup, 29
    Easter Pizza Casserole, 240
    Escarole Stew, 296
    Finochio Ripieni con Salsicce (Sausage-Stuffed Fennel), 286
    Gorgonzola Polenta Cakes with Braised Broccoli Raab, 168
    Green Bean Bundles, 292
    Grilled Broccoli Raab and Alfred Risotto, 142
    Grilled Vegetables, 288

Parsley Peas, 294
Patate Fritti (Fried Potatoes), 286
Pecan Broccoli, 291
Roasted Butternut Squash Stew, 283
Roasted Carrot Risotto, 141
Roasted Garlic Smashed Potatoes, 282
Roasted Red Peppers, 287
Rolled Squash, 289
Sauteéd Beets with Shallots, 293
Vegetable and Bean Sausage, 224
Vegetable Broth with Roasted Rigatoni, 28
Vegetable Stock, 16
Vegetarian Lasagna, 123
Verdure al Forno (Baked Vegetable Casserole), 284
Wilted Kale with Dried Currants and Walnuts, 281
Venison
    Marinated Venison Roast, 229
    Venison Bean Ragout, 232
    Venison Kebabs, 230
    Venison Meatballs, 208
Verdure al Forno (Baked Vegetable Casserole), 284
Vitello alla Francese (French-Style Veal), 242
Vitello Brasato (Braised Veal), 243
Vitello el Forno (Baked Veal), 236

Walnut Pasta, 118
Walnut Pesto, 73
Whitefish Sausage, 223
Whole-Wheat Flatbread, 81
Whole-Wheat Focaccia, 94
Whole-Wheat Pasta, 102
Wilted Kale Salad with Roasted Shallots, 38
Wilted Kale with Dried Currants and Walnuts, 281
Winter "Fruited" Chicken, 246

Zucchini
    about, 183
    Grilled Vegetable Frittata, 183
    Momma Theresa's Zucchini Cake, 309
    Rolled Squash, 289
    Zucchini Patties, 295
Zuppa di Pesce (Fish Soup), 19

THE EVERYTHING SERIES!

BUSINESS & PERSONAL FINANCE

Everything® Budgeting Book
Everything® Business Planning Book
Everything® Coaching and Mentoring Book
Everything® Fundraising Book
Everything® Get Out of Debt Book
Everything® Grant Writing Book
Everything® Homebuying Book, 2nd Ed.
Everything® Homeselling Book
Everything® Home-Based Business Book
Everything® Investing Book
Everything® Landlording Book
Everything® Leadership Book
Everything® Managing People Book
Everything® Negotiating Book
Everything® Online Business Book
Everything® Personal Finance Book
Everything® Personal Finance in Your 20s
    and 30s Book
Everything® Project Management Book
Everything® Real Estate Investing Book
Everything® Robert's Rules Book, $7.95
Everything® Selling Book
Everything® Start Your Own Business Book
Everything® Wills & Estate Planning Book

COOKING

Everything® Barbecue Cookbook
Everything® Bartender's Book, $9.95
Everything® Chinese Cookbook
Everything® College Cookbook
Everything® Cookbook
Everything® Diabetes Cookbook
Everything® Easy Gourmet Cookbook
Everything® Fondue Cookbook
Everything® Grilling Cookbook
Everything® Healthy Meals in Minutes
    Cookbook
Everything® Holiday Cookbook

Everything® Indian Cookbook
Everything® Low-Carb Cookbook
Everything® Low-Fat High-Flavor Cookbook
Everything® Low-Salt Cookbook
Everything® Meals for a Month Cookbook
Everything® Mediterranean Cookbook
Everything® Mexican Cookbook
Everything® One-Pot Cookbook
Everything® Pasta Cookbook
Everything® Quick Meals Cookbook
Everything® Slow Cooker Cookbook
Everything® Soup Cookbook
Everything® Thai Cookbook
Everything® Vegetarian Cookbook
Everything® Wine Book

HEALTH

Everything® Alzheimer's Book
Everything® Diabetes Book
Everything® Hypnosis Book
Everything® Low Cholesterol Book
Everything® Massage Book
Everything® Menopause Book
Everything® Nutrition Book
Everything® Reflexology Book
Everything® Stress Management Book

HISTORY

Everything® American Government Book
Everything® American History Book
Everything® Civil War Book
Everything® Irish History & Heritage Book
Everything® Middle East Book

HOBBIES & GAMES

Everything® Blackjack Strategy Book
Everything® Brain Strain Book, $9.95
Everything® Bridge Book
Everything® Candlemaking Book

Everything® Card Games Book
Everything® Cartooning Book
Everything® Casino Gambling Book, 2nd Ed.
Everything® Chess Basics Book
Everything® Crossword and Puzzle Book
Everything® Crossword Challenge Book
Everything® Cryptograms Book, $9.95
Everything® Digital Photography Book
Everything® Drawing Book
Everything® Easy Crosswords Book
Everything® Family Tree Book
Everything® Games Book, 2nd Ed.
Everything® Knitting Book
Everything® Knots Book
Everything® Motorcycle Book
Everything® Online Genealogy Book
Everything® Photography Book
Everything® Poker Strategy Book
Everything® Pool & Billiards Book
Everything® Quilting Book
Everything® Scrapbooking Book
Everything® Sewing Book
Everything® Woodworking Book
Everything® Word Games Challenge Book

HOME IMPROVEMENT

Everything® Feng Shui Book
Everything® Feng Shui Decluttering Book,
    $9.95
Everything® Fix-It Book
Everything® Homebuilding Book
Everything® Lawn Care Book
Everything® Organize Your Home Book

EVERYTHING® KIDS' BOOKS

All titles are $6.95

Everything® Kids' Animal Puzzle & Activity
    Book
Everything® Kids' Baseball Book, 3rd Ed.

All Everything® books are priced at $12.95 or $14.95, unless otherwise stated. Prices subject to change without notice.

Everything® Kids' Bible Trivia Book
Everything® Kids' Bugs Book
Everything® Kids' Christmas Puzzle
& Activity Book
Everything® Kids' Cookbook
Everything® Kids' Halloween Puzzle
& Activity Book
Everything® Kids' Hidden Pictures Book
Everything® Kids' Joke Book
Everything® Kids' Knock Knock Book
Everything® Kids' Math Puzzles Book
Everything® Kids' Mazes Book
Everything® Kids' Money Book
Everything® Kids' Monsters Book
Everything® Kids' Nature Book
Everything® Kids' Puzzle Book
Everything® Kids' Riddles & Brain Teasers Book
Everything® Kids' Science Experiments Book
Everything® Kids' Sharks Book
Everything® Kids' Soccer Book
Everything® Kids' Travel Activity Book

KIDS' STORY BOOKS

Everything® Bedtime Story Book
Everything® Fairy Tales Book

LANGUAGE

Everything® Conversational Japanese Book
(with CD), $19.95
Everything® French Phrase Book, $9.95
Everything® French Verb Book, $9.95
Everything® Inglés Book
Everything® Learning French Book
Everything® Learning German Book
Everything® Learning Italian Book
Everything® Learning Latin Book
Everything® Learning Spanish Book
Everything® Sign Language Book
Everything® Spanish Grammar Book
Everything® Spanish Phrase Book, $9.95
Everything® Spanish Verb Book, $9.95

MUSIC

Everything® Drums Book (with CD), $19.95
Everything® Guitar Book
Everything® Home Recording Book
Everything® Playing Piano and Keyboards
Book

Everything® Reading Music Book (with CD),
$19.95
Everything® Rock & Blues Guitar Book
(with CD), $19.95
Everything® Songwriting Book

NEW AGE

Everything® Astrology Book
Everything® Dreams Book, 2nd Ed.
Everything® Ghost Book
Everything® Love Signs Book, $9.95
Everything® Numerology Book
Everything® Paganism Book
Everything® Palmistry Book
Everything® Psychic Book
Everything® Reiki Book
Everything® Spells & Charms Book
Everything® Tarot Book
Everything® Wicca and Witchcraft Book

PARENTING

Everything® Baby Names Book
Everything® Baby Shower Book
Everything® Baby's First Food Book
Everything® Baby's First Year Book
Everything® Birthing Book
Everything® Breastfeeding Book
Everything® Father-to-Be Book
Everything® Father's First Year Book
Everything® Get Ready for Baby Book
Everything® Getting Pregnant Book
Everything® Homeschooling Book
Everything® Parent's Guide to Children
with ADD/ADHD
Everything® Parent's Guide to Children
with Asperger's Syndrome
Everything® Parent's Guide to Children
with Autism
Everything® Parent's Guide to Children
with Dyslexia
Everything® Parent's Guide to Positive
Discipline
Everything® Parent's Guide to Raising a
Successful Child
Everything® Parent's Guide to Tantrums
Everything® Parent's Guide to the Overweight
Child
Everything® Parenting a Teenager Book
Everything® Potty Training Book, $9.95

Everything® Pregnancy Book, 2nd Ed.
Everything® Pregnancy Fitness Book
Everything® Pregnancy Nutrition Book
Everything® Pregnancy Organizer, $15.00
Everything® Toddler Book
Everything® Tween Book
Everything® Twins, Triplets, and More Book

PETS

Everything® Cat Book
Everything® Dachshund Book, $12.95
Everything® Dog Book
Everything® Dog Health Book
Everything® Dog Training and Tricks Book
Everything® Golden Retriever Book, $12.95
Everything® Horse Book
Everything® Labrador Retriever Book, $12.95
Everything® Poodle Book, $12.95
Everything® Pug Book, $12.95
Everything® Puppy Book
Everything® Rottweiler Book, $12.95
Everything® Tropical Fish Book

REFERENCE

Everything® Car Care Book
Everything® Classical Mythology Book
Everything® Computer Book
Everything® Divorce Book
Everything® Einstein Book
Everything® Etiquette Book
Everything® Mafia Book
Everything® Philosophy Book
Everything® Psychology Book
Everything® Shakespeare Book

RELIGION

Everything® Angels Book
Everything® Bible Book
Everything® Buddhism Book
Everything® Catholicism Book
Everything® Christianity Book
Everything® Jewish History & Heritage Book
Everything® Judaism Book
Everything® Koran Book
Everything® Prayer Book
Everything® Saints Book
Everything® Torah Book
Everything® Understanding Islam Book

All Everything® books are priced at $12.95 or $14.95, unless otherwise stated. Prices subject to change without notice.

Everything® World's Religions Book
Everything® Zen Book

SCHOOL & CAREERS

Everything® Alternative Careers Book
Everything® College Survival Book, 2nd Ed.
Everything® Cover Letter Book, 2nd Ed.
Everything® Get-a-Job Book
Everything® Job Interview Book
Everything® New Teacher Book
Everything® Online Job Search Book
Everything® Paying for College Book
Everything® Practice Interview Book
Everything® Resume Book, 2nd Ed.
Everything® Study Book

SELF-HELP

Everything® Great Sex Book
Everything® Kama Sutra Book
Everything® Self-Esteem Book

SPORTS & FITNESS

Everything® Fishing Book
Everything® Fly-Fishing Book
Everything® Golf Instruction Book

Everything® Pilates Book
Everything® Running Book
Everything® Total Fitness Book
Everything® Weight Training Book
Everything® Yoga Book

TRAVEL

Everything® Family Guide to Hawaii
Everything® Family Guide to New York City, 2nd Ed.
Everything® Family Guide to RV Travel & Campgrounds
Everything® Family Guide to the Walt Disney World Resort®, Universal Studios®, and Greater Orlando, 4th Ed.
Everything® Family Guide to Washington D.C., 2nd Ed.
Everything® Guide to Las Vegas
Everything® Guide to New England
Everything® Travel Guide to the Disneyland Resort®, California Adventure®, Universal Studios®, and the Anaheim Area

WEDDINGS

Everything® Bachelorette Party Book, $9.95
Everything® Bridesmaid Book, $9.95

Everything® Elopement Book, $9.95
Everything® Father of the Bride Book, $9.95
Everything® Groom Book, $9.95
Everything® Mother of the Bride Book, $9.95
Everything® Wedding Book, 3rd Ed.
Everything® Wedding Checklist, $9.95
Everything® Wedding Etiquette Book, $7.95
Everything® Wedding Organizer, $15.00
Everything® Wedding Shower Book, $7.95
Everything® Wedding Vows Book, $7.95
Everything® Weddings on a Budget Book, $9.95

WRITING

Everything® Creative Writing Book
Everything® Get Published Book
Everything® Grammar and Style Book
Everything® Guide to Writing a Book Proposal
Everything® Guide to Writing a Novel
Everything® Guide to Writing Children's Books
Everything® Screenwriting Book
Everything® Writing Poetry Book
Everything® Writing Well Book

We have Everything® for the beginner crafter!
All titles are $14.95

Everything® Crafts—Baby Scrapbooking
1-59337-225-6

Everything® Crafts—Bead Your Own Jewelry
1-59337-142-X

Everything® Crafts—Create Your Own Greeting Cards
1-59337-226-4

Everything® Crafts—Easy Projects
1-59337-298-1

Everything® Crafts—Polymer Clay for Beginners
1-59337-230-2

Everything® Crafts—Rubber Stamping Made Easy
1-59337-229-9

Everything® Crafts—Wedding Decorations and Keepsakes
1-59337-227-2

Available wherever books are sold!
To order, call 800-872-5627, or visit us at *www.everything.com*
Everything® and everything.com® are registered trademarks of F+W Publications, Inc.